THE ENGLISH BOWMAN IN THE HUNDRED YEARS WAR

THE ENGLISH BOWMAN IN THE HUNDRED YEARS WAR

THE SECRET WEAPON OF THE MIDDLE AGES

M. J. TROW

Pen & Sword
MILITARY
AN IMPRINT OF PEN & SWORD BOOKS LTD.
YORKSHIRE – PHILADELPHIA

First published in Great Britain in 2025 by
Pen & Sword Military
An imprint of
Pen & Sword Books Ltd
Yorkshire - Philadelphia

ISBN 978 1 03612 472 4

A CIP catalogue record for this book is available from the British Library.

Typeset in INDIA by IMPEC eSolutions
Printed and bound in England by CPI (UK) Ltd.

The Publisher's authorised representative in the EU for product safety is Authorised Rep Compliance Ltd., Ground Floor, 71 Lower Baggot Street, Dublin D02 P593, Ireland.
www.arccompliance.com

For a complete list of Pen & Sword titles please contact:

PEN & SWORD BOOKS LIMITED
47 Church Street, Barnsley, South Yorkshire, S70 2AS, England
E-mail: enquiries@pen-and-sword.co.uk
Website: www.pen-and-sword.co.uk

or

PEN AND SWORD BOOKS
1950 Lawrence Rd, Havertown, PA 19083, USA
E-mail: uspen-and-sword@casematepublishers.com
Website: www.penandswordbooks.com

Contents

Author's Note

The Hundred Years War

For convenience, historians often use shorthand. It would be laborious for the writer and tedious for the reader to have casual phrases explained minutely, so the casual phrases enter the discipline and stay. The Hundred Years War is a classic example. Technically, it is wrong. If we go from Edward III's claim to the French throne in 1337 to the English defeat at Castillon in 1453, it is actually 116 years. But there are so many truces during that time that we ought to rethink our shorthand.

From 1337 to the Treaty of Bretigny in 1360 should be regarded as a single war (although fighting was clearly not continuous throughout it). This could be called the Crecy/Poitiers War after the two major battles that characterized it. A second war began in September 1369 when Edward renewed his claim to the French throne and could be called (although it gives the Constable of France too much precedence) the du Guesclin War. Peace talks, royal marriages and other issues took place during the stalemate after du Guesclin's death in 1380. The third war began in 1414 when Henry V claimed the throne of France in August. This could be called the Agincourt War, after the English victory of 1415, which concluded with the crowning of Charles VII at Rheims and his taking of Paris in 1436. The war from August 1443 to Castillon ten years later might be labelled the Final War, in that only Calais remained to the English and there were no further claims to the French throne by English monarchs.

No doubt this sounds artificial, but no more so than the Hundred Years War, which gives us a completely distorted view of the time.

Chapter 1

The Bow

The use of the bow by early man is one of the milestones of evolution. Along with fire and the wheel, it transformed the way of life for hominids and marked yet another separation from the animals. Stones, sticks and even rudimentary spears came first, but the bow was far more complicated, because it relied on manufacturing skills, selection of the most suitable wood, the creation of a string and the complementary making of the arrow. A bow by itself was almost useless in hunting although it could be – and was – used as a club in battle.

Because the earliest bows were made of wood and wood rots over time, we have no surviving examples of any before the Middle Ages. The discovery and raising of Henry VIII's ship the *Mary Rose* in 1982 added immeasurably to our knowledge of these weapons because dozens were found stored in the wreck's hull. The ship sank in the Solent in 1545 but essentially the bows on board were identical to those used at Agincourt in 1415 and all the other battles covered by this book.

Arrowheads are a different matter. Made of sharpened flint and stone, examples have been found in North Africa dating from 50,000 years ago when much of Europe was still covered in feet of ice. At various places in the world, other minerals were used, such as jasper, chalcedony and obsidian. These would have been bound to wooden shafts with animal gut.

In areas where timber was scarce or not sufficiently supple to bend under the tension of the bowmen's arms, horn, bone and sinew were probably used in a variety of combinations. Country children living in Britain in the 1950s tried to make bows emulating the hero of a popular television series, *Robin Hood*, starring Richard Greene, and they were almost universally disappointed. The wood either snapped or the arrows travelled a disappointing few feet, usually missing the target entirely.

We know from Neolithic rock and cave paintings that early man hunted with bows – and the sort of game that the arrows brought down. In Cueva de los Caballos in Castellau, Spain, archers are clearly killing deer. They are on foot and stood no chance of outrunning a gazelle, so the bow was vital. We should be wary of artwork like this, however. The example from los Caballos shows the animals running *towards* the men, rather than away from them; they may have had some other, perhaps ritualistic, meaning.

The arrowheads themselves were probably used for hunting, although killing other men was little different from killing game. The simplest and oldest forms are leaf-shaped, with a sharpened point and sides. Later examples are barbed and tanged (see diagram) which ensured that the arrow stayed embedded in the animal which had no opposable thumb to remove it. Such arrows could be used in battle too, and removal of them from a wound, even by an experienced surgeon, would cause an even worse wound than that made by the original impact. But they slowed attacking bowmen up. Once an archer had fired, he could advance and retrieve his arrows, either from the ground or from the body of a target; a barbed head would make this more difficult.

One of the earliest descriptions of a bow we have comes from the Greek Homer, writing in the eighth century BC:

> [Pandarus's] polished bow was made from the horns of an ibex that he had shot. They measured sixteen hands spans. A bowmaker worked on them, joined them together, smoothed them and set a nock [retaining notch] of gold at each end. Pandarus strung the bow, opened his quiver, chose an arrow and fitted it to the string. He held the arrow nock on the string of the sinew and drew back the string to his breast until the

> iron arrowhead touched the bow. When he had drawn the great bow to full compass, he loosed the string, which sang the sharp arrow into the air.

All very poetic and we have to remember that Homer *was* a poet. Today, he would be a novelist and we cannot take everything he says literally. For instance, the gold fittings of Pandarus's bow are almost certainly an example of poetic licence. Joining two ibex horns together required great skill, but such a composite bow had the inevitable weakness that it might collapse. Above all, we should note two things in this description. First is that the arrowhead is made of iron, which had become standard long before the Middle Ages and second, the bow is pulled back to the chest, not the ear as in the Hundred Years War. Some experts refer to this as a short bow and the range of the arrow is far less than the English war-bows of the fourteenth century.

The type of bow used in the period covered by this book was made entirely of wood. Composite bows were favoured by the Chinese and Arabs and, despite the crusades from the late eleventh century which saw an exchange of technology among other things, Western Europe generally did not use bows of this type. The English bows of the Hundred Years War were long bows, although several historians dismiss this terminology. It was certainly not used at the time, but it does help us distinguish this weapon from the short bow of the ancient world and the crossbows used throughout the Middle Ages. From bow fragments found in Germany and Switzerland dating from the late Stone Age, we know that some bows were about 70 inches long, over the height of a man at the time, and taller than most bowmen of the Hundred Years War.

The oldest bow found in England (at Meare Heath in Somerset) suggests, according to radiocarbon dating, an age of 2690 BC. Incomplete, it was probably 6 feet long and made of yew, the most flexible and suitable of European timber. It is a flat bow (of the type used by Hollywood for all its medieval epics) which differs from the type generally used throughout this book. By 6000 BC, hazel, elm, oak, lime and ash were all found in Britain, the country much more heavily forested than today. All those woods were used to make bows, probably by the hunters themselves with their experience of what was required. We are a long way from Homer's professional bow makers, and further still from the Chinese workshops of the second century BC, where archaeologists have found caches of composite bows and various arrowheads. The preponderance of yew as the national material for bow making is reflected in still-extant place names: Youghal; Dromanure (yew hill); Mayo (yew field).

Robert Hardy, actor and bow expert, believes that the first effective military use of what today we would recognise as a longbow occurred along the Rhine in AD 354 when the Roman Empire was under pressure from various 'barbarian' tribes. At a clash at Neuss in 388, a chronicler describes the barbarian arrows 'falling as thick as if thrown by arcubalistae'. This was a siege engine, the manufacture of which the Romans excelled at, which fired arrows in volleys like a primitive machine gun. With respect to Hardy, there is nothing to tell us what sort of bows were used at Neuss, nor what specific tactics were employed by bowmen. The Romans were usually masters of any battlefield, but occasionally their professionalism slipped, and by the late fourth century their enemies had got the measure of them.

There is considerable disagreement about the use of the bow in the post-Roman period. The fourth to the ninth centuries used to be called the Dark Ages to symbolise the collapse of Roman civilization in the face of ignorant barbarism. The term has now disappeared in recognition of the sophistication of those newer cultures, but it holds good in that the historical record is relatively sparse. Various Viking sagas refer to the use of the bow in warfare, and the king Harald Bluetooth was said to have been murdered with an arrow up his backside, which, because he was bending over, exited through his mouth. Rather like Homer, we have to take the sagas with various quantities of salt.

References to bows are scattered here and there, often as weapons of murder. In 490, Clovis, king of the Franks, introduced the Salic law to what would become France centuries later. The fine for anyone using poisoned arrows (even if the arrow missed!) was 2,500 dinars, and 54 solidi for cutting off the fingers of a bowman. Traditionally, archers used their index and middle fingers to control the arrow against the bowstring. This explains Henry V's speech to his bowmen on the morning of Agincourt and (supposedly) the origin of the offensive V sign long before Winston Churchill popularized it back to front.

Offrid, the son of Edwin of Northumbria, was killed by an arrow in battle with the Mercians and the Welsh in 633, which is the first reference to Welshman as the progenitors of military archery in Britain. An eighth-century whalebone casket currently in the British Museum clearly shows a bowman defending his horse against attack. None of the assailants has a bow, but the defender has already brought down two men and riddled the shield of a third.

The first full-scale battle in which we hear of bows being used is Maldon, Essex in 991, when a Viking raiding party led by Anlaf attacked the marshes' defenders of Ealdorman Byrhtnoth. 'Bogan, waeron bysige' a contemporary poet writes in Old English ('bows were busy'). In the poem, the Northumbrian Ashferth 'wavered not at the war-play, but, while he might, shot steadily from his sheaf of arrows, striking his shield there or shearing into a man'.

The Exeter Book of the late tenth century is typical of Anglo-Saxon riddles. Number 23 reads:

Wob's my name, if you work it out;
I'm a fair creature fashioned for battle.
When I bend and shoot a deadly shaft
from my stomach, I desire only to send
that poison as far away as possible.
When my Lord, who devised this torment for me,

> releases my limbs I become longer
> and, bent upon slaughter, spit out
> that deadly poison I swallowed before.
> No man's parted easily from the object
> I describe; if he's struck by what flies
> from my stomach, he pays for its poison
> with his strength – speedy atonement for his life.
> I'll serve no master when unstrung, only when
> I'm cunningly notched. Now guess my name.

As riddles go, it's not very gripping. In fact, the clue is in the first word! Even so, it's fascinating. We need not take 'poison' too literally – the fatality of an arrow lay in its iron tip. 'The stomach' is of course the moulded 'belly' of the bow, composed of both sap and heartwood from the tree that gave the weapon its strength and tensile power. References to 'lord' and 'master' – the bowman himself – are borne out by later references in history. By the time of Poitiers (1356) the French had a commander whose title was 'Master of the crossbows'.

In the seventh century, the polymath Aldhelm describes the impact of an archer in battle:

> Just as the warlike bowman … is hemmed in by a dense formation of enemy legions, then, when his bow is tensed by his powerful hands and arms and arrows are drawn from the quiver … the throng, swollen with the arrogance of pride, their shield-wall having been shattered, turn their backs and flee headlong …

The shield wall was *the* defensive tactic of the Saxons and although a single bowman could not 'shatter' a line of overlapping limewood shields, the account gives us an idea of how feared the bowman was.

Maldon aside, evidence for use of the bow in battle is rare before 1066. In that year, the year of Stamford Bridge and Hastings (Senlac) it is almost non-existent. There is only one English archer shown in the Bayeux Tapestry that chronicles William of Normandy's invasion of England. He is shown smaller than the knights behind him, accentuating his lowly status and has no armour or other weapons. Despite the persistence of the legend that King Harold Godwinson was killed with an arrow through his brain (the needlework is confusing at that point) the lack of reference to bowmen indicates that they were not considered important in the battle's outcome. That said, the Tapestry was made by nuns four years after the battle and their knowledge of events came from only one source, Bishop Odo, who fought at Senlac.

Historian Jim Bradbury (*The Medieval Archer*, 1985) has analysed the tactical use of archers on both sides at Hastings. The evidence is conflicting and Bradbury seems bent on re-interpretation to an alarming degree. He plays down the impact of the heavily armoured Norman knights and doubts various near-contemporary accounts. What cannot be ignored is that the English fought exclusively on foot (as they still did in the Hundred Years War) and were completely unused to massed cavalry charges on the field of battle. Neither can the fact that Godwinson's army was exhausted and depleted by casualties. They had fought victoriously at Stamford Bridge near York and marched all the way south in record time to face William. A fresher army might well have won the battle.

Most of the Norman archers on the Tapestry are shown in the borders (which also show mythical beasts and a man exposing himself to a woman!) and the fact that four bowmen are shown together in one scene does not imply the volley fire of the Hundred Years War period. There is only one mounted bowman and he is shown in the rout at the battle's end, not the fighting itself. The Tapestry's evidence of the bows themselves is also contradictory. On one hand, they appear large (the height of a man) which makes them longbows, but on the other, they are being fired from the chest (short bows). The bottom line for bowmen and Hastings at least according to the Tapestry, is that in at least two instances, the arrows are stitched on the wrong side of the bows; they would simply have fallen off.

In the post-Conquest period, evidence grows that the longbow was coming into greater use. In the civil war between Stephen and Matilda in the twelfth century, Stephen was also plagued by the Scots, always using English weakness to extend their penchant for cattle and land stealing. Near Northallerton in August 1138, they came unstuck. King David of Scotland, with an army larger than the English, had allowed his troops to ravage the north; although the usual list of atrocities, slashing the stomachs of pregnant women, hacking priests to death at their altars and bashing babies against walls was the stock-in-trade of Medieval chroniclers, rather like the 'video nasties' of a much later generation: actual *evidence* is distinctly lacking.

The English formation at the Battle of the Standard as it came to be known, was in some ways the blueprint for nearly all the clashes of the Hundred Years War. The bowmen and the billmen were ranged at the front (rather like the artillery in later battles) interspersed with knights on foot who also formed the second division. The third division was composed of cavalry, heavily armoured knights in great helms and mail ready to turn a retreat into a rout.

David's men of Galway led the attack which was, as usual, wild, loud and disorganized. For years before (and indeed after) the Standard, the Scots relied on their ferocity, shouting and ragged appearance to overcome their enemies. It was like this at Neville's Cross. Against them, the English bowmen stood, balanced with legs apart and fired volley after volley into them, some firing flat into the front rank, others high into the air so that those behind felt the impact too. The Scots fell back, as one chronicler, Aelred of Rievaulx wrote, 'like a hedgehog with spines'. Another chronicler, John of Hexham, summed it up – the Scots were 'destroyed by arrows'. The whole thing was over in less than two hours and the English cavalry were not even involved. Military historians argue over the role of bowmen in various engagements before 1337. The Standard was perhaps unique in that it was won almost exclusively by bowmen (as was Crecy in 1346 and, by and large, Poitiers ten years later) but other infantry played their part as (again, Standard is unique) did mounted knights. But the use of archers en masse, as a means of stopping an enemy in his tracks, was the face of warfare in the future. To say, as Jim Bradbury and Tim Newark do, that the bowmen only won battles when they were massed and defending a protected position is rather like saying that the RAF won the Battle of Britain in 1940 because they shot down more Luftwaffe planes than they lost themselves.

What is interesting about the earlier Middle Ages is the emergence of geographical areas which became noted for archery skills. In the English counties, Cheshire was one such focus and in particular, Macclesfield Forest. Today, the area is popular with hikers tramping over the peaks and its tiny villages are still remote and scattered. In the twelfth and thirteenth centuries, the moors were covered in trees, belonging to the Earls of Chester and the foresters there were able to select the finest woods for their bows. The other group famous for their archery were the South Welsh, although their role may have been exaggerated by the prolific accounts of the chronicler Giraldus Cambrensis (Gerald of Wales). He had a Norman name – Geraldi de Barri – and was born at Manorbier Castle in 1147. In 1188, he wrote an account of his travels throughout Wales, still then often at loggerheads with the English Marcher lords such as the de Braose, Despenser and Mortimer families who held the castles the Normans had built to keep the Welsh out.

Cambrensis tells the story of arrows that penetrated the 4-inch-thick timber of the gates of Abergavenny Castle in 1182. This would have required a longbow with a 100lb draw weight. He also describes the effect of such a bow against one of William de Braose's knights. He was:

> wounded by an arrow that penetrated his thigh [encased in mail armour] the part of the saddle known as the alva [nearly half an inch thick] and mortally wounded the horse … The bows

> the Welshmen use are not made of horn or ivory or yew, but of wild elm … they are rough and lumpy, but stout and strong nevertheless, not only to shoot an arrow a long way, but also to inflict very severe wounds at close quarters.

The implications here are that composite bows – horn and ivory – were known about and that yew was the best wood available. Welsh bows were not pretty, but they were pretty deadly!

It is very difficult to be certain of the origins of the longbow. In the Hundred Years War, it is called the war bow, the great bow or simply the bow. The man who fired it was an archer or a bowman, but just as often he was referred to as a forester, a reminder that bows were primarily and historically used for hunting. By the outbreak of hostilities in 1337, the bow was made of a single stave, round, with a central area in a 'D' section shape and tapered at each end. The outer edge (furthest from the bowman) was the sapwood which had the distinctive 'elastic' qualities. The part of the bow nearest the archer was the heartwood. Unlike today, children would be taught to use their right hands for everything, as the left was associated with the devil. So the bowman gripped the bow's 'handle', halfway along its length with his left hand and fired the arrow with his right. The bows of the Hundred Years War were approximately 6ft in height, but some were longer, and shorter examples of 5ft 8in have been found. Such bows were designed to be drawn back to the right ear rather than the chest.

Unfortunately, artistic representations do not give us clear pictures of these bows. We have already discussed the shortcomings of the Bayeux Tapestry. A thirteenth-century painting of the death of St Edmund, allegedly shot to death by Viking archers in 870, clearly shows a longbow (because of its length) but it is equally clearly being fired from the chest. A bad sketch in the margin of a document in the National Archives is of a Welsh bowman of the twelfth century. Again, this is chest-fired, the doodle is appallingly bad and the cloak wrapped around the bowman would make drawing a bow virtually impossible.

A thirteenth-century work from Trinity College, Cambridge shows a surgeon removing a barbed arrowhead from a victim's back. The surgeon is sitting on a chair and his patient is crouched over with his head in the doctor's lap. Forceps are being used to prise out the iron and, astonishingly, there is no sign of blood. There would have been no anaesthetic available as early as this and in reality, the wounded man would be pinned to the table by four others, to keep him as still as possible. With the resultant blood loss and risk of infection, it was most unlikely that he would survive.

In 1298, Simon de Skeffington was murdered by a bowman whose name remains unknown, but the case gives us one of the most detailed examples of bows in the period:

> With an arrow from a bow, the arrow being barbed with an iron arrow-head 3" long and 2" broad and the fletch [flight] of the said arrow was made of ash three quarters of an ell long [about 33 inches] and 1" thick, the said fletch being feathered with peacock feathers and the bow being of yew and the bowstring of hemp, the length of the bow being one ell and a half [about 67 inches] and in gross circumference 6" thick, with a length of bowstring of a fathom and a half [6½ft] and in thickness half an inch and with that arrow gave him a blow on the left side of the breast, 3" from the said breast, descending 2" and the depth 6" so that he immediately died of the blow.

Most historians agree that the 'father' of the longbow was Edward I. After the long and unsatisfactory reign of his father, Henry III, which saw the rise of a popular revolt under Simon de Montfort, Earl of Leicester and led to the creation of the House of Commons, Edward took an iron grip on his country, morphing into the kind of successful warrior king admired at the time and since. Ambitious, a natural soldier and tired of raids into his kingdom by the Welsh and the Scots, he determined to put them both in their place and very nearly succeeded.

It is not usual for former enemies to be so impressed with a leader that they become his fastest friends. The 'barbarian' Batavians became specialists for the Romans in fording dangerous rivers. Polish lancers did sterling work for Napoleon after he had defeated them. A cohort of Mamelukes from Egypt became his personal bodyguard on and off the battlefield. No one was more loyal to the British Raj than the warlike Sikhs of India's North West frontier. So, the Welshmen of Gwent went over to Edward I. Further north, Llewellyn ap Gruffydd, who became the last native Prince of Wales, had allied with de Montfort and his rebellious barons. For Edward, it was payback time.

Gwent provided 800 bowmen in 1277, Macclesfield a further hundred. They were the equivalent of the Rifle Brigade in the Peninsular War (1808–14), chosen men with a skill born of long years of practice at the butts and in the forests. There were glitches along the way. In that year of 1277, four bowmen arrived to fight for the king; one had a bow and twenty-five arrows; one had only two arrows; one had no arrows at all; and the fourth had nothing but a bowstring! This is an example of the Poor Bloody Infantry throughout time – we will look at the kind of men who became bowmen later. The recruits were trained to stand sideways, legs apart to give them balance and to place their arrows in the ground by their feet or stuffed into quivers and belts at their waists. The stronger the man, the more powerful the bow and the faster the rate of fire. It was a self-fulfilling prophecy.

Relative to the slower and clumsier crossbows, popular with Italian mercenaries such as the Genoese and Pisans, longbows and their arrows were cheap to manufacture. Even the best bows cost 1s 6d in the early fourteenth century and poorer ones only a shilling. Any general worth his salt has to factor in the costs of a campaign and the cheapness of bows worked in Edward's favour. Prices from 1300 to 1305 quote two arrows for a farthing (a quarter of a penny), casks for housing arrows were 8d.

It was under Edward that any kind of uniform first appeared for the bowmen. Men who followed their lord under the feudal system wore his livery, that is a coloured 'jack' with a family badge sewn onto it – the maunch (sleeve) of Hastings, the bull of Clarence, the bear and ragged staff of Beauchamp. Others were given coats of green and white and still others carried the red cross of St George on their breasts – the same flag that has been associated for decades with football hooligans on the terraces of Europe, as if the terrifying bowmen of England had come back!

The king ordered 25,000 recruits to join him at Winchester for the Welsh campaign – the best were trained as bowmen, the others as billmen. All played their part, but the higher pay of the archers reflected their value on the battlefield.

The war against Wales was a dazzling success, the chains of castles built around the coast a testament to Edward's brilliance and England's power. Prince Llewellyn was killed at Orewin Bridge in 1282 and when, according to legend, the defeated Welsh demanded a prince who could speak no English, Edward lifted his shield on the still being built ramparts of Caernarvon Castle and on it he carried his newborn son, Edward, a Prince of Wales who spoke no English. The story is almost certainly apocryphal, but it speaks volumes for the colour of the times as well as that of the later antiquarians who invented it.

When it came to Edward I's wars against Scotland, the picture was less rosy. The king was older, more tired and the little boy on the shield at Caernarvon did not impress as his successor. Scotland was altogether tougher than Wales; its geography and climate were bleaker. Perhaps its people were more resilient. But one thing they did not have was bowmen.

The first classic clash of arms at which English archers proved formidable was Falkirk on 21 January 1298. Edward I's campaign to right the wrongs of William Wallace's victory at Stirling Bridge the previous September had achieved little because he could not find the elusive 'guardian of Scotland' who avoided battle against the English at all costs. Scotland was riven with tribal animosities and not everybody was a fan of Wallace. Two Scots earls defected and gave Edward the guardian's position. Wallace had perhaps 10,000 infantry, organized in the field in schiltron formations, everyone armed with long spears. His cavalry of 200 was negligible, as, it proved, were his bowmen.

'I have brought you into the ring,' Wallace told his men, 'now see if you can dance.' The bottom line was that they could not. Edward's knights easily demolished the Scots cavalry, who turned tail and ran. Likewise, Wallace's feeble archers were trampled by the English destriers.

It was now that Edward unleashed his own bowmen. Over 80 per cent of the infantry were Welshmen and a good proportion of his 12,000 were bowmen. The first two divisions of mounted knights made little headway against the schiltrons, but the Scots were now exposed to wave after wave of arrows. The tight Scots formation were a gift to the bowmen. Many of Wallace's men had little or no armour and they fell 'like blossom in an orchard when the fruit has ripened … bodies covered the ground as thickly as snow in winter'. They were mopped up by Edward's cavalry, hacking them down as they ran.

The Scots had never seen such devastation, nor had they witnessed the impact of massed bowmen. The bow itself was not a secret weapon, but in the hands of thousands, it was unbeatable. At Bannockburn, it did not go so well. Robert the Bruce now led the Scots (Wallace had been executed in London in 1305) and had dug pits prior to the battle in 1314 into which the unsuspecting English cavalry charged headlong. The king of England was now Edward II, nothing like the soldier his father was and the men commanding the army itself (Edward was not there) squabbled between themselves about precedence. There would be no repeat of Falkirk and the lesson for the bowmen was that, caught in the open, they were vulnerable to attack. If they could change front to meet enemy charges, all well and good, but at Bannockburn that was not possible.

Under Edward II, the number of archers was increased. For every one man-at-arms there were ten bowmen, with all the technical backup of bow and arrow manufacture that that implies. Likewise, for every hobelar (light horseman) there were two archers. The three together made up a 'lance' which is often how the size of Medieval armies was calculated. The government increased bowmen's wages and for the first time paid for their armour (usually helmets and arm braces). On condition that they signed up for a campaign, criminals in prisons were released and pardoned, 215 in December 1324 alone.

Edward III, of course, was a military throwback to his grandfather and Scottish incursions over the border, involving cattle theft and raids on villages, continued to be a constant irritation. The new king (Edward was crowned at the age of 14) signed a treaty at Northampton with the Scots which guaranteed that no English army would invade Scotland by land. It said nothing about the sea, however, and in 1332 a force of 500 knights and men-at-arms and 1,500 bowmen landed on the Scottish coast and marched on Perth. They met the Earl of Mar with his 10,000 at Dupplin Muir.

Unusually, Edward attacked them in a night raid, which not only lost the Scots a large number of men, but dented their confidence. By dawn, the English were drawn up in a single division with bowmen angled on their flanks. It was a cul-de-sac of death, an obvious trap, but the Scots advanced anyway and the archers released volley after volley from both sides. Men floundering were unable to escape the fusillade and many were suffocated under the press of bodies. The *Lanercost Chronicle* claimed that the piles of dead were the height of a spear. As the Scots fled, the English cavalry routed them. Wary of casualty numbers as we must always be, the estimate is 76 Scottish knights dead, including Mar, and 1,200 men-at-arms. As usual, the billmen were not counted. The English side lost thirty-three knights and, astonishingly, only one bowman. The speed of the arrow attack meant that the Scots could not reach them. The success at Dupplin was repeated at Halidon Hill on 19 July 1333.

The bows used there and for the next century were made of yew, ash and elm, as we have seen. Brazil wood was acceptable too and that came from India via Persia (today's Iran and Iraq) and on to Western

Europe. According to Giraldus Cambrensis, the Welsh used wych elm predominantly. 'As for Brassell, Elme ad Ashe,' wrote Roger Ascham in 1571, 'experience doth prove them to be but mean for bows and, so to conclude, Ewe of all other things is that whereof perfect shooting would have a bow made.' Ascham was the tutor to the young Elizabeth I before she became queen and was writing thirty years after the *Mary Rose* sank in the Solent with its huge bow cargo, but essentially, he was talking about the weapon used by the Goddamns in the fourteenth century.

Ascham had comments to make, too, in the treatise he wrote in 1545, on arrows. Fifteen kinds of wood were used for the shafts, the most common being brazil, hardbeam, oak, ash, blackthorn, beech and birch. Ascham preferred ash for military use because it was heavier than willow and 'gives a good strype' (a hard blow). The heavier the arrow, the greater the penetration (as with the bolts of a crossbow). When Robert Hardy wrote the first edition of his book *Longbow* in 1976, there was only one arrow left in England which was believed to be genuinely Medieval. It was found in the chantry chapel of Henry V in Westminster Abbey and is made of ash. The iron arrowhead is the most common type used, the London Museum's No. 16, although many experts today doubt that it is genuine.

Hardy explains why so few bows and arrows have survived from the Hundred Years War. Bows in particular were very ordinary looking. They could not be decorated like metal weapons, e.g. swords, axes and daggers. A simple curved piece of wood, however deadly in the right hands, is just a curved piece of wood. Today's bows, with their ornate curves and complex sights are works of art, but that cannot be said of the fourteenth-century versions. It was not the Christian custom to bury grave goods for an after-life with the dead, so we have no examples from tombs or burial sites. And bows do not last long. Wood rots and the life of a bow on campaign must have been very short. Once it had cracked or split, it was thrown away as firewood or even rubbish.

The Hundred Years War produced a huge demand for such weapons. Increasingly, supplies of English yew were used up and much of the timber was imported from Spain, which in itself created problems when the Castilians allied with France and the Black Prince went to war against Enrico of Trastamara. We know from the existence of family names like Bowyer, Fletcher and Arrowsmith what large numbers of craftsmen were involved in manufacture. They selected the best woods from local forests or further afield, splitting the logs and allowing them to season for three or four years. The logs were further split to staves, carefully preserving the sapwood nearest to the bark. The bowyer would plane and shape the stave with the 'D' section in the middle and tapering ends. It was important that the middle was kept thick and solid because a bow that bends at the centre will cause the arrow to jump as it is fired. Aboriginal and Native American bows sometimes had this problem.

Most bows had nocks carved into the ends to take the bowstring, but some had nocks made of horn or bone fitted over the wood ends. On campaign, these were probably a liability and would often break off or slip, causing problems to the bowmen in action.

What can we learn about the bow from the *Mary Rose*? In the ship that sank in the Solent (almost certainly from being overcrowded with bowmen!) the bows and arrows were stored in boxes alongside a barrel of tallow candles. This was amidships just to the rear of the mainmast. It is highly likely that the archers themselves, clustered in the castles, fore and aft and on the main deck, were carrying their bows and a supply of arrows at their waists.

The number of such weapons on board is proof of the ongoing importance of English military archery nearly a century after Castillon and after artillery was beginning to dominate the battlefield. Henry VIII, powerfully built and a champion jouster in his own right, did a great deal to continue the tradition. In 1509, 'his grace shotte as strong and as great a length of any of his garde'. Even though the humble bowman was several places below the knight in the social order, squires aspiring to knighthood had to be proficient with the bow too. In the twelfth century, Richard de Clare, the Earl of Pembroke, acquired the nickname 'Strongbow' for his prowess with the weapon. Henry's 'garde' were the newly created Yeomen of the Guard, the Beefeaters. At the high-level 'summit conference' of the Field of the Cloth of Gold in 1520, he hit bull after bull (the white centre of the target) at ranges of over 240 yards. He had already bought 40,000 yew bows from the Doge of Venice (rather ironic bearing in mind the Italian penchant for the crossbow) and had appointed Henry Southworth and Henry Pikeman Surveyors of the Bowmakers and Keepers of the Bows at the Tower of London. All in all, Henry's fleet had 2,940 yew bows at its disposal.

Individual bows were discovered on the *Mary Rose* over several years but they were so badly damaged that it was not possible to decide what kind of nocks they had, wooden or horn. Since 1979, more than 2,000 arrows have been retrieved, along with 138 bows and 12 bracers, leather straps to protect wrists and forearms from the kick of the bowstring. There is nothing more painful than the string ripping back into position against the skin, as any amateur archer will tell you.

According to the Anthony Roll, a fleet inventory from 1546, each ship carried 250 bows, six gross of bowstrings (864 of them) and 400 sheaves of arrows (possibly as many as 4,000). It is likely that these weapons were used to defend the ships as well as for use on land. In two Acts of Parliament, in 1512 and 1541, the enactments of Edward III were repeated. Every man, unless 'decrepid or maimed' was to practise archery and every father had to ensure that his boy of 7 acquired skills with a bow and to use it until he was seventeen. By that time, every man must own his own bow.

And the memories of the Goddamns were long, as were those of their enemies. In 1590, Philip de Commines wrote in his memoirs that, 'the English are the flowers of the archers of the world.' Thirty years earlier, in a report to the Doge, Giovanni Michel wrote: 'owing to the general use made of [bows] by all sorts of persons without distinction of grade, age or profession, that it exceeds all belief … they draw the bow with such force and dexterity … that some are said to pierce corselets and body armour.' And the armour of 1560 was incredibly strong in comparison with the mail and beginnings of plate in the Hundred Years War.

Interestingly, although archery was still clearly important, the wages of the bowmen had barely changed; they still got 2d a day.

There are no examples of leather finger guards for the bowmen of the *Mary Rose*, although leather goods have survived in quantities and we know that other nations used them and had done for centuries. Perhaps the bowmen's skin was tough enough without or perhaps there was an air of snobbery involved in not using them. The boxed arrows were tied in clumps of twenty-four and have proved very difficult for conservators to maintain. The flights have gone and the wood is very fragile. All the arrows excavated were 2ft 6in long with an average diameter of ½in. Stains where flights were attached indicate that the flights were about 6in long. The wood used was poplar (aspen) or willow, which may indicate a meanness on the part of the government to spend too much money. Neither would it have impressed Roger Ascham. Every army in recorded history has always complained about the inferiority of its weaponry, from bows to keyhole bombs. Many of the arrows were stored in circular leather spacers to prevent the flights from being crushed together. Those spacers seem to have been used by bowmen in battle, probably tied to their belts, rather as modern infantry would carry spare ammunition clips for their rifles.

The *Mary Rose* Trust employed experts in a variety of fields to examine the weapons recovered. P.L. Pratt, Professor of Crystal Physics at Imperial College, London, was in charge of testing the bows themselves. Having been immersed in seawater since 1545, it was not possible to test the originals, so exact replicas were made by bowman/carpenter Roy King. In expert hands, these bows could fire arrows to hit targets 275 yards away. John Levy, Professor of Wood Science at Imperial, advised on the timber makeup of the bows, assisted by Doctor B.W. Kooi of Gröningen University. Dr P.H. Blyth contributed to Hardy's revised *Longbow* book on the design of the ship's bows including the efficiency of the arrows' release. Peter Jones considered the devastating effects of arrows hitting armour and men at various ranges.

When the *Mary Rose* was raised, my immediate interest was directed to the men on board, large numbers of whom would have been bowmen, perhaps the great-grandsons of those who had fought at Crecy, Poitiers and Agincourt and using the same weapons. Surprisingly little was made of them because the wreck was also a gravesite and modern sensibilities baulked at unnecessary intrusion. But these skeletons have a story to tell.

On Sunday, 19 July 1545, the *Mary Rose* was making all speed to protect Henry VIII's flagship, the *Grace à Dieu* from a French attack. Its commander, Vice Admiral George Carew, yelled to his uncle Gawaine aboard the *Matthew Gronson* that he had on his own ship 'the sort of knaves whom he could not rule'. This enigmatic phrase has perplexed historians ever since. Did he have a crew on the verge of mutiny? And if so, why? A potential answer emerged in the early 1990s with DNA profiling. Studies of the bodies recovered from the *Mary Rose* found that a high percentage of the sailors were Spanish. Bearing in mind the fearsome reputation of the Castilian fleet during the Hundred Years War and the very real terror of the Armada in 1588, this would make sense. Carew had a communications problem with his men.

Many of the bodies found in the wreck were on the upper decks and castles, meaning that they were armed and at action stations when the ship went down and that it sank very rapidly. Those found below decks were probably the sick and wounded. Writing before a complete study of the bodies had been carried out, underwater archaeologist Margaret Rule focused on two of the bodies, both of them, in all likelihood, bowmen. The bodies were found on the starboard side of the forecastle. Both were in their twenties, one 5ft 7in tall, the other over 6ft. Their bows would have been as tall as they were. The older man, at 25, suffered from a dietary deficiency which manifested itself in bad teeth and a slight deformity of his lower left leg. Intriguingly, his spine and arm bones were twisted and thickened implying constant use of the bow in practice at the butts. The taller man had concretions around the spine which probably came from a quiver of arrows at his belt.

As this book went to press, an article appeared on the bones of many of the *Mary Rose* crew, claiming that their right clavicles were larger than those of most sixteenth-century bodies. The conclusion by one archaeologist was that this was caused by the overuse of the right arm in the process of working the ship; clearly, hauling sail involves the use of both arms so this is a spurious theory. Much more obviously, the large clavicles belonged to archers, whose arms were overdeveloped by extensive use of the bow.

Relatively little work has been done on battlefield remains from the Medieval period. The bloodiest battle of the Wars of the Roses, Towton in 1461, still has a number of mass graves containing the bodies of bowmen, but the site is on private land and no comprehensive excavation has yet been carried out. From the bone development of the two *Mary Rose* bodies, it is likely that bowmen could be identified from billmen or men-at-arms. In the case of the 600 or so English dead at Agincourt, Henry V ordered that their bodies should be burned so we have no evidence of any kind from that source.

Chapter 2

'The Hurling Time'

'Take a fat cat, flay it well and draw out the guts. Take the grease of a hedgehog, the fat of a bear, resins, fenugreek, sage, honeysuckle gum and virgin wax and crumble this and stuff the cat with it. Then roast the cat and gather the dripping and anoint the sufferer with it.'

Thank God for fourteenth-century medicine! This complex and unlikely (not to say vicious) remedy, collected by an early twentieth-century medical historian, G.C. Coulton, was for quinsy. It was not a remedy for the Black Death because there was no cure for the Black Death. And the Black Death came to Bristol in 1348.

Almost exactly two years earlier, Edward III had won the astonishing victory over the French at Crecy and England was riding high in terms of its successes in what historians much later called the Hundred Years War. No one was ready for the apocalyptic disease that would wipe out between a third and a half of Europe's population over four years. Historians William Naphy and Andrew Spicer (in *The Black Death*, 2000) claim that there was a precedent for this. The plague of Justinian in 541 was almost certainly the same disease and it recurred cyclically over a 200-year period. This ignores the fact that man's experience of life – and death – is confined to their own generation and that of their parents. The only people who *may* have had knowledge of Justinian's outbreak were academics and clerics in the scattered universities and abbeys of the Middle Ages. And their knowledge was irrelevant, in that there was no cure for the disease in Justinian's time either. At first, the people of Bristol were on their own and were only joined later by the terrifying speed of the plague's spread and its horrifying death toll.

Bristol was an important port under the Normans in the late eleventh century and as such was particularly vulnerable to disease brought in by ships from the east. Originally named Briegstowe (the place of the bridge) by the Saxons, its twelfth-century castle had housed two kings who, over time, had fallen foul of their barons, Stephen in the twelfth century and Edward II in the fourteenth. It was already supplying warships and troops for Edward III's war (several of them would have fought at Sluys eight years before the plague came) to the extent that in 1373, the king granted the town a charter with the status of a county.

There is no record of the name of the ship that brought the plague, nor specifically where it came from. It may have come from France and no doubt led to rumours (as wild and numerous in the fourteenth century as today) that the French had sent it deliberately. The notion of germ warfare is a twentieth-century one, but the idea that disasters of all kinds could be inflicted on a nation by its enemies was far older. It could have come from Genoa or Venice, the leading maritime city ports of the Mediterranean. Beyond that, it was almost impossible to guess. Merchants themselves knew the trade routes that ran south to Libya, Egypt and the Holy Land; north to the myriad German states, Poland and Muscovy (today's Russia). The very few more widely travelled would have known that some goods came in ships from Cathay (China) although the travels of the Venetian merchant Marco Polo had only been written forty years earlier and were not widely available. The totally spurious travels of the English knight John Mandeville (actually a Frenchman) lay twenty years in the future.

Wherever the plague had come from, Bristolians were soon aware where it had arrived. The crew of the cog that drifted into Bristol harbour were dying. Medieval historians today cannot agree on the *exact* type of bacterium but the most likely is *Yersinia pestis*, named after the scientist Alexander Yersin, who first identified the microbe in Hong Kong in 1894. Whole books, not to mention erudite medical papers, have been published on this. Was it bubonic plaque that is carried by *Ceratophyllus fasciatus*, the rat flea? If so, it resulted in fever, black painful swellings in the armpits and groin (buboes, hence bubonic) and death. It *was* possible to survive, but the rate was very low. Was it pneumonic, an even more deadly strain because it was transmitted orally by breathing over another person? Today, the much-maligned black rat (*Rattus rattus*) associated with spreading the disease is often given the benefit of the doubt; the larger brown rat (*Rattus norvegicus*) now in the frame. Still other medical men believe that the disease that came to Bristol was not plague at all, but the cattle disease anthrax, in that various descriptions of the symptoms in the 1340s do not fit modern medicine perfectly. We know, of course, that bacteria have the ability to adapt and develop, so differing symptoms should not surprise us at all.

The actual cause of the plague, fascinating though the subject is, is irrelevant as far as we are concerned. All men at the time knew was that the cog's crew were ill. Some of them were probably lying dead in their hammocks below decks, their pale skin blotchy with buboes. Others, no doubt praying fervently, would have tried to find salvation of some kind. These men might have been from Bristol, but if they were not, they would have no idea how to find a doctor. Such men, apothecaries, were few in number and expensive. They had no more idea how to cure the disease than the cat-killer quoted at the beginning of this chapter. There was a surer way to find a solution – turn to God. Wherever the crew had come from, if they were Western Europeans, they shared a common religion with Englishmen. They were all Catholics and the Mass was spoken in the universal language of the Catholic Church – Latin.

And so, the terrible creeping infection spread, out from the docks of Bristol, along the winding cobbled streets via the taverns and the brothels, perhaps to St John's Church at the top of the climb later called Christmas Steps. There, perhaps, a well-meaning, terrified and uncomprehending priest, with shaved head and rosary, would offer what he could, culminating in the last rites.

The pestilence, as the disease was known at the time, took a terrible toll in England. There was no official census until 1801 so any populations statistic can be no more than informed guesswork. A probable figure is around 5 million in England in 1300, forty years before the Hundred Years War broke out and nearly fifty years before the plague hit. A century later, it was half that. The difference – and there has never been so great a difference – was due almost exclusively to the plague.

Britain was a country we would barely recognize today. The great arteries of the motorways did not exist until the 1960s – major, tarmacked roads that preceded them were essentially a feature of the very late nineteenth century. Before that, the cities, towns and scattered villages that housed the human population were linked by paths and 'highways' that sometimes dated from pre-Roman times. The cities were identifiable because they had cathedrals run by bishops – seventeen of them in the fourteenth century. Although in many ways the Church dominated, the city was the centre of trade and the craft guilds, trained men (rarely women) who had served their apprenticeships and now worked as masters, elbowing out competition in a way the nineteenth-century trade unions tried to do. They were crowded, unhygienic places, with no awareness of the link between disease and dirt. The first Act of Parliament that we could equate with a hygiene act was not passed until the reign of Richard II in 1388, during what was a lull in the Hundred Years War. It was to the cities and towns that plague-carrying carts travelled, carrying fleas, rats and mortality in their freight. In the year that Edward III died (1377), London had an estimated population of 40,000, making it easily the largest city in the country. York came next, with 12,000 and Bristol, where the plague landed, 10,600. At the bottom of the league, in terms of numbers, was Winchester, with 2,300. All these centres could be reached by water, along the extensive river network, so that the plague came waterborne as well as by land.

Villages and hamlets housed a handful of families, almost all bound to the land by virtue of their work and the feudal system (see below) brought over by the Normans after 1066. The whole year for those settlements was geared to the harvest – a failed crop meant the very real risk of starvation. There was no welfare state, no health service and nothing to act as a safety net for a people essentially living by subsistence. Such a population was particularly vulnerable to an outbreak of the pestilence.

The chronicler Jean Froissart, from whom we shall hear again, assumed that 'a third of all the people in the world' died from the plague. He had no accurate way of knowing that the pandemic hit the Islamic world too, from what today is Iran and Iraq to southern Spain (then called Al-Andalus) but the horrific figure was the same there too. Because of the nature of the disease and the calling of those expected to cope with it, the plague did not strike uniformly. It was no respecter of rank, age or sex. The cleric William Langland wrote *The Vision of Piers Plowman*, probably in the 1370s (the translation below by Siegfried Wenzel) –

> So Nature killed many through corruptions,
> Death came driving after her and dashed all to dust.
> Kings and knights, emperors and popes;
> He left no man standing, whether learned or ignorant …
> For God is deaf nowadays and will not hear us.
> And for our guilt he grinds good men to dust.

In August 1348, as the plague reached Bristol, 15-year-old Princess Joan, the daughter of Edward III, sailed into Bordeaux harbour in France, in the fiefdom of Gascony then owned by the English. She was on her way to Spain to marry Pedro, the *infante* (heir to the throne) of Castile. There were four ships with the princess's entourage, fluttering in the summer sunshine with the brilliant heraldry of Edward's arms, quartered for England and France. Lord Robert Bourchier accompanied the girl. Her father was too busy with the war, and her mother the queen, Philippa of Hainault, never left England except to visit her family in the Low Countries. With the princess too were 100 bowmen, many of them veterans of Crecy, whose attendance was necessary so near to hostile France and whose presence, to anybody in the know, meant that no one would tangle with them.

The princess's party, unaware of the situation in Bristol, were horrified to see the corpses lying piled for mass burial on the docks at Bordeaux and were sickened by the smell. The visitors swept past to the castle, where at least they did not have to witness the horrors of the quayside. Robert Bourchier died of the plague on 20 August, his body blackened with buboes. On 2 September, Princess Joan followed him. Edward III's plans for an Anglo-Spanish alliance to hem in the French fell apart at a stroke, apart from the human tragedy of losing a daughter.

Bourchier's body was brought back to England for burial, bringing with it the bacillus that had killed him. On 25 October (St Crispin's Day, later a seminal date in the Hundred Years War), Edward sent the bishop of Carlisle to bring the princess's body back too, but it was too late. The mayor of Bordeaux, Raymond de Birquale, had ordered the dock area to be burned to destroy the plague. Had this been done earlier and had it been controlled, this *could* have been effective, but it was too late and the fire roared out of control. Joan's body was cremated along with so many others, among them, no doubt, a number of her anonymous archer escort.

The following year, another high-profile Englishman, William of Ockham, died of the plague too, but in Munich, where the disease was raging as fiercely as in England. Ockham was perhaps the most influential of late Medieval philosophers, but his controversial views on the Church and poverty did not detract from the fact that he was a member of the Franciscan order, many of whose brethren were in the front line against the plague. As we have seen, the Church had no practical answers. The plague was seen as God's displeasure with man's wickedness and the only answer was fervent prayer and attempting to lead a pure life. In what was a predominantly superstitious age, Church ceremony and the last rites were everything. So plague victims without number were dragged to churches or parish priests, friars, monks and nuns were expected to spend time comforting the dying and giving absolution to the already dead. Accordingly, the death rate among the clergy rocketed. Half the monks at Peterborough Abbey died by 1350. Of fifteen nuns at Henwood in Warwickshire, only three survived. In the bishoprics of York and Lincoln, 40 per cent of the clergy perished. In Herefordshire, the figure was 50 per cent.

Whole villages, in extreme cases, disappeared. Today there are hundreds of uninhabited Medieval settlements scattered over the country, where there were no longer peasants to till the fields or milk the cows. The churches stood empty and there was no one left even to toll the funeral bell. At Ashwell church in Hertfordshire is a unique and harrowing inscription, crudely carved onto a wall in the nave – *Expente miseranda ferox, violenta Superest plebs pessima testis*, MCCCL. (Miserable, wild, violent, the worst people alone survive to bear witness 1350.) The plague returned in 1361, 1368–9 and 1390–1. Fifteen per cent of the population died in the early 1360s; 10 per cent more by the decade's end. This drop in fatality was not obvious at the time as a shell-shocked population tried to come to terms with what was happening.

In one respect, we have the edge over our recent ancestors. The Industrial Revolution, unplanned and at first unregulated, led to the outbreak of diseases like cholera, smallpox and tuberculosis. Society learned to live with all that and eventually to find cures. A vaccine was found too for COVID-19, but in experiencing it, our generation can *almost* grasp the dread of the pestilence of the fourteenth century. The figures of course do not compare. In the UK, the excess deaths from COVID and related complications reached an estimated 170,000 (0.26 per cent of the population). The elderly, infirm and vulnerable anyway with other ailments, were deemed most at risk and the rise in infection in care homes was inordinately high (compare this with priories and abbeys in the fourteenth century). Western Europe in the twenty-first century had relatively excellent healthcare, with scientifically trained doctors and nurses. Their opposite numbers in the fourteenth century believed that the disease was caused by planetary influences if not over-influenced by the over-arching fear of God's wrath. What was totally different was the solution. COVID was combatted by workable science (even if Donald Trump, then president of the United States, went all fourteenth-century by recommending drinking bleach!). The British vaccine was rolled out first and was arguably the most efficient, Oxford University scientists doing immeasurably better than their fourteenth-century counterparts, one of whom, John Gaddesden, recommending that women who were overtly sexual should travel and exercise frequently. Though pointless, this was at least less extreme than the regimen that opened this chapter.

What was also different was who was held to be responsible for finding a solution. With the creation of the National Health Service in 1948, everybody assumes that, ultimately, it is the government that finds cures, solves problems and generally bales us all out. This has only been the case in general terms since the 1870s when prime minister Benjamin Disraeli began to 'gas, water' and tax Britain in what were the beginnings of the nanny state; the actual Welfare State followed shortly afterwards. In the fourteenth century, each man was responsible for his own destiny. There were laws, proscribed by parliament, and there was royal policy, but nobody expected the kings of the Hundred Years War period, Edward III, Richard II, Henry IV, Henry V and Henry VI to provide solutions to the plague.

So it was the government of Boris Johnson that cracked down on COVID, shutting schools and shops, emptying the streets, using the police to catch curfew-breakers and creating a lockdown which would have been unthinkable and unworkable in the fourteenth century. That is not to say that local governments sat idly by. The republic of Venice, supposedly impregnable across its scattered islands and protected by the sea, nevertheless had an astonishingly high death rate.

Guards patrolling the walls of Florence fixed their crossbows at visitors venturing too near the town. Within some towns, infected houses and whole streets were quarantined (from the Italian word *quarantine*, forty days, that had Biblical echoes), lockdowns far more draconian than anything Boris Johnson dreamed up.

We shall look at the far-reaching results of the plague later and we shall find that out of the panic and chaos, some good, astonishingly, did come. But *at the time*, none of this was apparent and it looked like the end of days. In parts of France and Germany, but not England, terrified penitents called Flagellants roamed the countryside, chanting, singing and whipping themselves and each other to atone to God for man's sinfulness. What they were actually doing, of course, was spreading the plague still further, carrying it from town to town and village to village. Various town corporations and lords of manors gave instructions to their heavies to shoot them.

Because of the relatively limited movement of most people in the fourteenth century and the fact that news spread far more slowly than today, most Englishmen were not remotely aware that what they were going through was happening everywhere. In 1348, John VI Cantacuzenos, the emperor of Byzantium, wrote, 'The plague attacked almost all the sea-coasts of the world and killed most of the people. For it swept not only through Pontus, Thrace and Macedonia, but even Greece, Italy … Egypt, Libya, Judea, Syria …' The Muslim world was far more stoic than Christendom, believing as it did in *kismet* (fate) and Allah's will. That did not make the outbreak any less violent or the fatalities fewer, however. Ibn al-Furat was in Cairo in 1347 – 'The deaths had increased until it had emptied the streets … I only saw lamps burning in a few of the shops … the horror of this is too long to recount …'

An anonymous Flemish chronicler described, in January 1348, a scene that cannot have been unlike Bristol months later:

> Three galleys put in at Genoa driven by a fierce wind from the east, horribly infected … When the inhabitants … learnt

> this and saw her suddenly … they infected other people, they were driven forth from that port by burning arrows and divers engines of war, for no man dared touch them.

Giovanni Boccaccio, writing *The Decameron* in 1349–51, has a series of horror stories about survivors of the plague escaping from Florence. He hedges his bets as to the outbreak's cause – 'whether disseminated by the celestial bodies or sent upon us mortals by God in His just wrath' – he cannot say. Bodies piled up in Florence, whole families thrown onto over-laden carts. There was a total breakdown of law and order and the norms of behaviour. Boccaccio believed that over 100,000 people died in the city between March and July. While this is clearly an exaggeration, it illustrates the sense of doom and hopelessness that haunted all Europe. Francesco Petrarch, along with Boccaccio, one of the greatest writers of the later Middle Ages, lived in Parma. Here and in nearby Reggio, an estimated 40,000 died. In Siena, Agnolo di Terra wrote despairingly in 1348, 'And no bells tolled and nobody wept no matter what his loss, because almost everyone expected death … and people said and believed "This is the end of the world".'

Most poignant was the account of the Florentine Giovanni Villani. In 1363, when the second outbreak struck, he wrote, 'In the midst of this pestilence there came to an end …' and he stopped in mid-sentence because it was here that the plague killed him.

In April 1348, a Bruges resident told friends that he had seen the effects of the disease in Avignon, the home of the schismatic Pope Clement VII. Seven thousand houses were locked and boarded up and, in a field near Our Lady of Marisoles, 11,000 bodies were placed in a mass grave. The existing cemeteries in the town were already full. There was an outbreak of panic here, with thousands arriving daily, the Flagellants. They were accused of bringing with them bags of dust, a poison which they threw into wells. In many towns and cities, especially in the German states, the Jews were routinely blamed for the pestilence. There were no Jews in England after the 1290s when Edward I expelled them and in European cities they lived in ghettoes. The leading rabbis were tortured in Chinon, France, and claimed that the disease was part of an orchestrated plot to overthrow Christianity. Those who believe that anti-Semitism was a peculiarity of the Nazi state would do well to read these appalling fourteenth-century examples. In Avignon, the relatives of the sick threw them bread and left. Priests could not be found to carry out the last rites and rough men from the mountains near Provence were paid a small fortune to bury the dead.

One of the rare instances of Flagellants in England took place at Michaelmas (September) 1349 when about 600 of them arrived from the Low Countries. Stripped to the waist, they congregated at Paul's Cross outside the cathedral's doors wearing caps marked with a red cross. Each man carried a three-tailed whip and they processed in single file around the cathedral cloisters. The sudden arrival of these people caused terror and they were accused of robbery and murder. It was a mark of how desperate societies had become by 1349 that Ralph of Shrewsbury, Bishop of Bath and Wells, lamented that so few priests were available that laymen administered the last rites and even (he almost wrote it in a whisper) women!

Friar John Clyn of the Friars Minor in Kilkenny, Ireland, wrote, shortly before he died, that he hoped his writing would not 'perish with the scribe and the work fall with the labourer, I add parchment to continue it, if by chance anyone may be left in the future and any child of Adam may escape the pestilence and continue the work thus commenced.'

Of course, the children of Adam did survive and there was a future, however grim the picture must have seemed at the time. In 1978, author Barbara Tuchman wrote: 'The end of the age of submission came in sight. To that extent, the Black Death [a much later term for the pestilence] may have been the unrecognized beginnings of modern society.'

Thirty-three years after the plague ships sailed into Bristol, the peasants of Kent and Essex went on the rampage. Risings like this were not new, neither were they unusual, but the sheer size of the peasant army rattled government and society in general. For the first time, the people had an ideology and a cause.

'When Adam delved and Eve span, Who was then the gentleman?' ran the sermon of John Ball, the rabble-rousing excommunicated priest who was the philosopher of what some have seen as a crypto-Socialist working-class movement 600 years before Karl Marx wrote his *Communist Manifesto.* In some ways, the Revolt of the summer of 1381 was in direct response to the pestilence. The abnormally high death rate had robbed the land of its usual workers, with crops unharvested and livestock abandoned. Those who survived filled the gaps where possible but it was now, suddenly, a seller's market and the peasants demanded ever higher wages because they knew that the landowners needed their services. The feudal system of the Normans, whereby a villein worked for his Lord and received land to till in exchange, was breaking down anyway and a cash economy – 'bastard feudalism' – was starting to replace it.

Appalled by the avarice, as they saw it, of the people, Edward III's government passed the Statute of Labourers in 1351, in an attempt to put the clock back to the pre-plague situation, 'First, that carters, ploughmen, drivers of the plough, shepherds, swineherds, draymen ad all other servants, shall take the liveries and wages accustomed in the twentieth year [of Edward's reign, i.e. 1347] or four years before.'

In modern terms, the free market economy was over. There was nothing approaching democracy in fourteenth-century England. When the legal documents talked of the Commons, in a parliamentary sense, they meant the burgesses and knights of the shire as opposed to the lords who had always advised the king. No one had the vote in the modern sense of the word and actual power lay in the hands of a tiny minority.

The other factor that led to the Peasants' Revolt was the war itself. As we shall see in later chapters, Edward III had spent a small fortune on pressing his claim to French lands and the finances for all military expeditions came then, as now, from taxation. There had been two tax increases in the early years of the new boy king Richard II and the third – the Poll Tax – was introduced in November 1380. The purpose of the tax was, in part, 'the safety of the realm and … the keeping of the sea' and everybody, male and female, over the age of 15, was liable for a charge of three groats (1s at the time). Genuine beggars paid nothing.

In the fourteenth century, the collection of taxes had to be done by hand and face to face. Mayors, bailiffs and constables knew who was eligible for payment in their areas and made house-to-house demands or rounded up people on the village green. Not for nothing were tax collectors seen as 'the baddies' in countless stories in the Old and New Testaments; they routinely rooked people and raked off their share, passing on only a fraction to central government. Some went further, taking heavies with them to browbeat awkward locals, molesting wives and daughters. On the other hand, a shady tax payer could easily bribe a collector and in that way, the 1381 tax was short by £18,000. This was apparent by March, collectors riding into towns, hammering on doors, demanding payment. The folk memory of William I's survey of 1086–7 may have kicked in. This was called the Domesday Book because it appeared to ignorant, illiterate people that the day of God's judgement was at hand. Not only had he sent the plague but here he was, in the livery of the king's men, demanding money with menaces.

Letters began to circulate in the villages and towns of the south-east. Those who could not read (the vast majority) had them read out, in whispers and after dark. They were signed John Sheep, Jack Straw, Jack Carter, John Nameless and Jack Trueman. Some of the men who read those subversive tracts would have been the bowmen who had won the king's victories at Crecy, Poitiers and Najera. They had heard of the Jacquerie in France and may even have seen them looting and pillaging at first hand. Their leader was 'Jacques Bonhomme' (Goodman John) and there were any number of Jacks ready to lead them in England. Jack Trueman's letter went beyond the gripes of a man who thought he was being over-taxed – 'Falseness and guile have reigned too long.

Truth has been set under a lock and falseness reigns in every flock … Sin flares as wild flood … God gives redress, for now is time.'

This was the rhetoric of John Ball. The chronicler Froissart records him preaching in churchyards because he was not allowed to preach from the pulpit. 'My good people, things can't go well in England … until all property is in common and there are neither villeins nor gentlemen but one united people … We are all descended from the same father and mother, Adam and Eve.'

Rebel he may have been, revolutionary even, but Ball, like virtually every other peasant, did not blame the king for the taxes or the country's other woes. Even when large and dangerous numbers of rebels were camped at Blackheath overlooking London, he told his followers, 'Let us go to the king. He is young and we will show him our miserable slavery. We will tell him it must be changed or else we will provide the remedy ourselves.' To Froissart – and most literate contemporaries – John Ball was mad; today, of course, he would be extraordinarily run of the mill.

When the Revolt erupted at the end of May, Ball was in gaol in Maidstone, put there by one of the arch-villains of the time from the peasants' point of view, Simon Sudbury, the Archbishop of Canterbury. In the minority of the king (Richard was only 14 when he was crowned), men like Sudbury held huge influence over all aspects of government and in this he was ably supported by the most hated man in England, the king's uncle, John of Gaunt. His opulent palace of the Savoy, along the Strand of the Thames' north shore, would become *the* target of the mob in the weeks ahead.

The actual violence first broke out at Brentwood in Essex, a little village a day's ride north-east of London. It was 30 May and Thomas Bampton had come to collect the taxes due. The people of Fobbing, one of the outlying villages on the Essex marshes, refused to pay a penny more than they had already. A scuffle broke out involving two thugs Brampton had brought with him and the tax collector ran for it, his attackers, more terrified than buoyed by what they had done, hiding out in local woods until hunger forced them out. The mood in Essex grew ugly, the men and even some women from the scattered villages joining the rabble army that was growing. Whether any of these men were the king's bowmen is not known, but every peasant in the Middle Ages carried a knife and knew how to use it. They also had access to an arsenal of farming tools that could easily become weapons – billhooks, scythes, sickles, hammers and awls. On the road, they scared the living daylights out of people of property.

The government sent Sir Robert Belknap, Chief Justice of the King's Bench, to open a court at Brentwood and punish the wrongdoers. He barely had time to empanel a jury before an armed mob crashed into the court, dragged Belknap from his dais and made him swear that he would never hold court again. Three of his clerks were decapitated, their heads impaled on poles carried by the mob. As to the jurymen, they died too and their homes were burned to the ground. The contemporary *Anonimalle Chronicle* says, 'It was their purpose to slay all lawyers and all jurors and all servants of the King …' As with any rebellion, some of the motivation was probably personal, an act of revenge for wrongs real or imagined, but never before had this level of motivation and solidarity been seen in England. Like the pestilence, it seemed at once unprecedented, terrifying and unstoppable.

The response from central government was feeble, probably because no one could believe what was happening. The king himself, although he would show enormous courage in the weeks ahead, was completely out of his depth. Sudbury and Sir Robert Hales, the Lord Treasurer, effectively ran the country, along with the Earls of Warwick and Oxford and the Percys, among whom was the Earl of Derby. Others, like Thomas, Earl of Buckingham, were in Plymouth organizing yet another military campaign in France. John of Gaunt, himself fully absorbed in trying to make himself king of Spain, was in the north. None of the great peers was in London and London quickly became a hotbed of clandestine revolt.

About the only man capable of withstanding a peasant march on London was Sir Robert Knollys with a retinue of loyal men-at-arms and bowmen. But the rumour mill told him that he was more needed to defend London than to make the day's march to Brentwood. Likewise, the three most powerful men in the corporation of London, the merchant and ex-mayor William Walworth, the wool-millionaire and current mayor Nicholas Brembre and yet another ex-mayor, John Philpott, had no jurisdiction in Essex.

Meanwhile, the mob was growing on the road, hundreds turning into thousands. The 'men of Kent were up in the Weald' on 4 June and assembled at Dartford. Mindful of the risk of news spreading to France and the likelihood of a French raid on the coast, the peasants of coastal villages were told to stay put and not join in the Revolt. This was clearly the decision of some sort of central leadership and it cannot have come from Ball, still in prison as he was.

The peasants' first target was Rochester Castle, a huge fortress on the Medway whose keep is a formidable sight, even today. A rag-tag army of riff-raff, carrying bows and billhooks could not possibly take it – could they? In half a day, Sir John Newton, commanding the garrison, surrendered and the castle was in peasant hands, its dungeons emptied, its food supply and valuables distributed among the looters. The next day, they marched on Maidstone and released John Ball. Their leader was by this time Wat Tyler; as historian Maurice Collins says, 'In exactly six days' time, he was master of England.'

The fact that Tyler was elected leader implies that he had some sort of military training and experience. According to Froissart, he had fought in France under Richard Lyons and he may have taken to highway robbery on his return (which, as we shall see, is what many ex-soldiers did in France). He was also a mob orator – 'the idol of the populace' according to the contemporary *Chronicon Angliae.*

Over the following days, manor houses were torched. Servants were given the choice of joining the rebels or dying. Any legal papers – probably *any* papers – were burned. Prisoners were released, even cattle forced from their pens to roam at will. Pilgrims on the road to Canterbury were stopped and forced to take an oath upholding 'King

Richard and the Commons of England'. The mob forced its way into the cathedral during Mass, looking for the hated Archbishop. But Sudbury was hiding in London and the monks were left unmolested. Several of the rebels even prayed at the shrine of a previous murdered archbishop, Thomas Becket, before they resumed their march on the capital.

Terrified chroniclers estimated their numbers at 60,000 which has to be an exaggeration, but certainly no one had seen numbers like it. 'They hastened like mad dogs through Kent' wrote John Malverne, and the poet John Gower (a keen archer, by the way) wrote of them as lunatic clowns – 'Says Willie "I'll back you whatever the crime." Grig steals while Dawey shouts. Lorkin is happy to be right in the swim. Hudd strikes, Jubb smashes, Cobb threatens, Jack snatches. Hudd boasts himself better than any lord. Ball prophesies as if possessed by a devil.' How many of these fictionalized characters once drew a bow for England?

By 12 June, the rebels were camped in a ramshackle settlement on Blackheath, open common land to the south-east of London with a clear view of the walled city with its cluster of church spires and its formidable castle, the Tower. Messengers were sent to parlay with them, but Tyler was in no mood for small talk. His demands, reasonable to him and his people, were ludicrous in terms of the fourteenth-century power base. He wanted an end to serfdom, although there may have been more to it. So far, there had been no serious attempt to stop the rebels who must have known by now that the bulk of the country's fighting men were away in France. That was the day that Sudbury resigned the chancellorship – all too little, all too late.

There was news that rebellion was spreading, from the prosperous wool country of East Anglia and the scattered settlements, yet to be truly industrialized, of the Midlands and the North. Trying not to panic, William Walworth, the Lord Mayor, closed the drawbridge that stood on London Bridge (the only one over the Thames then) and doubled the guard on all the city's gates. The Tower itself had primitive cannon and 600 men-at-arms, but they were for the protection of the king, not to safeguard London. And nobody knew how many Londoners secretly sided with the rebels. The capital had always been restless – everybody had their gripes.

Southwark, south of the river, was attacked the next day. The Marshalsea prison was broken open and its prisoners released. The prostitutes known as the Bishop of Winchester's geese (he owned much of the land in the area) were only too happy to throw in their lot with the rebels. Archbishop Sudbury's Lambeth Palace was burned to the ground and his fabulous library destroyed. This was mindless anarchy with illiterate peasants targeting literature and the literati – any clerk caught in the streets was likely to be lynched. One of Wat Tyler's demands when he met the king a couple of days later, was that 'masters of grammar schools … would never again teach grammar to children' according to the chronicler Thomas Walsingham in *Historia Brevis* (1381).

The idea was for Tyler to meet Richard at Greenwich along the river but, according to Froissart, the mob were so unruly – 'like men without power to reason or sense to behave' – that this was considered too dangerous and the royal barge swung back the way it had come. Tyler wrote to the king with a hit list of men whose heads he wanted. Sudbury and John of Gaunt were the first.

Historians are divided over whether Tyler was insane or not. We have seen many such rabble-rousing insurgents over the centuries, men with no experience of *realpolitik* who are all defeated when the going gets too rough. The point, in the context of this chapter, is that there had never been anything like the Peasants' Revolt and it fed into the madness of the time. John Ball's final oration to his 'troops' at Blackheath was laughable in its naivete – the barons must be killed, the lawyers, anyone who opposed the will of the people. With equality achieved, all would be well. Such was the irony of the situation, that the peasants intended to make Ball Archbishop of Canterbury, thereby continuing the hierarchical status quo against which they were rebelling!

By midday on Thursday, 13 June, Alderman Walter Sybyle, in whose ward the Bridge lay, opened the drawbridge and let the rabble in. Many Londoners were pleased to welcome them and the behaviour of the rebels could have been worse – indeed, would have been, had London resisted. The principal targets were John of Gaunt and Robert Hales, who had proposed the hated Poll Tax. Accordingly, the Savoy and the headquarters of the Knights Hospitallers in Clerkenwell were destined to be destroyed – the respective leaders owned them. The Savoy, regarded as the finest house in England, was burned down, but its sumptuous contents – furniture, tapestries, books and silver plate – were destroyed rather than looted. Tyler was trying to pretend that his cause had nothing to do with theft. The Temple (today the Law Courts) was destroyed too, as was the Priory of St John in Clerkenwell. How much of this destruction and the looting that followed later was directed at the Church is difficult to say. It was here that large numbers of Flemings living in the City were found and butchered. Foreigners were generally held to blame for a country's ills. The usual target (as in the plague aftermath) was the Jews, but of course they were virtually non-existent in England. The Lombard bankers, who had financed Edward III's war against France, were targeted too. There is no record of any stand being made by Londoners themselves. Newgate and the Fleet prisons had been 'liberated' adding to the chaos in the streets; the criminal classes had no cause to fight for except their own greed and rapaciousness.

The rebels now made for the Tower itself and this immediately raises the question – how many professional soldiers did Tyler have at his command? Artistic depictions from the time and slightly later show the peasants as well-armed as the king's retinue, which is extremely unlikely. They are also drawn up in divisions or 'battles' as if ready for action. No doubt weapons and some armour would have been stolen along the way and any bowmen or billmen who had fought in France would have the rudiments of battlefield formations in their heads. Laying siege to a castle as strong as the Tower was a different matter. The peasants had no cannon and a headlong attack on foot against walls 30ft high and (in places) 20ft thick would achieve nothing.

That night, there were fires everywhere – the Savoy, St John's and the Temple, roaring into the night. The Tower was encircled by the peasants who had pitched camp along the Embankment and on Tower Hill. A war council was held in the Tower, with Sir Robert Knollys, Bertucat d'Albret, a Gascon *condottiere* (mercenary) who had fought under the Black Prince at Najera, and the Earl of Salisbury, a veteran of Poitiers, decided that their little garrison was too small to launch a counter-attack. The final solution was for the king to parlay with the peasants a distance from the Tower, to allow Sudbury and Hales to slip away.

The appointed place was Mile End, far enough away to give the Tower a breathing space. It was largely open country then (even in the nineteenth century it was known as the Mile End Waste) and there would be plenty of room for the estimated 100,000 rebels to hear the young king's promises. We have no idea of the size of the king's entourage, but if he had his bowmen with him, they were unarmed. Crossing the open fields near the White Chapel, the Holland brothers, probably jostled by the crowd, pulled their horses out of the cavalcade and galloped away. There is no report of anyone firing arrows at them, which would have been logical had there been competent bowmen with the peasants. At Mile End itself, the mob was respectful. They carried banners of St George and knelt before the king, whose nerve that day was extraordinary.

Richard agreed to everything while the mood of the mob still seemed to be on his side. He accepted written petitions of grievances from all over the rebellious counties and promised that, in effect, the political and social structure of his kingdom would be obliterated. What would be put in its place, no one, probably not even Wat Tyler, had much idea. The king handed out royal flags and the peasants began to drift homeward.

Tyler and a band of unknown size went to the Tower, carrying the king's writ to execute Sudbury and Hales. The garrison, small and quite possibly sympathetic to the peasants' cause, opened the gates.

The 60-year-old Sudbury was at prayer in the White Tower's chapel when they grabbed him. He was hustled outside to Tower Hill, jostled and spat at. The *Chronicon Angliae* says that the mob sounded like demented peacocks, squawking for his head. He was forced to the ground, begging for mercy and the axeman took eight blows to slice it off. Robert Hales died soon after. The heads were carried on poles to the shrine of Edward the Confessor in Westminster Abbey and a red cardinal's hat was nailed to Sudbury's skull. The body was eventually interred in Canterbury Cathedral, and the embalmed head is still on display in St Gregory's Church, Sudbury in Suffolk.

The murder of Sudbury and Hales changed everything. The king was bundled by his people back to the Wardrobe, a fortifiable building near St Paul's. Richard's mother, widow of the Black Prince, was there too and the handing out of petitions continued. Richard was now considered King of the Commons in a way undreamt of only days earlier. It was now that Tyler unleashed his hounds. In the same way that military commanders like Edward III and the Black Prince gave carte blanche to their troops to sack towns and villages across France, Tyler probably gave the word and all Hell was let loose. Contemporary chronicles reported a massacre of Flemings in the Vintry north of the river. Mass beheadings took place along the Cheap, the City's busiest street, that ran east to west. Piles of headless corpses blocked what had once been the king's highway. Any foreigners were to be killed on sight. Tax collectors, lawyers, anyone who apparently did not back the peasants' cause, were beaten up and summarily executed. There were kidnaps and ransom demands and a thousand chances to settle old scores.

A second meeting with the king was set up, this time at the tournament ground of Smithfield beyond Aldersgate. After their rampage, many of the rebels had drifted home, leaving a hard core of what we can properly regard as revolutionaries, perhaps 30,000 of them. There was still no sign of rescue by the lords on their scattered estates, much less from the most powerful of them, John of Gaunt, who effectively, hid in Scotland. According to the *Chronicon Angliae*,

'It is credibly reported that Wat Tyler boasted ... that in four days' time all the laws of England would be issuing from his mouth.' This was pure dictatorship, far more extreme and draconian than the concept of Medieval kingship.

Both sides were ready for anything. A message had gone out, probably from Robert Knollys, that the citizens should be ready to back the king with armed force. Tyler's plan may have been to grab Richard and use him as a bargaining tool. The king and his entourage prayed at the shrine of the Confessor in Westminster Abbey before riding east out of the City. According to some chroniclers, the peasants were drawn up in the three 'battle' formations of most clashes of the Hundred Years War. There were definitely archers with them, but whether they presented the deadly front envisaged by Maurice Collins in his 1958 account is debatable. All young men practised with the longbow in fourteenth-century England, but not all of them were expert shots and only a relatively small number would have fired at anything but a fixed target. The *Anominalle Chronicle* wrote that Tyler rode a little pony close to the king's grey destrier, a huge warhorse, and treated him like an equal. He dismounted, half bowed and shook his arm. Laying hands on the Lord's anointed was a hanging offence, but it got worse. 'Brother,' he said, 'be of good comfort and joyful for you shall have within the next fortnight 40,000 more of the Commons than you have now and we shall be good companions.' Richard asked him why he and his men did not go home. Tyler said he had no intention of leaving without more charters, which the king had, in fact, already promised him.

It was a stand-off, neither side moving. Richard was consideration itself, calm, smiling. Tyler, ready perhaps to unleash his bowmen, took a drink of water and possibly spat it on the ground. He then swigged some beer while he decided what to do. He recognized a Kentishman among the king's entourage and demanded his dagger. Richard told him to hand it over and Tyler played with it, tossing it from hand to hand. He then demanded the squire's sword. As he approached him, Tyler told his standard bearer to behead the man. As the squire reacted, Tyler lunged at him with the dagger but Mayor Walworth urged his horse in front of the rebel. 'I owe the king no respect!' Tyler snarled. Walworth shouted back, 'Fellow, how dare you use such words before the king? You presume too far!' Tyler lunged upwards for Walworth's stomach but the mayor was wearing armour under his mayoral robes and the blade merely dented his breastplate. Walworth retaliated immediately, either with a shortsword called a basilard or a dagger, hissing, 'You stinking scoundrel' and drove the blade into Tyler's chest.

Quicker than it had begun, the Peasant's Revolt was over. It proved what an extraordinary hold Wat Tyler had on his followers. If the king's party could have identified and found him earlier, perhaps there would have been no revolt at all, certainly no sacking of London. Walworth stabbed the rebel twice and the squire Ralph Standish finished him off with his sword. Nevertheless, Tyler managed to reach his horse and clung on in the saddle for several more paces before he toppled off. There was chaos. Nobody in the peasant ranks seems to have seen what happened. In the cliché too often used in television cop shows in our own time, 'it all happened so fast'.

According to some accounts, arrows flew, but if they did, they had virtually no impact, which leads me to believe that Tyler's men did not contain the professional bowmen who form the core of this book. In one of those extraordinary moments that even a film script writer could not make up, Richard spurred his horse forward alone and called out to the frightened, bewildered mob, 'Sirs, will you shoot your king? I am your captain. Follow me.' The arrows stopped, some of the rebel units broke up. Richard trotted north to the open fields and most of the crowd, like the children of the Pied Piper, drifted after him.

Unforgivably, some of the knights in Richard's band turned back, leaving the king exposed. William Walworth was one of them, but he had gone to fetch Robert Knollys and his men-at-arms, which almost certainly contained a contingent of bowmen. The mercenary d'Albret was there to command them and by the time they marched through Aldersgate they were perhaps 7,000 strong. The rebels dithered. Jack Straw was Tyler's number two but he proved to be not up to the job. John Ball was a priest and had no experience of the sharp end of rebellion. The dying Wat Tyler had been taken to nearby St Bartholomew's Hospital. Walworth found him, dragged him outside and decapitated him. Just as Sudbury's head had become a terrible token of contempt for the government, now Tyler's was impaled on a lance and Walworth carried it out to Priory Fields where the mob, effectively, had the king as their prisoner.

Knollys and d'Albret were outnumbered nearly three to one but the professionalism of war-hardened soldiers was worth its weight in gold. The peasants were encircled and Richard was rescued. The rebels threw down their weapons. The sight of Tyler's head unnerved them and many sank to their knees, begging for forgiveness. Knollys wanted them slaughtered. He had been killing Frenchmen for years and had seen the lawlessness and brutality of the mob called the Jacquerie first hand. The king and more generous counsel prevailed and they were allowed to go home.

Walworth, the merchants Nicholas Brembre and John Philpott were knighted by Richard, along with Ralph Standish who had brought Tyler down with his sword.

'No kingdom,' wrote Froissart, 'was ever in such peril as she was on that occasion.' Reprisals were not as severe as they might have been – unlike those of the Jacquerie in France – although John Ball and Jack Straw were both hanged. Straw left a confession that the destruction of all aspects of government was the final aim – Lords, the Church, the laws – all would have been swept away to create some sort of brave new world run on a county basis; a sort of federal hell 400 years before the Declaration of Independence. Essentially, nothing changed and the status quo was restored. The charters, signed by the king, were ignored as being obtained under duress. 'Villeins you are,' the king told the St Albans rebels in June, 'and villeins you shall remain.'

Seventy years after the Peasants' Revolt, Gregory, Lord Mayor of London, wrote of that period, 'That tyme was Syr Wylliam Walworthe made knight in Smethe Fyllde, for that he slew the Chefteyn of hern which were rysers. And thys was called "the hurling tyme".'

In fact, the whole of the fourteenth century and the early part of the fifteenth could be called the hurling time. The impact of Lollardy is difficult to determine, but it was certainly another example of the chaos that had suddenly erupted. The Lollards were heretics (the name comes from the Dutch word meaning 'mumblers') who rejected a number of the tenets of the Catholic Church and despised its wealth and corruption. Their leader was John Wycliffe who was expelled for his views by Oxford University in the year of the Peasants' Revolt, but there were similar leaders and movements in the Italian states. The movement denied transubstantiation (the miracle of the body and blood of Christ that occurred at communion) and ridiculed the superstition of the cult of relics, out of which, of course, the Church made such a fortune. 'If the cross of Christ, the nails, spear and crown of thorns are to be honoured, then why not Judas's lips, if only they could be found,' one argument ran.

The only prominent figure to defend Wycliffe was John of Gaunt, brother of Edward of Woodstock, the Black Prince, but since he was out of England after 1386 attempting to make himself king of Castile, effectively Wycliffe was on his own. Under Richard II and Henry IV, the government tightened the law. *De Heretico Comburendo* in 1401 equated heresy with treason, the most serious case in the book.

In 1413, shortly before the Agincourt campaign, John Oldcastle led a Lollard rebellion against his friend, Henry V. Oldcastle was Lord Cobham after 1409 and two years later commanded an army in France, forcing the Duke of Orleans to raise the siege of Paris. Outed by the Church, he went into hiding, but was caught and hanged in 1417, his body burned as it dangled at Smithfield.

What effect Lollardy had on the rank and file of ordinary people cannot be known with certainty. Conceivably, troops serving under Oldcastle may have influenced him, but they have left no record.

In England, the pestilence so upended the routines of civilization and terrified three generations that extraordinary outbreaks of terror like the Peasants' Revolt were perhaps inevitable. In France, the same disease caused the same havoc, but the rising of the Jacquerie was not a direct result of the plague but of the effects of war. and it was the Hundred Years War that forms the ongoing backdrop to this extraordinary time in history.

We have seen that both the peasants and the lords had bowmen in their retinues, hard men who had been trained to kill and to seek solutions to every problem through violence.

As historian Maurice Collis wrote: 'The battles in France were not won by knights but by the archers. An English army with enough archers could march anywhere. The archers were the commons. But not only had the commons won Crecy, Poitiers and Najera by archery, they themselves had created archery.' Such men, hitherto downtrodden and ignored as mere 'cannon-fodder' before there were cannons, now realized their own importance and began demanding their rights. The French called them 'the Goddamns', because of their blasphemous profanity on the march and the havoc they brought with them. Such men did not just win battles; they were in many ways the creators of twenty-first century Britain.

Chapter 3

Leopards and Lilies

The battle was over. As the Duke of Wellington said of Waterloo eight centuries later, 'Next to a battle lost, there is nothing so terrible as a battle won.' About 8,000 men had died at Senlac, 7 miles from the coastal town of Hastings that would give the battle its famous name. Most of them lay piled on top of each other along the half-mile front of the English on the ridge where Battle Abbey now stands. They lay thickest around the banners of the Fighting Man and the Dragon of Wessex, both symbols of the loser that day, Harold Godwinson, the last king of the English, the man who had been appointed by his predecessor, Edward the Confessor and chosen by the parliament called the Witan.

The winner of the battle was William the Bastard, the illegitimate son of the Duke of Normandy. He walked his tired horse along the ridge as the night descended on that short October day and saw the bodies of his knights, who had ridden too fast and too far in the twilight into a deadly criss-cross of ravines that the Normans now called Malfosse, the evil ditch.

It is rare that a single battle changes the course of history and in that October of 1066, William had no way of knowing that there would be no more major battles to fight. His claim to the English throne was spurious, although the pope backed him, and had sent his gonfalon standard with the pontiff's blessing. From now on, for several centuries, the king of England would be a stranger in his own land. He did not speak the language of his people and, depending on his temperament, ruled perhaps 4 million people with an iron rod.

The usurpation of a foreign king remained a problem in England for years to come, but it also created an awkward international situation.

William was king of England, literally owning all of it himself, but back home he was merely Duke of Normandy, one part of the much larger kingdom of France. Under the feudal system of government that the Normans brought to England with them, a symbiotic relationship existed. The king in effect rented out great estates to his tenants-in-chief, largely the men who had ridden with him at Senlac – Roger le Bigod, Odo of Bayeux, Robert of Mortain among them. They became dukes and earls with their own castles and private armies. They in turn lorded it over knights, lower down the social order but still classed as *pugnari* in the Middle Ages – those who fight. The knights in turn were socially superior to the freemen, who were given small parcels of land in what was a rural society and an agricultural economy. We have their names and the value of their mills, rents and land under the plough from the Domesday Book, a tax survey ordered by William twenty years after Hastings.

In exchange for lands and rents, William demanded 'knight service'. His barons must report to him two or three times a year, usually at Christmas and Easter and give him any advice he asked for – advice he was not bound to take. They also undertook to provide him with soldiers should the king require them – the knights who formed the heavily armed cavalry, the billmen and the bowmen who made up the infantry. In theory, such men served for forty days, but in practice, especially when the king took his army overseas, it could be much longer.

The feudal system looks clumsy and vague to us, used as we are to a cash economy, personal ownership of property and professional armed forces, but it worked for 500 years. In fact, it was not until the Hundred Years War that forms the core of this book that the system began to break down.

But the clash of interests between duke and king presented problems. In England, William was absolute. There was no parliament to cause him problems and, at a stroke, he could take away the titles and lands of a troublesome baron. In France, however, he *was* a troublesome baron, who saw himself, despite the Europe-wide feudal system, the equal of the king of France.

History, as it was taught in the nineteenth century, was all about kings and queens and family trees. Umpteen cultural revolutions since then have focused on lesser mortals and other, more complex, issues, but there is no getting away from the fact that foreign policy, like everything else in the Middle Ages, was decided by rulers. Because of war, marriage and even personal whims, territory and allegiances changed hands like small change. If we fast forward from 1066 to the twelfth century, we arrive at the reign of Henry II, Curtmantle, the 'king of the North Wind'. The man's energy and ambition were legendary and his marriage to the former queen of France, Eleanor of Aquitaine in 1152, sent Henry on a quest to increase the size of his demesne. He grabbed so much territory, with the aid of his highly talented soldier son Richard (later the Lionheart) that by 1189, the kings of England held more land in France than the French king. From Gascony in the far south with its frontier in the foothills of the Pyrenees, eastward from the Bay of Biscay to Auvergne, north via Agenois, Perigord, Limousin, La Marche, Berri, Poitou, Anjou, Marie, Touraine, Normandy itself and the Vexin, all of it belonged to the kings of England, today called the Angevins.

The term itself comes from Anjou, in that Henry II was the son of Geoffrey, count of that territory. Confusingly, many standard textbooks refer to Richard II, the young king of the Peasants' Revolt, as being the last of the Angevins. His successor, however, who usurped the throne in 1399, was Henry Bolingbroke, who became Henry IV and was also, like Richard, a grandson of Edward III. Convention dictates that Henry IV is regarded as the first of the Lancastrian kings, but this is an attempt to simplify history and is not strictly accurate.

The family name of all Angevins was Plantagenet, although this was not generally used until the fifteenth century. Heraldic legend (responsible for a great deal of nonsense) is that Geoffrey of Anjou, involved in several wars as he was in his day, wore the broom flower

(*Planta genista*) in his cap as an early example of uniform. It is not altogether convincing.

By the fourteenth century, the little, parochial demesnes that made up France under the feudal system were fast becoming obsolete and there was a move to the concept of the nation state. Increasingly, as Edward I subdued first the Welsh, then the Scots, England in particular was becoming a powerful country, although it would arguably be centuries before it was as wealthy as France. Even though the vassal states listed above were administered by locals, be they Normans or Gascons depending on the area, it was now accepted that these were part of England, separated from the mainland by the Channel.

Under Richard I, England's gains in the French territory had been impressive, but his brother John lost swathes, so that he was mockingly called Lackland. In John's day, the duchy of Aquitaine, inherited from his mother, filled the geographical centre of France, but John was not the soldier his elder brother was and he had great difficulty holding it all together, especially against his nemesis (as he had been Richard's) Philip Augustus, the French king. Philip had launched an attack on Aquitaine while Henry II was still alive and the old man (as he was in the mid-1180s) ceded territory to him. Richard could have stopped Philip (he was easily the ablest general in Europe at the time) but put most of his energies into the Third Crusade (1189–92) with Philip as an unlikely (and untrustworthy) ally. By 1204, John was forced to hand Normandy over to the French king, effectively breaking the pattern of fealty that had existed since the Conqueror's time. So detested was John and his mercenaries that even Gerald of Wales (Giraldus Cambrensis) spoke admiringly of 'the fierce courage of free Frenchmen'.

By the early fourteenth century and the accession of Edward III, nothing had really been resolved in terms of the dichotomy between the king of England being a vassal of the king of France. Pride and reputation played their part, as did the personalities of the kings involved. The role of king in both countries was twofold, as is apparent in the royal seals attached to various documents. On one side the Lord's anointed sits on his throne, the crown on his head, his orb and sceptre in his hands. In this capacity, he is the lawgiver, the decider of policy, the fount of all wisdom as the Old Testament told men that Solomon had been. On the other, he was mounted on his destrier, with drawn sword, helmet and shield displaying the gold leopards of England on a red background. These were actually lions, but in heraldic terms, if the animals faced the observer, they were technically known as leopards. In this context, the king was commander-in-chief, the leader of his soldiers and he was expected to lead them in the field. The French king had exactly the same dual roles – only the heraldry was different. The king's shield carried the lilies (fleur de lys), gold on a blue background.

The French royal family had its problems. In 1303, Edward II had married the princess Isabel. This made him the son-in-law of Philip IV and brother-in-law to his three sons. By February 1328, all three had died childless and, under French law, Isabel, as a woman, could not rule her country. Had that been possible, the French crown would have slid sideways, by default, to Edward II. But he too was dead, murdered, it was rumoured, in Berkeley Castle with a red-hot poker forced up his anus as a final, grotesque insult to a man who was almost certainly bisexual. The French throne, therefore, passed to Philip of Valois, Charles IV's nephew. But, by virtue of his own lineal descent, Edward III had a claim to the French throne too.

It must have been an awkward part of Philip's coronation, at Rheims, to realize that his rival would arrive any moment to pay him homage. In the event, Edward kept him waiting, not turning up until the following year. Edward's position in England was that he was contending with the plots of his mother, Isabel, and her lover, Mortimer, but the young king's steel in moving decisively against them established him as a shrewd politician and, ultimately, one of the great kings of the Middle Ages. Mortimer was arrested and drawn and hanged as a common felon at Tyburn, at the western end of today's Oxford Street. As for Isabel, she was 'retired' to Castle Rising in Norfolk where she eventually took the veil, dying in 1358.

Just as Edward I had done, Edward III imposed his will on the ever-rebellious Scots. Robert the Bruce's death allowed Edward to appoint Edward Balliol as the Scots king and that was a signal to wage war. On the morning of 19 July 1333, a vastly superior Scots force under Archibald Douglas advanced up the slope of Halidon Hill near Berwick. The English army was drawn up into three 'battles' (divisions) with a screen of longbowmen across its entire front. The *Lanercost Chronicle* wrote that the Scots 'were so grievously wounded in the face and blinded by the host of English archery that they were helpless and quickly began to turn their faces from the arrow flights and to fall'. Halidon Hill was a blueprint for the great victories of the Hundred Years War – Crecy, Poitiers, Najera and Agincourt.

For a generation, the Scots stayed out of England, but the defeat did lead to an unholy alliance with the French. The 'auld alliance' would manifest itself on and off until the English victory at Culloden in 1746 and it meant that throughout the Hundred Years War, kings of England had to watch their backs constantly.

Revisionist American historians like Norman F. Cantor of New York University, depict Edward and his son, the Black Prince, as dinosauric monsters bent on destruction and mayhem. The Prince of Wales is dismissed as an 'exact copy of his ruthless, devious and greedy father', who was a 'horrible old man … clutching his venereal mistress [Alice Perrers]'. Cantor does have the grace to admit that this was not how contemporaries saw him, so we wonder why a distinguished historian is measuring a fourteenth-century ruler by the mores of the twenty-first.

In fact, both Edward and Philip tried very hard to sort out their impasse by legal, peaceful means. Edward employed bilingual scholars at his court in the 1330s, but the problem was that the French king did not regard the English as his equal but as an underling. A century earlier, Philip Augustus, warring with Henry II, Richard I and John, laid claim to the English throne, which made little sense, but now that the pope was at Avignon, the religious heart of Europe was in French hands too.

Another key issue was trade. The sea-lanes of the Channel took English wool (far and away the largest export) to Flanders, where Flemish weavers monopolized the woollen industry. Wool, along with grain and salted fish, was also shipped to Bordeaux in the south. Half of Edward's revenue came from this trade, which meant that the ports and the sea must be available at all times. It was no accident that the first full-blown action of the Hundred Years War occurred in the harbour at Sluys, while both armies were on board ship. Many chroniclers at the time (and some historians since) have seen the *casus belli* of the conflict as some rather silly spat over chivalry. In fact, it was to do with land, money and economics. By 1337, the French were building an extensive fleet, complete with Genoese and Castilian galleys (which, in fact, would prove to be of limited use in the wild waters of the Channel) based at Rouen to hit English merchant vessels. Before the creation of modern communications and the discovery of the Americas, *all* British trade that was not home-based was with Europe – there was no other realistic choice. If Philip had actually attempted to blockade England, before Edward stopped him, his plan might just have succeeded.

The English plan was to continue the process begun by Henry II of making alliances with France's enemies, especially Burgundy in the north and its near neighbour, the Holy Roman Empire. It would be another six centuries before Napoleon proved that the area was neither holy nor Roman and he broke up the empire by defeating it in battle, not once, but several times. In the fourteenth century there was no Belgium. Bruges was in Flanders, Brussels was German. There would be no Germany until 1871, merely a collection of some 300 states, each with its own ruler, economy, culture and army. It was of huge help to Edward that his wife. Philippa, was a princess of Hainault, which automatically gave him an ally, money and men. In a move which would be echoed by William Pitt, prime minister in the 1790s, England was rich enough to buy co-operation and coalitions. Edward had a knack of persuading people, like the Lombards and the Fugger family, the billionaires of the stock market before such a thing really existed, to lend him cash. Philippa's brother-in-law, the Duke of Brabant, got £60,000 (a complicated calculation to do, but this could correspond to more than £6.5bn today). The Emperor, Louis IV, made the English king vicar-general, which was not an ecclesiastical rank, allowing him to command troops and raise taxes on all territories west of the Rhine. By outmanoeuvring the merchants into buying English wool, France's ally Flanders was left isolated.

At home, in readiness for war, Edward moved his headquarters from York to the Naze near his fleet and reorganized the Exchequer and the Chancery, vital departments handling money, so that ready cash was available to him on campaign. The king was careful to get parliament's backing at each step on the road to war, even though he did not strictly need it. Parliament, in its modern sense of Lords and Commons debating issues, controlling taxation and the armed forces, did not exist. The Lords were the tenants-in-chief, Edward's advisors (and his generals). The Commons, knights of the shire, represented the towns and the small landowners. Neither group could push the king around – that story belonged to later centuries.

Despite precedent being squarely on Edward's side, various groups whinged about the changes he had made once he was in France. The Council threatened to resign. Inflation was rampant after years of good harvests and the king flooding the market with silver – Spain would have the same problem in the sixteenth century. With the Prince of Wales, the future Black Prince, only a child, Edward gave power to John Stratford, Archbishop of Canterbury. Stratford's problem was that, like all Medieval archbishops, he was the servant of two masters; he worked for the king and the pope. And the pope lived at Avignon. He was effectively a French puppet and bombarded Stratford with missives demanding a truce between the two countries.

By February 1340, Edward was forced to come home to plead with parliament to fork out more cash. They agreed, but only on terms favourable to them – a foretaste of things to come.

Technically, the war had begun in 1337, but hostilities did not occur until a year later. The south coast of England was particularly open to attacks and even invasion. Philip's army was not large, nor strong enough to invade, but it could certainly raid and pillage, which was designed to humiliate and annoy. In 1338, Portsmouth and Southampton were both hit; Folkestone and Dover the following year. This was piled on top of Philip's invasion of Gascony (English territory) in 1336 and led to Edward ordering his heralds to create the joint arms of the leopards and lilies on his standards which were to remain for 200 years.

There is very little information on the French raid on the Isle of Wight, but it was mounted by a fleet commanded by David II of Scotland, evidence that the alliance with France was already working by 1338. Portsmouth was under threat as well, already well established as one of the cinque ports vital to England's defence and a busy trading centre in its own right. Much later defences ringing Portsmouth's harbour make it impossible to imagine what it looked like in the 1330s. The fleet that landed there under the command of Nicholas Béhuchet destroyed most of the town – only the church and hospital survived. Southampton was a cinque port too and in 1338, much of the town above the Bargate was ransacked by a French, Genoese and Monegasque army led by Carlo Grimaldi who used the loot he acquired to establish his independent demesne of Monaco, out of which his family continues to make money. As a result of the destruction, Edward III ordered the building of the impressive town walls, much of which still stand today. In these slightly more enlightened days and in the spirit of European rapprochement, Southampton is twinned with Le Havre. Folkestone had no actual harbour until the nineteenth century, but its role as a rich port made it a natural target for the French and an easy one. Much more difficult was Dover, with its massive castle built in the reign of King John. The French had had a crack at this over a century earlier, during the Barons' War which coincided with John's death. Louis VIII's army was beaten back by 400 bowmen firing down from the famous white cliffs, but the

French held the town for three months before being dispersed. The raid in 1339 was less organized and successful.

How did Jean Froissart, the best-known chronicler of the period, view the opening moves of the war? He says that attempts at negotiations with the French at Valenciennes failed and that Edward called a parliament at Westminster which lasted three weeks. The wisest counsel given to the king was that he 'could not delay revoking his homage to the King of France and [make] a declaration of war on him and all his adherents'. Today, such declarations are made by telephone and computers. In the fourteenth century, the Bishop of Lincoln was sent with an official document dripping with royal seals and ribbons. It was the equivalent of the chivalric throwing down of a gauntlet. Burgesses from London, York and Coventry (then effectively the country's third largest city) offered 300,000 nobles a year to fund the whole thing.

In view of the attacks on the south coast, the men of Cornwall, Guernsey, Wight, Hampshire and Sheppey, all very much targets, were exempt from defending anywhere but their own ground. In addition, they should 'train their children in the use of arms and archery'. In fact, archery was to take a central place in the English mindset rather as the paranoia of a Fifth Column did in Winston Churchill's war 600 years later. 'No one in the realm on pain of decapitation, should practise any game or sport other than that of shooting with bow and arrows.' The craftsmen making those bows should be cleared of their debts. If only today's practitioners and followers of the 'beautiful game' had listened! No horses were to be shipped overseas without the Chancellor's permission and, oddest of all, 'It was also ordained … that every lord, baron, knight and honest citizen of the larger towns should make every effort to instruct their children in the French language, in order that they should be more efficient and feel more at home in the wars.' No doubt, when the Goddamns were sacking a town, stealing its wine and raping its women, this bilingualism would be much appreciated.

The Bishop of Lincoln duly gave Edward's declaration of war to Philip VI and one of his secretaries read it out. This was in Paris in early November:

> Since it falls out that … we are heir to the realm and crown of France by a much closer degree of kinship than yourself, who have entered into possession of our heritage and are holding it … by force … we give you notice that we shall claim and conquer our heritage … by the armed force of us and yours and from this day forward we and ours challenge you and yours to rescind the pledge and homage which we gave you. And now we place our domain of Ponthieu … under the protection of God, not under yours, since we consider you as our enemy and adversary.

The French king smiled at Lincoln, thanked him and told him that Edward's note required no answer. He then gave the bishop safe conduct out of Paris and out of France. This was diplomacy fourteenth-century style. Philip did not rise to the bait. The ball was now in Edward's court and an English expeditionary force was sent to defend the Scheldt estuary, considered important because it was a landing place in the communications between England and Hainault. There was no fighting.

Edward crossed to Hainault himself in the following summer, this time with an army. Again, Lincoln took a renewed challenge to the French king and it is from this incident that war actually broke out. It was a green light for pirates and freebooters to attack English towns. Froissart describes the attack on Southampton:

> As soon as Sir Hugh Kieret [Hugues Quiéret] and his companions on the seas heard that the challenges had been sent and war had opened … they were jubilant. They set out with their fleet, which carried at least a thousand fighting men

> of various kinds [crossbowmen and billmen] and sailed for England, coming into Hantonne [Southampton] harbour one Sunday morning when the people were at mass. The Normans and Genoese entered the town and pillaged and looted it completely. They killed many people and raped a number of women and girls, which was a deplorable thing. They loaded their ships and vessels with the great plunder they found in the town which was rich and well-stocked and then went back on board …

When Edward came back from Hainault a second time, he received petitions from the towns that had been sacked. It was time he took the war to the French.

Chapter 4

Neville's Cross: 17 October 1346 St Ignatus' Day

The 'auld alliance' was a headache for England. Throughout the Medieval period and beyond, ragged armies of Scotsmen routinely crossed the border and raided the north of England. Towns like Berwick changed hands with monotonous regularity and the efforts by Edward I at the turn of the thirteenth/fourteenth centuries had not resulted in a permanent peace. The alliance with France effectively opened up a second front by the Scots, who responded in 1346 to a specific request from the French king, Philip VI, to lend their support.

Edward III and his army were in France in October and it was the perfect opportunity for the Scots to take advantage of the French connection and invade England again. The Scots army was perhaps 12,000 strong. We have to be wary of numbers quoted in Medieval battles. They invariably come from chroniclers who were not there at the time and were often writing months or even years after the events they describe. Twelve thousand is a powerful force by fourteenth-century standards and may have included the camp followers, some of whom would have been women, in the total.

Their commander was King David II, the only surviving son of Robert the Bruce, a national hero who had made a fool of Edward II's attempts to keep Scotland in check. David had been in exile between 1334 and 1341, sheltering in the welcoming arms of the French, but five years later was prepared to try his luck and perhaps get some revenge. The Scots' battle tactics, honed under the Bruce and William Wallace, the 'guardian of Scotland', was based on the schiltron, a rectangular mass of infantry carrying long spears, that was strong enough to withstand a cavalry charge of heavily armoured knights. What the Scots did not have was much cavalry of their own. Neither did they have anything resembling a strong body of bowmen.

Edward III and his key commanders may have been absent in France, but the north of his kingdom had plenty of men who had been holding the borderlands called the Marches for years. While the whole of England was in theory liable to the fourteenth-century equivalent of conscription, the maritime areas and the north of England was exempt. Ralph de Neville, Henry Percy and William de la Zouche, the Archbishop of York, commanded the English. It will surprise modern readers to find a senior churchman directly involved in military operations, but de la Zouche doubled as Warden of the Marches, the castles that defended the frontier. There was a long history of churchmen 'doing their bit' for their king in the Middle Ages. Under these there were perhaps 700 men-at-arms and as many as 10,000 bowmen.

On the morning of 17 October, William Douglas, leading member of a notorious fighting clan, raided Kirk Merrington and its surrounding villages as a routine part of what the French called a *chevauchée* (horse ride). There was thick fog in the hills and valleys west of Durham and Douglas seems to have been particularly lax in that he was unaware how close Neville's army was. According to the *Lanercost Chronicle*, a 'history' of northern England compiled by various monks of Lanercost Abbey in Cumbria between 1201 and 1346, the first the Scots knew of the problem was 'the trampling of horses and the shock of armoured men' looming out of the mist. The raiding party, probably composed of less than 500 hobelars (light cavalry), panicked and had little time to warn King David's camp at Beaurepaire Priory (today's Bearpark) of the sudden threat. Two monks who did carry a message of impending doom were believed to be spies and were executed.

Neville took up a position on high ground between the rivers Weir and Browney, on a narrow ridge marked by an Anglo-Saxon cross, one of several that ringed the ancient city of Durham as boundary markers.

Having tramped over the battleground, I can agree with all battlefield historians who say that this was no country for cavalry. The hobelars could cope, but the heavier destriers of the knights would not be able to manage more than a trot over such terrain and that would make a mounted charge impossible.

Accordingly, Neville drew up his three divisions of billmen (infantry) with his knights (cavalry) behind them. Across the front of the whole army was a screen of bowmen, each man armed with a longbow of yew and a short sword or dagger. Each man carried at his belt a quiver of fifty arrows. Simple mathematics tells us that, given the likely numbers, 10,000 arrows would have been released in the first volley. We know that Medieval bowmen could fire up to twelve shafts a minute, so that within sixty seconds, 240,000 arrows would have hit the Scottish lines. It was possible that, despite the long experience of English and Welsh bowmen over the previous century, for many of them at Neville's Cross, this was a baptism of fire. We know that some groups hung back in indecision faced with the intimidating appearance of the Scots' advance.

David of Scotland had no inkling of the disaster that awaited him. He calmly ordered his breakfast and said he would finish it 'when he had slain the English at the point of the sword'. His army advanced across Crossgate Moor with the Browney (little more than a stream) to their right and Baxter Wood along its meandering curve. Today, the modern A167 runs right through the battleground heading north to Chester-le-Street and it has changed the lie of the land beyond recognition. In 1346, the countryside would have been open moorland, grazed by sheep, with ridge and furrow arable fields around the scattered hamlets.

The original commander of the vanguard (the first wave) was Patrick Dunbar, Earl of March but seeing the English position and that he would have to attack uphill, asked David to let him lead the rearguard instead! All in all, this did not inspire confidence. Command, therefore, fell to John Randolph, the Earl of Moray, on the right who pushed his schiltrons forward too fast and got into difficulties. The high ground around the Downey forced Moray into the centre where his troops became hopelessly entangled with David's central division. This meant that well over half the front line were floundering in what was a still a wet and foggy field and they made a perfect target for the bowmen.

As we shall see in later chapters, these men's fathers had cut their teeth against the Scots. They had routed them at Falkirk and Halidon Hill, but the enemy had learned nothing from these encounters. Bending their yew bows to full stretch, the gut strings pulled back to their ears for maximum range and impact, the bowmen let fly and kept on firing. It is no exaggeration to say that the impact of those archers was as devastating as the machine gunners of the Western Front in the First World War. In neither case was the bow or the machine gun a new or 'secret' weapon, but few people had met the massed firepower of either weapon before and they had no answers to make. The *Lanercost Chronicle* says that, 'the archers of England were quick and light and shot with good aim and skill and so fiercely that it was a terror to see.'

If an enemy could get close to the bowmen, they were vulnerable. Individually, a single man with a bow could achieve little and a large force of determined Scots would have charged them down. The left division under Robert, the High Steward (the title later became the surname Stewart), and the dithering March tried to reach the bowmen but the English cavalry, in reserve, were unleashed on them and halted the Highlanders in their tracks. The Scots' left and right divisions, riddled with arrows, had effectively broken, leaving David's central 'battle' exposed. The bowmen fell back behind their men-at-arms for protection and were unleashed again as David's attack wavered.

The king himself was found, once his army had broken and fled, hiding under a packhorse bridge over the Downey. Still a fighter to the last, he knocked two teeth out of the jaw of John de Coupland who had captured him. David had been wounded twice in the face by arrows. One was removed, but the unskilled surgery of the day meant that the second one had to be left in situ. It gave him headaches for the rest of his life, but it was little short of a miracle that infection did not kill him. He was kept a prisoner in England until 1357 when he was finally released by Edward III for 100,000 marks (£78 million in today's currency).

In that short October day, the English pursuit lasted well after darkness fell and the Scots limped home as best they could. The chances are that even when the rout ended, the defeated were not safe. It was payback time for the villagers who had been at the receiving end of looting, pillage, rape and murder so often along the border. Hexham Abbey had been destroyed by David's army before the battle; Carlisle and Durham had paid a fortune in protection money to be left alone. In the treaty that followed Neville's Cross, there was an uneasy peace that lasted for nearly forty years.

Lord Neville replaced the Saxon cross on the battlefield with a new one to commemorate the dead. Once again, numbers are unreliable. Contemporary chroniclers give 1,000 dead for the Scots, but modern experts have trebled that. They included many of the Scots nobility. As for the survivors, anyone worth it was held to ransom, the traditional money-making scam which acted as a bonus for the victors. Edward III was furious about this; he wanted the nobility kept as prisoners so that their leadership in any future hostility would be limited. Anyone not worth a ransom was murdered, traditionally by having their throats slit, work probably carried out by the bowmen.

These men were rewarded for their skill as winners of battles. We know that the Lancashire contingent were paid a £10 bounty per man (£11,700 in today's currency). They had been sent forward ahead of the main host to fire into the Scots' lines, provoking Moray into a precipitous charge. They had demolished the first ranks of all three Scottish divisions. And they finished off the stragglers at the end.

By the time Neville's Cross was fought, news would have reached both the English and the Scots armies that an even greater victory had been won, largely again by the bowmen, at Crecy in France on 26 August. In these two engagements, only weeks apart, the bowmen of England, whom the French called the Goddamns, had won their place in history.

Chapter 5

'The Favoured One': Edward III

Kings' reputations depend on their strong governments at home and their successful foreign policy. The strong kings of England in the Middle Ages are those who made the name of England stand for something on the international stage – Henry II, Richard I, Edward I, Edward III, Henry V. The last two made their names in, and largely as a result of, the Hundred Years War and in terms of his long reign, the most outstanding is Edward III.

Although there is a great deal more to the man than his leadership in war, it is in this context that we have to view him in this book: Edward the general is more important in this context than Edward the king.

No English king in history has been so closely linked with the concept of chivalry and chivalry itself is so complex an idea, varying from country to country and even man to man, that trying to define it causes huge historical problems. The bowmen who formed at once the backbone and the 'secret weapon' of Edward's armies had no direct role in the chivalric ideal, but they were always on the fringes of it and, in England at least, central to that ideal's success. Ironically, it was not the lords and knights, the practitioners of the knightly code, that won Edward's battles but the bowmen who almost certainly had a very different take on life.

Like most other ideas, chivalry has been hijacked by later generations. Arthur, probably a sixth-century Romano-British warlord, became, in Edward III's own day, a Medieval king, complete with a castle (Camelot), an order of worthy knights sitting at a round table and undertaking dangerous and noble tasks, the greatest of which was the search for the Holy Grail, Christ's cup at the Last Supper. In the nineteenth century, the novelist Walter Scott wrote rattling 'boys' yarns' like *Ivanhoe*, *Castle Dangerous* and *Quentin Durward*, distorting and simplifying the *real* chivalry of the Middle Ages.

In 1884, the French scholar Léon Gautier drew up the Decalogues, essentially the commandments of knighthood, in his book *Le Chevalerie.* How do they fit what we know of Edward III's reign? First, Gautier cites an unswerving belief in the Church and obedience to her teachings. This was not as straightforward as it sounds. The fourteenth and fifteenth centuries were marred by the Great Schism of the Papacy – yet another chaotic disaster for the age of calamity, the 'hurling time'. There were two popes – one in Rome, the other in Avignon. In fact, for a short period, there were *three.* This schism was political, rather than spiritual, but it weakened the papacy and muddied the waters in terms of loyalty. The pope *was* the Church; if his role was compromised, where did that leave the knightly code of unswerving belief? As we have seen, Lollardy would make an impact on the religious situation too, although how far this was evident during the period of the war is debatable.

Defence of the Church was Gautier's second commandment and is obviously linked to the first. The same problems apply and while warring kings like Edward, Philip and later Henry V could forbid the sacking of churches and killing of priests, we know that the rank and file of the Jacquerie and the free companies had no such qualms; churches offered a soft target with their unarmed priests and their gold and silver plate. Gautier's third point is respect and pity for all weakness and steadfastness in defending them. This was tied in with the songs of the troubadours and *minnesängers*, the professional minstrels who performed at royal and noble courts, the rough equivalent of rock stars today. Yet we know that rape and sexual assault were the all-too-common results of chevauchées, raids on the countryside, which Edward and his knights, as well as their French counterparts, encouraged.

Gautier's love of country is difficult in Edward's reign. It was the Hundred Years War that arguably created the concept of the nation state that was England. Wales had recently been incorporated by Edward I, but in 1402 Owain Glyndwr claimed to be the rightful prince of Wales and rebelled against Henry IV, allying with the French in the process. As we see throughout this book, Scotland was outside the English remit until 1707 and still caused waves after that. Ireland was, in all senses, 'beyond the Pale'. France was even more fragmented, the powerful dukes fiercely independent of Paris and more interested in feathering their own nests than following commands of their king. On the battlefield, Edward's arms were the quartered leopards and lilies but those bowmen who did not stand under their individual lord's banner fought under the red cross, which was not the English flag but the device of a rather obscure Armenian saint, George. When the English captured Rouen in 1418 they planted a number of flags to mark the victory. At the castle, they set up the Trinity; at Pont Caux, 'a banner of the Queene of Heven' (the Virgin Mary); and at Pont Martvile, the flag of St George. Oddly, the king's banner went up last. Gautier's 'refusal to retreat before the enemy' was often conveniently ignored. As we shall see, there was a lucrative living to be had capturing enemy knights and holding them to ransom. To that extent, and that extent only, war was a game, but dying was not part of it. At Crecy, Poitiers, Najera and Agincourt, the greatest clashes of the war, the French fled the field every time. And perhaps it goes without saying that the bowmen who won these battles were poor men – nobody ransomed them. They simply had their throats cut.

The sixth point of the Decalogue was largely irrelevant to the Hundred Years War; it was unceasing and merciless war against the infidel. The thorny issue of the Holy Land – Outremer (the other side of the sea) – arose because three major creeds – Christianity, Islam and Judaism – all saw Jerusalem as the holiest place on earth. As long as everyone was allowed to worship there, all was well and good, but when the Seljuk Turks invaded the area in the twelfth century, Christians rushed to liberate it. The First Crusade of 1099 was the only genuinely successful one, but the Templars and the Hospitallers failed to hold the city and subsequent crusades were launched to win it back. The ideal was never abandoned by the papacy. In fact, one reason why the popes of the fourteenth century were unable to forge a peace between England and France is that they were constantly plotting to send another relief force to the Middle East.

To add to the confusion, in the late fourteenth century, crusades were also launched against the pagans of Eastern Europe. When Geoffrey Chaucer, the poet and customs officer, wrote *The Canterbury Tales* in the 1380s, he listed the campaigns of his fictional knight – 'In Lithuania had he fought and Russia'. By this time, the Ottoman Turks were encroaching on Christian Europe too. Several English knights, including perhaps Henry Bolingbroke, the future Henry IV, fought them at Nicopolis in 1396.

The feudal system was enshrined in the chivalric code by obedience to one's lord. This was largely adhered to in the Hundred Years War, although clashing with that was the idea of *diffidatio,* the right to rebel if a lord was considered to be at fault. A number of earlier English and French kings fell victim to that and it was to re-emerge in England in the form of the Wars of the Roses (a later term) two years after the fall of Castillon.

'Loyalty to the truth and to the pledged word' was another chivalric virtue. Oaths were taken very seriously – they are still used in various forms in courts of law today. In taking them, a man was making a solemn pledge, not just to another, but to God. Generosity in giving was another ideal, one that both Edward III and his son, the Black Prince, carried out assiduously. When Edward, disguised as a humble knight, fought in a tournament in Sir Walter Manny's retinue in 1348, he eventually defeated a Frenchman, Eustace de Ribeaumont. That night, he not only entertained the French at a sumptuous banquet but gave the man a pearl chaplet worth a small fortune in appreciation of his courage. He also set him free without ransom.

Gautier's final point – championship of the right and the good against evil – is, of course, in the eye of the beholder. In what was a simpler age, when issues tended to be more black and white than today, 'good' and 'Godly' went hand in hand. Were the French, to Edward III, the forces of evil? Life may have been simpler but was not *that* simple! In fact, two of the outstanding examples of chivalric honour in this period were shared equally by the English and French.

Jean le Bon was the king of France defeated and captured by the Black Prince at Poitiers in 1356. He was taken back to England as a prisoner but was treated with extraordinary civility by the Prince, who served the king at dinner but would not sit with him because 'he was not worthy to seat himself at the table of so great a king, or of so valiant a man as he had shown himself that day'. This was not hypocrisy on Edward's part; neither was he mocking Jean. He meant every word of it. Jean's ransom was 2,000 nobles (£666 at the time, £560,000 today) and his escort to England consisted of 500 men-at-arms and 2,000 bowmen. While Jean rode his grey destrier through London's streets, the Black Prince was mounted on a little black hackney. Jean's son Philip came with him and he was often visited by various French noblemen.

After considerable haggling, Jean's ransom was settled at 200,000 gold crowns and a sizable slice of French territory. He left behind another son, the Duke of Anjou, and returned to Paris. Anjou, however, had none of the honour of his father and broke his parole, fleeing the country. Outraged by this, Jean voluntarily returned to London where he died in 1364.

A similar example of chivalry comes from 1380 on the death of Bertrand du Guesclin, Constable of France. At the time he was laying siege to Chateauneuf-de-Randon, held by a mixed Anglo-Gascon garrison. The castle's English commander promised to surrender if relief had not arrived by 12 July. It did not, but du Guesclin died of natural causes the next day, which effectively freed the commander from his oath. In fact, so that du Guesclin's last campaign should not end in failure, the commander kept his word, surrendered the castle and placed its keys in du Guesclin's dead hands.

It was the creation of the Order of the Blue Garter in January 1348 that is most closely linked with Edward III:

> Tie about the leg for thy renown this noble Garter, wear it as the symbol of the most illustrious Order, never to be forgotten or laid aside, that thereby thou mayest be admonished to be courageous, and, having undertaken a just war … that thou mayest stand firm and valiantly and successfully conquer.

The concept of a just war was still being discussed in military and political circles throughout the twentieth century, although where the Hundred Years War fits into that concept is debatable.

The original Order was confined to the king, the Black Prince and twenty-four knights. Perhaps, bizarrely for the time, the Order allowed a handful of women. One of the best known was Alice Chaucer, the granddaughter of Geoffrey, the poet, who was actually Comptroller of Woollens, Hides and Wines in the reign of Richard II. The poet himself fought as a young man in the French war, being taken prisoner in Brittany and was ransomed by Edward III. Alice too had links with the war. her first husband, John Philip, was killed in Henry V's army attacking Harfleur in 1415. Her second husband, Thomas, Earl of Salisbury, was killed soon after the siege of Orleans in 1429. Her third husband, William, Duke of Suffolk was executed at sea in 1450; Alice was only 24 at this time and had more than earned a right to the Garter, if only by virtue of her grief and the upheavals in her life. For modesty's sake, women wore their garter on the left forearm as it was not seemly to show off legs.

The famous motto of the Order – *Honi Soit Qui Mal Y Pense* (evil to him who thinks evil) – was said to date from a ball held at Calais when the garter of Joan of Kent, the daughter of Edmund of Woodstock, fell off. Sniggering courtiers were silenced by the king's line which became the Order's motto. Joan, like Alice Chaucer, was involved in the Hundred Years War too, only more directly. At Neville's Cross (see Chapter 4) in October 1346, the Countess of Salisbury (as Joan was then) was present with her husband, rallying the troops as the English bowmen annihilated the Scots. The Garter motto story may be no more than legend, but it fits the pattern of a larger-than-life king from another age.

Edward III's running of the war, especially in its early stages, was very good. It was helped, of course, by a number of highly capable captains, like John Chandos, Walter Manny and the Black Prince himself. The king's strategy was to bring the enemy to a confrontation in the open as soon as possible, confident as he was of the edge his bowmen gave him. Later commanders like du Guesclin used guerrilla tactics, fighting a war of manoeuvre, if only because France's track record in open combat was not only deplorable, but did not noticeably improve. It was only the advent of artillery – and arguably, the lack of an effective royal military commander – which led to the reversal of fortunes that in turn led to Castillon.

Napoleon was acutely aware of the role that luck played in warfare. In appointing a general as a Marshal of France, he would ask, 'Is he lucky?' He already knew the man's abilities, but luck was a different matter altogether. It was luck that in early summer 1340, the wind that blew the English fleet across the Channel was the same one that kept the Franco-Genoese fleet virtually trapped in the Zwin estuary.

But luck alone cannot win wars. Edward was a pragmatist despite the high-flown veneer of the chivalric ideal. He clashed at first with his parliament, expecting them to fund his foreign adventures. By 1341, however, he had back-tracked and worked well with them for the rest of his reign. He broke two Italian banking families, the Peruzzi and the Bardi, but royal revenue was expanding. And the war helped. Ruinously expensive though it was to keep men in the field and having literally to hock his crown twice in ten years, two royal ransoms (of the kings of France and Scotland) brought in £280,000, four times the annual GDP.

The king's handling of military finances reached an apogee by the 1360s. Everybody was paid, marking the end of the land-based feudal system and the beginning of a cash economy. Edward Balliol, king of Scots, got 50 shillings a day; the Black Prince £1; the bowmen of Cheshire 2d.

Hand in hand with that went the king's popularity. A good king won battles and increased his people's reputation overseas. His foot soldiers no doubt grumbled, as foot soldiers will, but there are no recorded mutinies, and desertions were infrequent. Edward had an innate sense, which cannot be taught or learned in a classroom, of the best ground to confront an enemy and to use it effectively if, as often, his numbers were small. It was in no small measure down to him that the supplies to the army were well maintained. An army can only live off the land up to a point – and French chroniclers describe whole swathes of territory that had become a wasteland after the locusts of a foreign army had passed over it. Much of the materiel of the war came direct from England, especially since, after Sluys, Edward had command of the seas. The excellent English river network brought supplies of all kinds. The eastern parts, like London, Harwich and Kings Lynn covered the troops in Flanders. Portsmouth supplied Normandy; Bristol and Plymouth supported Aquitaine.

Something that is often downplayed is Edward's grasp of propaganda. He pushed his claim to the French throne to the limits; even when his troops were sacking towns and villages, their commanders did all they could to persuade the locals that the English cause was just. Throughout the 1340s, Edward's Goddamns raided castles, villages, abbeys and churches. This may have thrown his knights into confusion over their chivalric vows but it does not seem to have bothered the rank and file. Whether these attacks on churchmen (and women) and property were a sign of a latent anticlericalism is difficult to decide. Peer pressure and spur of the moment decisions probably played their part.

The French chronicler Jean le Bel wrote:

> When the noble Edward first gained England in his youth, nobody thought much of the English, nobody spoke of their prowess and courage … Now, in the time of the noble Edward, who has often put [the French] to the test, they are the finest and most daring warriors known to man.

Chapter 6

'Wooden Horses': The War at Sea

The first problem for the English in invading France was crossing the Channel. The French called this vital seaway 'La Manche' because it looked like a sleeve (itself a heraldic design in the Middle Ages). At its narrowest point the Channel is only 21 miles wide, but that strip of water, despite – or because of – its sudden squalls and often terrifying weather, has sometimes been almost all that saved Britain from invasion. It proved no deterrent to the various raids on England's south coast; neither did it stop Edward III and Henry V from taking impressive armies overseas in support of their claims to the French throne.

One of the oddest things to us today, in a country that produced Francis Drake, Walter Ralegh, Martin Frobisher, not to mention Horatio Nelson, is that English kings in the Hundred Years War had no navy at all. Various authorities will contend that the British navy was founded by Alfred the Great to counter the Viking longship threat of the ninth century, but that is pushing the envelope considerably. There was no official navy in the fourteenth century and no Admiralty to run it. Instead, the building, fitting and provisioning of ships was the responsibility of the Chancery and the Exchequer. Admirals themselves were actually lords of the realm appointed by Edward and Henry to command troops at sea. They had no experience of naval warfare; in fact, naval warfare as we know it did not exist.

There were no specific warships anywhere in Europe at this time. The largest cargo and passenger carrying traders of the fourteenth century were the cogs and the hulks and both were adapted for war use. The cog was a flat-bottomed, clinker-built vessel, the planks of which, usually of oak or elm, overlapped and had to be regularly inspected for leakage. It had a single mast and a single square sail. Ships of this design were new in the Hundred Years War. They had probably been developed along the Frisian coast early in the century, replacing the older knarr, which was essentially an open longship of Viking appearance. Unlike the knarr, the cog relied on wind-power and had no oars, the vessel's movement controlled by a central stern rudder. The hulk was larger and had seen variants in use since the tenth century. It had a huge side oar to effect manoeuvrability and may have been carvel built, that is, the hull planking abutted rather than overlapped. Sadly, there are no example of either type in the archaeological record and it is not until Henry V's reign that we have a clearer view of the warship. Galleys (ships with oars on both sides as a means of propulsion) were used in the Mediterranean and by various Lords of the Isles off Scotland, but they proved unreliable in the open sea of the Channel and never gained popularity among the English.

Edward III would have done deals with harbour masters via his own people to obtain cogs and/or hulks as troop transports in 1340 and later. For war use, fore and aft castles were fitted, on the bows and the sterns which were effectively firing platforms for the bowmen. Of these, the term fo'csle (forecastle) is still in use in the Royal Navy. We know that Edward had his own warship, the *Christopher*, but names of others are now lost. Perhaps, among the transports that sailed in 1340 were the *Seynte Mariecog* out of Winchelsea or *La Cristiane*, *Le Blythe* and *Le Porteur* from Weymouth. If these names sound confusingly French, it is because polite society, from the court on down, used French as their formal language.

We know, too, that Henry V had four great warships, all of them in service by 1416. They were the *Grace Dieu*, the *Trinity Royal*, the *Jesus* and the *Holigost*, all reflecting the piety (and perhaps superstition) of the age. Henry had thirty ships, half of which were armed with cannon. The *Grace Dieu* was found rotten and destroyed in the mud of the River Hamble in Hampshire in the 1930s, but a more recent discovery (1974) of the *Holigost* gives us a fuller record.

Originally, the ship had thirteen anchors, later reduced to one huge one, with its own name, the *Marie Tynkstowe*. It was a carvel, a new type that would morph in time into the ship of the line of the Armada period. The three ships that Christopher Columbus took to the New World in 1492 were carvels. The *Holigost*'s master was Jordan Brownyng, but in all other respects, sailors' names have vanished. The *Holigost* had a crew of 200, although how many of those were actual sailors is debatable. According to the manifest, there were fourteen bows on board, six crossbows, weapons and armour, as well as 2,000 arrows. There are no details of the guns, but the ship carried gads, iron darts lobbed onto enemy decks to kill soldiers, and grapnels, hooks which could be used to drag an enemy vessel nearer. The *Holigost* was boarded by the French during the siege of Harfleur in August 1415 and badly damaged. In action once again two years later, she drove off the French fleet at Chef de Caux and broke the back of French sea power for half a generation.

From 1420, all four of Henry's great ships were in dock along the Hamble, but it was hardly dry. Three years later, the *Holigost* was leaking badly, despite Brownyng, who lived on board, working night and day to keep her afloat. Welshman Davy Owen was sent below the waterline to carry out repairs, the first time that such an operation had been recorded. By 1452, the *Holigost* had 'sunk in the sea and in this way [was] broken'. She was almost a metaphor for English aspirations in the war itself.

There were no effective maps available. The first known, the Gough Map of the British Isles, dates from 1360 and is very approximate. Even so, it was a one-off, huge and pinned to a wall. Regular traders, fishermen and sailors who plied the Channel, relied on observation, folklore and experience. Navigation took place by sun and stars. The compass was unknown and the astrolabe, although available in the Arab Mediterranean for generations, was a novel gimmick that might or might not catch on. The poet Geoffrey Chaucer, was so smitten with this gadget that he wrote a treatise on it for his son. Most sailors, traditional and superstitious, left the thing alone.

So the army that crossed towards Sluys in June 1340 was in many ways amateur. Its commanders were experienced and trusted under their king and it was assumed, as always, that the rank and file, the bowmen and the billmen, would do their duty, rise to any occasion and generally behave themselves. But none of that, of course, could be guaranteed.

According to the chronicler, Jean Froissart, the fleet sailed from the Thames Estuary on 22 June. He had no idea how many ships there were, but every cog and hulk would have been draped with the colourful heraldry of the lords and knights on board. They would have made an impressive sight, bows dipping in the summer sea, flags snapping from the rigging, steel-helmeted men, some of whom may never have seen the sea before, cramming the rolling decks. Bizarrely, although this would continue to be a tradition for centuries in British armies, there were a number of ladies present, the wives of lords, knights and London merchants, all anxious to grovel at the queen's court because Philippa of Hainault was in Ghent. Edward had a special bodyguard for them, 300 men-at-arms, to keep them safe.

Although he is the best-known chronicler of the period, Froissart *does* make mistakes. The English fleet sailed from the Orwell, not the Thames. Modern research contends that there were 66 registered ships, but an actual total of 120 to 150 would seem reasonable. All in all, there were 1,300 men-at-arms and 1,000 bowmen. The role of the archers at sea, as on land, was to cover the flanks of the main army and provide devastating fire power from the fore and aft castles. Sluys was essentially a land battle fought on the water.

Edward's fleet weighed anchor off Blankenberge, today a seaside resort, having crossed the Channel in a day. There was no chance in that limited time frame for fresh water to sour, food to rot or tempers to fray. It could take three days or more to make the crossing and in the twelfth century, the Breton nobleman Herve de Leon took fifteen days to travel from Southampton to Harfleur.

The French fleet, strung out across the estuary, blocking the English advance up the Zwin to Bruges, was larger and still more impressive. Unlike Edward, Philip had a regular, professional navy; in fact, in secret plans captured after Crecy, the English discovered that a full-scale invasion of the south coast had been planned and the fleet stood ready to carry it out. To be fair to Edward, he had done his level best to reduce the odds. In the tit-for-tat build up to what would be the first major clash of the war, the English had hit the French fleet anchored at Boulogne in thick fog. With the bowmen firing blindly into nothingness, they nevertheless scored huge successes. Eighteen galleys were destroyed along with twenty-four other ships. This was in January and there had not been time to make up the deficiency. Philip had been forced to commandeer ships in the same way that Edward had to and his slowness led the bowmen to send their arrows into Frenchmen at Dieppe, Le Tréport and Mers. At Sluys, Philip had perhaps 19,000 men, easily outnumbering Edward, but his much-boasted 'Great Army of the Sea' had only 500 crossbowmen and the Genoese pirate Pietro Barbavena was down to six galleys. Like the English fleet, the French had fitted castles and crows' nests to their ships and, to make the Zwin unreachable, had roped and chained the vessels together in three lines. Rain and wind on the night of the 23rd had hopelessly battered this formation, so that the lines were intermingled and the rear had no hope of joining battle. The Admirals Béhuchet and Quiéret were still trying to sort this out when the English struck.

It was 24 June, St John's Eve. Edward could see that the French had placed their largest ships in the front line, including his own *Christopher* and *Cog Edward*, stolen off Waleheren in September 1338. There was a braying of horns, the usual means of signalling by sea, and the French advanced. The *Christopher* was bristling with crossbowmen, their iron kettle hats flashing in the sun, but they would have to get within 200 yards of the English to inflict any damage. The longbowmen had a 100-yard advantage and they made it tell.

The king and his lieutenants, the Earls of Northampton and Huntingdon, saw Barbavena's galleys rowing out of line. They feared a flanking move and the reserve of archers, three cogs packed with longbowmen, gave chase. When they eventually closed, the castles of the cogs were higher than the galleys and long before the murderous iron-tipped beaks could smash a hole in hull timbers, the deadly arrows rained down. One bowman, a Londoner, remembered afterwards that it was like watching hail in winter, volley after volley thudding onto the decks, skewering men and pinning them to the timbers. The Genoese had never seen anything like it.

Elsewhere, the French front line was being decimated. Edward had created units, not unlike the lance on a land battlefield, of three ships, one of men-at-arms, the others full of bowmen. The arrows cut down the crews and fighting men of the *Christopher*, the *Cog Edward* and so many more, while the men-at-arms in the centre threw their iron-spiked gads and grappling hooks and hauled the hapless French ships to more open water, where the hand-to-hand slaughter began. Men wounded by arrows, bleeding and in pain, lurched helplessly on the rolling decks. Crossbowmen did not have time or space to handle their weapons into position, their bow stirrups slipping in blood.

One galley got through and, shamefully, its target was one of the ladies' ships. It must have been obvious on that clear summer's day, even as the light began to fade, that the men on board were only a bodyguard and they knew perfectly well that butchering women in battle was no part of anybody's military creed. Nobody except the Barbary pirates who made up most of Barbavena's rabble. Even the French regarded the man as sub-human.

News spread, almost certainly from watchers on the river banks and the coast, that the French were losing the day and from everywhere, Flemish ships of all shapes and sizes crowded their sails and made for the estuary. It was well and truly dark before the isolated third line of the French (the first two had been destroyed) tried to break out. They discovered that English bowmen could shoot as well in the night as in the day and flickering torches gave them excellent light. Only seventeen ships got away.

Twenty-four vessels blazed into the night; the English had captured one hundred and sixty-six. There would be no more raids on wool merchants for a while and the sea roads belonged to Edward. Half-drowned sailors and soldiers, bleeding and shocked, reached the shore, only to be clubbed to death by locals, keen to loot what they could; it was the way of the world in the hurling time. Bodies were washed up by the tide for days and burials were brief and rudimentary. Froissart, at heart perhaps a Frenchman despite his English connections, wrote that the French commanders – Quiéret, Béhuchet and even Barbavena – were good and courageous knights. Edward III disagreed. Béhuchet was hanged from his own masthead like a common felon. Quiéret was beheaded for his outrageous attack on unarmed civilians off Walcheren two years earlier.

Edward stayed on board his ship during that short summer night (it was Midsummer's Day) with so much musical celebration, of drums and trumpets and cymbals 'that God's own thunder would not have been heard above it'. The next day, he celebrated Mass at the Church of Our Lady at Aardenburg before riding on to Bruges for a joyful meeting with the queen.

The heroes of the day, in time-honoured tradition, were the nobility and the knights – the Earls of Derby, Pembroke, Hereford, Huntingdon, Northampton and Gloucester; Lords Reginald Cobham, Felton, Brandeston, Stafford, Percy; the knights Henry de Flanders, John Beauchamp, Walter Manny – their names would become household words in the months and years ahead. Of the nameless bowmen who had actually made the victory happen ... nothing.

But if there was euphoria in the English camp at Bruges, the same could not be said of Paris. At first no one could find the courage to tell the French king the result of Sluys – 'the terrifying shout ... above the wooden horses' as the chronicler Geoffrey le Baker put it. In the end, Philip's jester got the short straw and explained the grim news via a riddle – 'Why are the English less brave than the French? Because they wouldn't jump into the sea in full armour like our gallant knights.' It must have gone down like a lead balloon. Barbavena might have got away from the English but he could not escape the French. He was arrested for desertion in the field (not actually accurate) and served a year in prison. The Goddamns joked that if the fish in the Zwin could speak, it would be in French because so many of their men lay in the mud of the river's bottom.

Winston Churchill might have called this 'the end of the beginning' but it was not even that. Until battle could be joined for real on dry land, the war would drag on and ten years after Sluys, it all happened again. Sporadic French raiding on the south coast continued. The Flemish pirate John Crabb joined forces with the Scots and it was not until 1352 that he was grabbed at sea by Walter Manny and his roving days were over. Such piracy was a two-way street; the Englishman John Hawley was wreaking havoc along the French coast too.

It was piracy that led to the next naval clash, off Winchelsea on 29 August 1350, St Adelph's Day. This time the enemy was Spain, not France. Spaniards had, for decades, been attacking English merchantmen and a large band of them, moored at Sluys that summer, got wind of the fact that the English planned to waylay them on their return home. They stocked up with bows, mercenaries, even artillery. Edward summoned the usual army from the Cinque Ports and elsewhere and his fleet carried the pride of his nobility. His sons, Edward of Woodstock (already the hero of Crecy four years earlier) and John of Gaunt, later Duke of Lancaster, sailed in the same ship. They all waited at Dover for the Spanish fleet to be sighted. Both fleets had siege weapons on their decks, mangonels and trebuchets that hurled stones onto the enemy, scattering men and smashing timbers.

We have a vivid description of Edward on the foredeck of the *Salle du Roi*, dressed in black velvet with a beaver hat, ordering his band to play a German dance tune that John Chandos had recently brought to England. He insisted that Chandos join in with the singing and it may have been a relief to many that the observer in the crow's nest shouted, 'Ship ho!' And as the single sail turned into many, the scout called down, 'God help me! I can't count them.' The trumpets blasted out the signal and the English fleet moved out into the Channel. The whole episode, which came to be known as *Les Espagnols-sur-Mer* (the Spaniards on the Sea), was watched by the queen and her ladies of the court from the Dover headland. The tradition of what the Germans called *schlachtenbummler* (battle walkers) which we associate with the Crimean campaign of the 1850s and the American Civil War of the next decade, has a long history.

Off went Edward's beaver hat, to be replaced by the iron bascinet he habitually wore in battle. Everybody else followed suit. The bowmen looked to their weapons. During the day in August, there was no fear of wet bow strings or warped arrows. It is highly likely that the core of the king's archers were experienced men who had fought with him at Crecy and even at Sluys. Shooting on a moving deck was a different skill set from dry land, but the sea was calm that day and there were few problems. Edward turned to the *Salle*'s master, the recently appointed Robert of Namur – 'Lay me alongside the Spaniard who is bearing down on us, for I will have a tilt with him.' Like his son the Black Prince, the king was an expert jouster but this phrase sums up how all European commanders saw naval engagements – they were land battles on water.

The irony of the moment was that the Spaniards could have avoided a fight altogether had they wanted to. The wind was behind them and Edward's fleet, coming from a standing start, as it were, could probably never have caught them. Just like two knights colliding in the lists, the *Salle* and the Spanish commander's vessels rammed into each other, the Spaniard's forecastle shattering and scattering men into the sea. The *Salle* was seriously damaged and leaking, men-at-arms furiously baling out with whatever they could find while the bowmen poured fire on the enemy. Edward insisted that he wanted to capture the Spaniard, but was forced to let that one go and went for another.

Generally speaking, the Spanish fleet was composed of larger ships that sat higher in the water. They may have been carvels and hand-to-hand fighting with bills, swords, daggers and grappling hooks broke out between several vessels. Since the *Salle* was in danger of sinking, it was vital to take the enemy ship and get on board. The entire Spanish ships' company were thrown into the sea, many riddled with arrows like so many pin cushions.

The fight had begun late in the day and the Spanish crossbowmen, at close quarters able to find their marks easily, were inflicting terrible damage on the English ships. Elsewhere, the Black Prince's ship was grappled to a big carvel and was holed in several places. The day was saved by the redoubtable Henry of Lancaster, who had fought at Sluys. He pulled his ship to the other side of the Spaniard, yelling his battle cry 'Derby to the rescue!' (he was Earl of Derby too!) and boarded the Spaniard from starboard. Once again, the defeated troops were consigned to the deep. We have no idea how many men on either side could actually swim. In Nelson's day, when we have far more detailed information, a high percentage of sailors could not. The Black Prince took over the Spanish ship, no doubt with profuse thanks to Henry of Lancaster, and sailed off looking for more action.

This simple 'boys own' event must have raised complications. The enemy ship did not carry *any* English heraldry and even though the Prince had his own banners on board and his bowmen in their distinctive green and white, such switching of ships (the king, of course, had done it too) must have caused confusion, if not chaos.

As dusk fell, Edward was back on the *Salle du Roi*, grappling with a larger Spaniard. The enemy ship was big enough to drag the *Salle* off as a prize (which, with the king of England on board would have been a mighty prize indeed). In the panic, an Englishman, perhaps a bowman called Hanekin, leapt onto the enemy deck and hacked at the grappling ropes with his sword. Thus freed, the *Salle* slid away from her would-be captor.

The Spaniards lost fourteen ships; the others vanished into the night. The retreat was sounded in the English fleet and the ships put in to Winchelsea and Rye. Celebrations went on for days.

The last major naval clash of the Hundred Years War took place off La Rochelle on 22 June 1372, St Paulinus' Day. Under the terms of the Treaty of Bretigny twelve years earlier, the thriving seaport, vital to England's wine trade, came under English control. That did not mean that the majority of Frenchmen were happy and by the summer of 1372, a French army under Bertrand du Guesclin was laying siege to it.

Edward III was, by this time, already in the grip of his long dotage. He slept a lot, drank too much and was increasingly under the thumb of his pushy mistress, Alice Perrers. This was also, as bad luck would have it, almost the last time that Edward, the Black Prince, would function effectively. Both men would be dead by 1377. The king's plans seemed to be, although he was often unclear about it, to mount a huge campaign to secure Aquitaine, at which the French had been nibbling for some time. Perhaps as an advance part of that, John Hastings, Earl of Pembroke, was given £12,000, thirty-two ships and seventeen barges (for towing bowmen and materiel) and told to lift Du Guesclin's siege. His force was small – twenty-four knights, fifty-five squires and eighty archers as well as two free companies under Hugh Calverley and John Devereux. Pembroke was Duke of Aquitaine, so he perhaps had more incentive than most to hang on to his territory.

The chroniclers are very vague about the fleet that sailed from Plymouth, with numbers of ships ranging from fourteen to thirty-six (neither figure, of course, tallying with those above).

The Castilian fleet facing them was there as a result of the ever-changing alliances during the war; the king of Castile, Enrico of Trastamara, had stuck a deal with the French. The first day was a series of half-hearted skirmishes, although Pembroke was quickly aware that the Castilian navy both outnumbered and outmatched his own. In fact, it was possibly the most impressive in Europe. The galleys were faster and more manoeuvrable than Pembroke's hulks and the Castilians had mounted extra-tall castles on them so that fire power rained down on English decks. The Goddamns no doubt fought back bravely, as they always did, but firing 'uphill' was always fraught with difficulties. On the second day, the fast-rising tide caught several English ships aground on sand banks and the Castilians had their own 'secret weapon' that the English had possibly never seen before. They used their height advantage to pour oil onto English timbers, then set ships alight with flame-tipped crossbow bolts. Of the approximated 800 deaths in the English fleet, most were caused by severe burns.

La Rochelle was the worst defeat the English had suffered. Pembroke had little choice but to surrender, his entire fleet destroyed. English control of the Channel ceased to exist and French raids on England continued as before, Gravesend in the Thames estuary blazing in 1380. Du Guesclin took La Rochelle and Gascony, as the only English territory in the south began to slip away.

Although there was to be a brilliant re-awakening of English fortunes under Henry V, the sea war against the French was a dwindling spectacle; from the high of Sluys to the depths of La Rochelle, there is (if you are English!) a depressing inevitability about it. Back in the glory days of 1340, Edward III had a gold coin struck to commemorate Sluys. It showed the king standing on the deck of a cog, the arms of England and France all around him. Around the rim runs the legend *IHC Transiens Per Medium Illorum Ibat* (Jesus, passing through, then went his way). Had there been room on the coin, Edward should have added, 'And he had a few bowmen with him.'

Chapter 7

The Chevauchée

The most consistent tactic of the Hundred Years War was the *chevauchée*, practised by both sides in the conflict. It literally means a horse ride and refers to the marauding advance into a territory to loot, pillage and terrify the inhabitants. The English used it as a ploy to force the French to give battle, especially in the early years when they knew they had the edge in the field. Such raids drove down morale and led to unrest, as with the Jacquerie in 1358 and, to a lesser extent, the Peasants' Revolt in 1381. It could be argued that the Blitz of civilian populations in the Second World War had a similar purpose, not to provoke the British government into an open fight (that was already happening, especially at sea and in the air) but to encourage the people to overthrow Churchill's government and sue for peace.

Nothing like that actually happened in 1940–2; neither did it in the Hundred Years War but in that conflict, the chevauchée could (and did) lead to the acquisition of territory.

The first chevauchées were carried out, as we have seen, by the French in their attacks on the south coast in 1338. This was not an unprovoked act of aggression as, technically, war had been declared the previous year. The raids certainly caught England napping, however, with fifty French ships sneaking into Southampton's harbour on a Sunday morning when the town was at church. Guards patrolling the walls must have seen this activity, but by the time the alarm was raised, the French had landed and their cannon smashed the flimsy masonry then in place. The whole area behind the walls (the Medieval street pattern is still obvious) was burned, up to and beyond the internal gates, now known as Bar. Homes, workshops, inns, brothels, churches, all of it was attacked as the French troops ran riot. The walls had no siege engine defences and, astonishingly, it was not until the 1360s that the new walls ordered by Edward III were completed. A second chevauchée in 1377 posed a more serious deterrent for the French and they raided Portsmouth and the Isle of Wight instead. Southampton Castle was strengthened and re-fortified in that decade by architects Henry Yvele, John Polymund and John Sandes and the gunports they built were the first to be seen in England. By 1382, in common with most of the larger towns, Southampton had its own cannon and later improvements to the walls included God's House Tower (1417), while Henry V was conducting his own chevauchées in France, and Catchcold Tower (1439), both of which proved that artillery was now the key to siege warfare.

The problem for the vulnerable areas on both sides of the Channel was that they could not easily be defended. In Britain, as elsewhere in the Roman empire, soldiers built temporary forts on the march and permanent ones which became legionary bases. These were well built and maintained (as were later Medieval castles) but beyond the camp/castle wall, towns grew up in a ramshackle, unplanned way that did not take defence into account. Often in the chevauchées of the Hundred Years War, a town was destroyed but its castle held out, necessitating a siege of whatever duration. In the meantime, the local population had to cope as best it could. If the people had not had time to get to the safety of the castle, their choice was to scatter into the forests or come to whatever terms they could with their attackers. Outlying villages and hamlets were still more vulnerable. While most towns had watchmen and even militia, rural areas had nobody. The local lord had a retinue of fighting men, but their numbers were small and the manor houses, even the fortified ones, were not capable of withstanding a determined force. In several cases, the lord and his retinue were already absent, with the king's army elsewhere.

Froissart, along with other chroniclers, describes dozens of chevauchées and while they might all exaggerate the killing and destruction, we only have the vaguest mention of this. There are no known accounts of people who actually faced the arrival of the Goddamns, bent on slaughter as most of them were.

'There must have been four thousand men-at-arms and ten thousand archers,' he wrote of the army that sailed from Southampton for the Crecy campaign, 'without counting the Irish and Welsh who followed his army on foot.'

This was the reality of Medieval warfare. Kings gave harsh orders involving life and death (in this respect, both Edward the Black Prince and Henry V were far harsher than Edward III) and underlings carried them out. Whereas a knight might have enough respect for the rather hypocritical laws of chivalry with regard to women and children, the common soldier had none. A Goddamn might think of his own wife and child back home and hold back from butchery, but in the heat of the moment, who knew what might happen? In a very different war and in a different time, the village of My Lai in Vietnam was razed to the ground and its inhabitants massacred by men who had wives and children too. The implications of Froissart's Irish and Welsh are those of pure snobbery and racism. The idea was that the Celtic fringe was even more barbaric than the English soldiery. Such men, from the bogs and mountains, spoke an incomprehensible language, were barely civilized and carried murderous knives. How much control would Edward III, in 1346, have over such people?

Because of the distances involved and the need for speed to catch communities unaware, most of the chevauchées involved cavalry, lightly armed hobelars on saddle horses called palfreys rather than the huge, 17-hand destriers of the knights. Even though men-at-arms and bowmen normally fought on foot, they almost certainly rode as part of a chevauchée. It is likely that even the smallest chevauchées, of perhaps 1,000 or 2,000 men marched in battle formation, with three divisions interspersed and flanked by bowmen. The archers probably covered the rear as well and formed a screen at the front to guard against attack. The roads in France were as bad as those in England, the best of them originally built by the Roman legions 1,400 years earlier. With no accurate maps and only rare and probably not very accurate road signs, actually *finding* a particular site was difficult and most villages were probably attacked just because they happened to be on the way to a target town or castle.

The artwork of the period is singularly unhelpful in this regard. The painting itself, for example for the book of psalms belonging to the Duc de Berry called *Les Riches Heures*, is superb and the figures generally realistic. A large number, now housed in the Bibliothèque Nationale in Paris, invariably show an elegant, many-turreted castle in the background, even when there was none there and the scale of building to man is usually hopeless. One or two show pillaging going on, incredibly well-dressed and armoured soldiers smashing barrels of wine or emptying pots and pans out of upstairs rooms or carrying chests. There is no sign of killing, or rape, presumably because the potential victims have long gone.

One or two examples of an army on the march raise more questions than they answer. In a fifteenth-century version in the Bibliothèque Royale de Belgique, we have an illustration from the *Chronique de Hainault.* It shows a ragged column of carts and wagons, with four wheels, each drawn by four horses. Men on foot provide flanking protection, but because this is a French or Burgundian army, there are no bowmen among them. What is fascinating is the central wagon which contains women, children and assorted furniture. They are clearly refugees and presumably are being escorted to safety.

Another painting in the Bibliothèque Nationale depicts Edward III's invasion of Scotland, although it is not clear which campaign specifically. Intriguingly, the only bowman in the picture is in the Scots army, bearing in mind what little faith David II had in them.

Edward III's army marching from La Hogue in 1346 hugged the coast, keeping the fleet in sight as far as possible. Froissart singles out the bowmen – 'Archers and foot soldiers marched … robbing, pillaging and carrying off everything they came across.' While a preponderance of booty slowed an advancing army down, looting was a perk of the soldier's trade and no Medieval commander (usually late with his pay) could afford to ignore it.

At Barfleur, the residents were so terrified at the sight of the Goddamns that they opened the town's gates without any attempt at resistance. The town was emptied of gold, silver and jewellery. Froissart says that, 'they found so much there that the very servants in the army turned up their noses at fur-lined gowns.' The men of Barfleur were roped together and herded onto the ships so that there could be no retaliation later. The Goddamns 'did whatever they pleased, for no one resisted them'. They sacked the town of Cherbourg and destroyed Valognes, leaving it a burned-out ruin.

From these and other towns, the English helped themselves to livestock, no doubt using their drovers-turned-bowmen to herd the sheep, cattle and pigs of Normandy which provided excellent fare. In all this, no one mentions anything resembling a scorched earth policy in the 1340s. Perhaps the locals had no time to initiate it or perhaps they hoped that the raiders would take another path and leave them alone. Froissart implies that the Normans had no experience of war and had no idea how to handle marauding armies. At Saint-Lo, so much cloth was stolen that the Goddamns could have made a fortune selling it on, had they had anybody to sell it to!

At Caen, the Goddamns found the two wealthy abbeys of St Etienne and the Trinity. One of them housed 120 nuns 'all fully endowed' (which meant that they were wealthy, rather than curvy). Annoyed at the resistance the inhabitants put up, Edward took the town and intended to slaughter all of them indiscriminately. He was restrained by Sir Godfrey de Harcourt who issued orders, as Marshal of the army, that there should be no fires, no murder and no rape, on pain of death. The punishment itself was by hanging, in the fourteenth century, a slow and grisly process by which a man was strangled to death. Even so, atrocities did occur and Froissart refers to the 'criminals without conscience' among the Goddamns.

The wholesale slaughter of citizens was a feature of the Hundred Years War. Had the French ever ventured further inland than England's south coast, they would no doubt have carried out the same atrocities. Most of us are appalled by this today, but it is little different from bombing raids carried out by all participants in the Second World War and is still going on elsewhere today. There was no such thing as 'legitimate military targets' in the fourteenth century and, as long as churches were by and large left alone, everybody else was fair game.

According to the chronicler Thomas Walsingham, a particularly awful atrocity happened in England in 1379 and it was carried out by Englishmen! Sir John Arundel, younger brother of the earl, was on his way to Brittany with a retinue of soldiers, the majority of whom were probably bowmen. They found a priory and the prioress, as she was bound to do, offered them shelter. In return, the troops got drunk and raped a number of the nuns before gate-crashing a wedding party and helping themselves to the presents and the bride. A number of women were taken on board ship and, to lighten the load in rough seas, were thrown overboard. Nobody but Walsingham records this incident and it is not listed in any official records. The point is that those who read it almost certainly believed it because this, for brutal soldiers, was the norm. Cock-fighting was a children's game. Horses and other animals were beaten into obedience. Everybody watched bull- and bear-baiting and children as young as 7 could be hanged for theft.

There are many today who believe that we live in more savage, dangerous and lawless times than in the past. Don't you believe it!

For three days, the English sacked Caen and sent their loot down the river to Ouistreham where the fleet was anchored. The booty, the prisoners and most of the ships returned home, with 400 bowmen on the fore and aft castles to provide protection. Edward's plan was not to waste good men and siege engines in actual warfare but to ravage the unprotected countryside. He halted at Poissy and burned the outskirts of Paris itself – Saint-Germain-en-Laye, Saint-Cloud, Boulogne,

La Montjoie and Bourg-le-Reine. King Philip fled to St Denis to organize his nobility for the head-on clash with the English at Crecy.

It was after this battle that Froissart describes the work of the camp followers – 'pillagers and irregulars, Welsh and Cornishmen armed with long knives'. Their job was to roam the battlefield and cut the throats of anybody still alive. Wounded men were a problem that a small army in alien territory could do without. Since the cut-throats had no notion of the value of ransom money, many of their targets were high-born Frenchmen whose lives were worth a fortune. They killed them anyway and the king was furious. In the mopping-up operations after Crecy, Froissart was told that four times as many died in the surrounding areas over the next four days than had gone down in the battle itself.

The English army continued after Crecy much as it had done before, burning Saint-Josse and Neufchatel, Etaples and Rue. This led on to the siege of Calais. About the only success the French had here was taking the well-guarded tower near the hill of Sangotte. It was held exclusively by the Goddamns, who rained their arrows down on wave after wave of attacks until they were all killed.

Henry of Lancaster burned Fauquenberg to the ground. The only building to survive was the thirteenth-century church of St Leger. The following year, the Goddamns were secretly furious because Edward III agreed to a temporary truce to give his army time to recover. That meant no more looting, at least for the time being. We have to remember that ordinary houses, shops, inns and brothels were timber-built in the fourteenth and fifteenth centuries. Only castles and churches were made of stone. In the dry summer months of a campaigning season, it was easy to torch whole streets and nowhere had anything resembling a fire service to put such conflagrations out.

In 1355, Edward the Black Prince launched a chevauchée that has been described as one of the most destructive in history. Setting out from what was effectively his capital at Bordeaux he marched to Toulouse, trying to bring Jean, the Count of Armagnac, to battle. Edward had already won his spurs at Crecy and, at 25, was a battle-hardened veteran. For all his reputation as a chivalrous commander he had a hard streak in him that some modern historians see as sadism. He got as far as Carcassonne and Narbonne, destroying towns and villages as he went. In a second foray early in the next year, he marched north towards Normandy, making money out of the chevauchées by capturing French lords and demanding ransom for their release. They left the countryside, says Froissart, 'broken and devastated behind them'.

With 7,000 men (nearly half of them bowmen) the Prince made for Bourges, the capital of the Duchy of Berry and a centre known for its alchemy. The town was not sacked, but Vierzon nearby was. King Jean's army, seriously outnumbering the Prince, was trailing him and the Goddamns clashed briefly with the French advance guard in the area of Romorantin, which Edward then attacked. We will look at this assault in a later chapter.

In a bizarre incident recorded after the battle of Poitiers, Froissart tells the tale of one of Sir Peter Audley's squires leading a raid on the village of Ronay. High Mass was being held in the local church and the squire marched down the aisle and emptied the holy wine from the priest's goblet onto the floor. When the priest protested, the squire slapped him across the face with the back of his gauntlet and blood sprayed onto the altar. The squire rode off with the chalice and silver plate, but as he did so, the horse went berserk in a field, whirling around in circles until both hit the ground with broken necks. They immediately turned to 'dust and ashes'. Witnesses were so horrified that they vowed never to rob a church again. 'I do not know,' says Froissart, his tongue presumably firmly in his cheek, 'whether they kept their promise.' And if you believe that …

Froissart describes the baggage that the chevauchées took with them. Apart from the tents, of various shapes and sizes, there were mills for grinding corn, ovens for baking, forges for shoeing horses. One particular outfit had 8,000 wagons, drawn by rounseys (all-purpose draught horses) brought over direct from England. They also had skiffs and other boats for fording rivers and fishing in lakes. When the king himself led a chevauchée (as Edward III did in September 1347) or a lord commanded (like John of Gaunt in 1373 and the Earl of Buckingham seven years later) the trappings of the court moved with them. Edward had thirty mounted falconers and sixty hunting dogs, to provide entertainment when there was little or no human quarry in sight.

John of Gaunt's 9,000 men (the numbers creep up over time) left Calais late in the summer of 1373 to halt the French fight-back by Bertrand du Guesclin, the Constable, who was winning town after town from the English. Du Guesclin was a past master at avoiding pitched battles and harassed Gaunt's army by isolating foragers and butchering them. At Moulins, struggling to cross the river there, the Goddamns lost much of their own baggage and nearly all the loot they had taken over the previous month. Among Gaunt's troops were 6,000 bowmen and a contingent of Scots fighting as mercenaries for the English during a period of truce between the two nations.

At Vaux, in harvest time, the Goddamns held farms and the larger villages to ransom under threat of burning the crops and happily collected the wine, flour and livestock that the villagers brought. After that, however, the sheer absence of a sizeable French army wore the English down. 'Let them go on,' the French king is supposed to have said to his war council. 'They cannot rob you of your heritage by fires and smoke. They will grow tired and crumble away to nothing.' This is a fascinating example of resistance mentality. In the Second World War, the assumption was made by both sides that saturation bombing would cause a collapse in morale and force governments to surrender. It had actually the exact opposite response – a determination to hang on in there. The French of the Hundred Years War had already learned this lesson 600 years earlier!

It is clear from events in the 1370s that the English had civilian craftsmen with them, men who could repair roads and rebuild bridges. The problem was time and the constant harassment from du Guesclin's riders. The bowmen were kept on constant alert in these situations to protect any engineering work that was going on. When two armies nearly collided, as at Epernay, both looted the area, pulling the locals in two directions to provide food, drink and shelter. Even so, by definition, the native population favoured the French and du Guesclin's men boarded comfortably in towns with roofs over their heads, while Gaunt's were in open country, passing through the poverty-stricken areas of Limousin, Ronergue and the Agenois. Men ditched their armour and starvation hit. By the time they reached Bordeaux, they had lost over half their horses. Six days had passed without any bread being available and men froze to death in the December cold crossing the mountains.

Equally disappointing was the Earl of Buckingham's expedition in July 1380. Thomas of Woodstock would later become embroiled in the murky and petty politics of Richard II's reign, but that summer he was on his way to the support of his ally, the Duke of Brittany. He laid siege to Nantes, but Brittany's force failed to turn up, leaving Buckingham outnumbered. He lamely accepted 50,000 francs to abandon the siege and the campaign.

The biggest chevauchées that never came off happened in 1386. 'Why shouldn't we go over to England for once,' Froissart has the French nobility saying, 'and have a look at the country and the people? We'll get to know our way about there, just as the English did in their time in France.' The French had, of course, had a very good look at parts of the south coast on several occasions since 1337, but this was a full-scale invasion. Taxes were raised, flour was milled, biscuits were baked at Tournai, Lille, Donay and a score of other towns. The fleet would sail from Sluys, various lessons having been learned since 1340. Charles VII's massive fleet, still bolstered by the Castilians, groaned with wine, salted meat, hay and oats for the horses, flour, vinegar, salt, onions, egg yolks beaten in barrels, and, no doubt, crossbows without number; everything necessary for such a campaign. Later attempts to invade England, from the Armada of 1588 to Hitler's Operation Sealion in 1940 had similar ideas.

By September, 1,387 warships and transports were assembled, the Hollanders and Zeelanders having been paid for their vessels in advance. The Constable of France, Olivier de Clisson, who had grown up at Edward III's court and until 1370 had fought for the English, was building another huge fleet at Treguier in Brittany. Rather as William of Normandy had brought collapsible wooden castles over in September 1066, so the French had portable timber fortifications to build temporary defences on English soil again. This would house the army's commanders and there were hundreds of carpenters and engineers on board to handle it.

'And those French soldiers,' Froissart wrote, 'to hear them talking, considered England to be already crushed and devastated, all her men killed and her women and children brought to France and held in slavery …' Heraldry dazzled everywhere, gold leaf decorating the ships' masts. Guy de la Trémoille paid over 2,000 francs for his vessels' artwork. Who paid for all this? The French taxpayer and they moaned mightily.

In England, there was panic. There was no attempt to hide troop movements on the French coast and the rumour mill went into overdrive. Religious processions were held in towns, prayers were offered up in cathedrals and churches. Others, with folk memories of Crecy and Poitiers, were casual to say the least – 'Let them all come … Not a bollock of them shall get back to France, by God.' Probably the Goddamns and their sons and grandsons shouted this loudest of all.

Ports and harbours were strengthened, from the Humber to Cornwall. Beacons were built or rebuilt on the coasts and the headlands. On clear days, the watchers in Kent could virtually see the French coast. Richard II's war council (the king was still only 20) decided to let the French land and roam the countryside for three or four days. This may have been foolhardy; the best time to stop an invasion was at the start as men floundered in the surf and before the horses were brought ashore. A kind of scorched earth policy was decided upon, with crops harvested and guarded, dead dogs in wells, rivers flooded. The bridge at Rochester was destroyed, slowing any potential attack on the castle. 'In England,' Froissart knew, 'there were 100,000 good archers and

10,000 men-at-arms.' Were it possible to put so many bowmen in any field at one time, no French army could stand against them.

Fisherman spies, ostensibly going about their legitimate business in Boulogne and Wishart, reported troop and ship movement to Simon Burley, the governor of Dover Castle, the largest in England. De Clisson left Treguier with seventy-two ships, loaded with provisions and bristling with men. The wind was with them at first, but off Margate it changed and strengthened and, not for the last time in British history, the great fleet was scattered. The wind drove isolated vessels into the Thames Estuary, where they were easily overpowered by the English. Among the spoils was the wooden fortress so lovingly crafted as headquarters for the French army. Ships, prisoners and loot were taken upriver to the delight of Londoners, who crowded the banks of the Thames, cheering and jeering in equal measure. Seven of de Clisson's ships foundered on the Dutch coast, but the Constable himself limped home after days of exhaustion.

At Sluys, the rest of the fleet dithered, exactly as they had done in 1340. By December, it was decided that a winter campaign would not work and the 'enterprise of England' (as the Spanish called the similar attempt in 1588) was called off. The chevauchée that never happened had cost France in taxation alone more than 3 million francs.

The last great chevauchée of the Hundred Years War, that of Henry V in his Agincourt campaign, is covered in other chapters. As the war progressed, sieges rather than pitched battles came to dominate and the whole strategy of the conflict changed direction. In 1435, Sir John Fastolf, a veteran of Agincourt, Verneuil and the Battle of the Herrings suggested to the government of Henry VI that chevauchées should be launched again, avoiding the mistakes of John of Gaunt and the Earl of Buckingham. But the French had motivated themselves by now, won a brilliant victory at Orleans and would not slip back into the bad old ways. Fastolf may have been right, but nobody was listening.

Chapter 8

The Siege

For all it is the pitched battles of the Hundred Years War that we remember, sieges achieved far more in terms of land gained and the enemy being forced to rethink their position. Sieges have not caught the imagination because they are slow and laborious, did not always work and only rarely provided acts of valour and derring-do, the raison d'être of the knightly class that undertook them.

In simple terms, if Edward III or the Black Prince or Henry V invaded France with an army, they were bound to come across castles and fortified towns and cities. Their choice then was straightforward: they could ignore the fortress simply by riding round it and carrying on or take the obstacle by whatever means. Ignoring the castle was risky, because there was now a garrison *behind* the advancing army, with all the uncertainties that that caused. Laying siege to an area effectively stopped the advance and gave time for enemy reinforcements to arrive. It was also expensive in terms of pay for the army and the cost of provisions.

By the middle of the fourteenth century, castles were complicated structures, cleverly designed to block attacks wherever possible. From the wooden pre-fabrication that William of Normandy brought over on his ships in September 1066, magnificent stone fortresses guarded every pass and major road throughout Europe. The castle was at once a status symbol and an effective means of control. When Edward I went to war with the Welsh, he built a chain of such castles around the coast, so that their garrisons could be supplied by sea, and along the border, where Marcher lords could easily keep in touch with their nearest neighbour only a few miles away.

The crusades had taught western Europe a great deal about tactics and defence and engineers with mathematical precision were hired by kings and lords to build fortresses that were all but impregnable. Today, with modern aerial warfare, keyhole bombing and drone missiles, castles are an irrelevance. Even by the late nineteenth century, the power of artillery, just developing in the Hundred Years War, meant that bombardments lasted for days and men took shelter underground, not in the high castles their ancestors had built.

After Poitiers, the French avoided open battle with the English whenever they could, relying on sieges and the guerrilla tactics of Bertrand du Guesclin and the free companies. There is a marked difference between castles proper and fortified towns. Most large settlements had walls and gates by the 1340s for security. Both were patrolled by armed guards and the gates locked at night. Even so, it was relatively easy to take a town; less so a castle.

A castle's walls were very thick (the base of the White Tower, the keep of the Tower of London is 20ft thick in places). Its walls were anything up to 40ft high, to make attacks by scaling ladders almost impossible. That said, castle walls, like town walls, were filled in many cases with rubble, which meant that they could not withstand a bombardment of cannon. Carisbrooke Castle in the Isle of Wight (besieged by the French in 1377) had to undergo a major rebuilding in the 1590s to repel a potential attack from the Spain of Philip II. Walls were dotted with bow-slits through which archers inside could fire on the troops below. The chances of a bowman on the ground, however expert, of hitting such a target, were minimal. The stone cannon balls of Edward III and Henry V battered the masonry, but could not topple a tower. For that, the only answer was undermining by special troops who dug tunnels under walls, propping them up with timbers exactly as coal-miners would in the centuries ahead. It was hard and dangerous work, but once the moment was right, the timbers were set alight and the whole wall/tower would crash down. That was the signal for a besieging army to haul itself through the gap – 'Once more unto the breach, dear friends, once more,' as Shakespeare makes Henry V say at Harfleur – and kill anybody they saw. For all that to happen, a lot had to go right for the attackers, and many commanders preferred to camp out of bow reach and wait for the garrison to surrender or starve or die of thirst.

When Edward III invaded France in 1340, he besieged Cambrai and Tournai, abandoning them both because they were too strong. He took a number of towns in the Crecy campaign, but could not take the castles at St-Lô, Valognes and Carentan. The action at Caen gives us an opportunity to see how the process worked. The English arrived by land and upriver, their ships bristling with bowmen and Edward ordered an attack on the Old Town.

Despite the generally acknowledged protocols involving chivalry, the sacking of a town was not part of that. Merchants, craftsmen and peasants were not gentle-born and there were no rules covering them. Shops were looted and burned, unarmed citizens were hacked to death in the streets. Women were assaulted, raped and left for dead. The citizenry tried to defend themselves by hurling stones and planks from rooftops, which infuriated Edward. The town surrendered after only hours, the townsfolk telling Sir Thomas Holland that they were particularly afraid of the English bowmen.

There are few clear accounts of bowmen in siege situations. If the Caen citizenry did not form units to withstand the attack, which is unlikely, then the massed arrow storm which became famous at Crecy would be pointless. No doubt individual bowmen shot and killed individual townspeople, but it was just as likely they did not waste arrows and instead used their bows as clubs or drew their swords and daggers once they were at close quarters.

Edward's next target was Calais in the far north, which he needed as a base for future operations. The Medieval town stood on an island, only 18 miles as the crow flies from Dover, dominated by its castle and the church of Notre Dame. During the siege, Edward had to break off to give battle at Crecy, but despite the totality of his victory, the siege dragged on into 1347. The castle was formidable, with double walls and a double ditch and was held by the stubborn Jean de Vienne. The commander sent out 1,700 of the town's paupers, throwing them on Edward's mercy. Other commanders, such as the Black Prince and Henry V would have butchered them, but Edward gave them a free meal and cash and sent them on their way.

During the eleven months that the siege lasted, the English brought over cannon and built siege engines, the tried and tested weapons used in sieges before gunpowder became genuinely effective. Siege towers or belfries were just that – timber-built structures on wheels, as high as a castle or town wall, which housed bowmen and men-at-arms on a number of floors inside them. They could be used to reach battlements for hand-to-hand fighting, to fire various ballistic weapons and as a cover for mining operations. Henry V took several on his Agincourt campaign. The towers were vulnerable to fire (bowmen regularly used flaming arrows dipped in tar for siege operations) and were covered in water-soaked ox-hides to counter this.

Ballistae were huge crossbows and had been used in warfare for centuries. They made no impression on walls but were deadly in sweeping defenders off battlements. Mangonels were stone-throwing machines with a wooden cup at one end of a pivoted arm, released when the string was freed. They could do considerable damage to walls, but the oddest and most horrific use of one was at Auberoche in 1345 when a pageboy brought a message from the beleaguered English garrison. The French reply was tied around his neck and he was catapulted over the walls to make a point. The garrison were appalled.

Trebuchets were more powerful than mangonels and relatively new to warfare. Dating from the thirteenth century, they could smash walls, gates, ships and any other obstacle with their counterweighted sling-arms hurling stones hundreds of yards. Depending on the number of operatives, a trebuchet could be fired quickly. In an earlier clash on the Tagus in the siege of Lisbon, 5,000 stones were fired in ten hours. In common with soldiery for centuries, the siege weapons were given names by those who used them. It would be fascinating to know if the bowmen had names for their weapons, but we have no examples of them. Under Edward I, fighting the Scots at Stirling in the 1290s, we have names for trebuchets like *Vicar, Parson, Segrave* and *Warwolf.*

Scaling ladders were notoriously vulnerable. They could be set alight, would not always take the weight of armoured men scuttling up them and could easily be pushed away from walls by defenders. At Pontorson, this was famously done by Juliéme du Guesclin, the sister of the Constable – and she was a nun! The most flamboyant use of a scaling ladder, however, was by the French Marshal Jean le Meingre, known as Boucicaut. To show how fit he was, the champion jouster of Europe somersaulted on the ground in full plate armour, climbed a ladder using his arms but not his feet and, at the top, stripped off to his mail shirt before doing it all again, one-handed.

Engines of all sorts, however, were only as good as the ground they stood on and the whole area around Calais in 1346–7 was marshy and unsuitable. Edward settled down for the duration. He built a camp, which developed into a town beyond the range of Calais' missiles. The Goddamns, already used to tents and sleeping rough, now had the luxury of huts, with a market and streets. Fresh fish was available from the sea, and bread, flour, ale, meat and above all, wine, was obtained from the neighbourhood. How far any of this was obtained through fair payment is debatable. As the war progressed, Edward became notorious for big borrowing and a failure to repay debts. For the bowmen, this was what war was all about. They were fed, had roofs over their heads and if pay was not always regular, they could live with that. French wine would have been new to most of them in the 1340s; Englishmen drank ale and cider at home.

Inside the town, the inhabitants were reduced to eating cats, dogs and rats. When a desperate message to that effect was intercepted by the English, Edward forwarded it to Philip VI! At night, the besieged lit fires along their walls, as if to keep their spirits alive. Every possible entry to the town was blockaded with ships and siege towers. Philip himself, though in his fifties, challenged Edward to personal combat. Although no doubt the Black Prince and dozens of English lords were keen to accept, the king declined; throwing away a huge advantage on a chivalrous gesture was not his style; he had yet to found the order of the Garter! The garrison threw the fleur de lys into a ditch at their contempt for the French army that turned up to relieve them, but achieved nothing.

Calais duly surrendered and the normally fair-minded Edward intended to carry out a wholesale massacre, always a possibility after a siege, especially a long one. No doubt the bowmen readied themselves for an orgy of killing. Eventually, the king was persuaded to execute a token six volunteers from the town, led by the wealthy merchant Eustace de Saint-Pierre. The other five were merchants too and reached a kind of immortality as the burghers of Calais. Stripped to the waist, with halters around their necks, they were jostled and jeered at by the Goddamns, until the queen intervened.

Several of Edward's captains, including Walter Manny, urged him to spare the six, but it was only the pleas of the pregnant Philippa that worked. Froissart makes a meal of the incident, waxing lyrical for seven pages. The burghers, who were all ultimately freed, found their place in the sun centuries later when the sculptor Auguste Rodin immortalized them in bronze. As the pestilence broke out on both sides of the Channel, thirty-six wealthy families and their hangers-on were moved into the city to form a nucleus of English power.

Ten years later, it was the turn of Breteuil, defended by the English. Bowmen behind their walls and barricades had the advantage because men on the ground below the arrow-slits were sitting ducks. King Jean brought massive siege engines with his own crossbowmen and archers on each of the three platforms inside. The moat was filled in to make a firm base for these, close enough to the walls to reach the battlements. The garrison used cannon and Greek fire (an early form of napalm) to burn the belfries. The operatives here were probably not bowmen, but the gunners, themselves a new breed on European battlefields. The first belfry was destroyed, but there was no relief force galloping to the town's rescue and the English surrendered.

There is no doubt that the wanton destruction of towns by the English, the Goddamns first among them, was a psychological ploy to terrify French citizens and wear down their morale. The chronicler Geoffrey le Baker got it right when he said that the Black Prince's attack on Romorantin 'ought to provoke the French to come'. The English knew that, largely because of their bowmen, they would have the upper hand in the field. The problem, after Poitiers, was in giving them no choice but to fight.

A section of the French army, having clashed with the English and been given a bloody nose, lived in the castle at Romorantin, even though the town had already fallen. The Black Prince sent John Chandos, one of his father's ablest lieutenants, to parlay with the castle's defenders. It was everybody's bad luck that the commander was Boucicaut, one of the most dazzling and determined Frenchmen of the Hundred Years War. Nobody was backing down. Froissart takes up the story:

> Early the next morning, all [the Prince's] fighting men armed themselves, including the archers. They stood along the banks of the moat, shooting so steadily that the defenders hardly dared show themselves on the battlements. Others launched out on doors and hurdles with picks and mattocks or bows and arrows in their hands. Reaching the foot of the wall, they hacked and hammered away at it.

Edward III had burned this town some twelve years earlier and this particular siege was unsurprisingly bitter as far as the French were concerned.

The defenders threw stones, flints and quicklime, which did considerable damage to the attackers below. The fighting went on all day. The Prince was furious and determined to take the castle with no quarter being given. The wiser heads among the Goddamns realized that frontal assault with arrows and ladders was not going to work. So, almost reluctantly, bombards and other cannon were hauled into position, and the walls blasted. Using Greek fire, the guns set the castle's timber and thatched roofs alight and the defenders panicked, surrendering unconditionally. The castle and town were destroyed and the Goddamns had a field day.

Underhand tactics were not acceptable in the code of chivalry, but both sides adopted them nonetheless. The English were holding La Rochelle in 1372 and the French mayor of the town told the commander, Philip Mansel, that he had received a personal letter from Edward III that the garrison should parade in the town square on a particular morning. The king's seal was genuine enough, but the letter was not and Philip Mansel could not read it; he was illiterate. The French even promised to give the English troops the back pay that was owed them. Mansel and his men fell for it and found themselves, outarmed and outnumbered by the townsfolk. The garrison surrendered and the French handed over La Rochelle to Bertrand du Guesclin. Since, as we have seen, much of the English fleet was also destroyed in this engagement, it was, all in all, a bad day for England.

As the war progressed, the actions became more atrocious and the casualty rate rose. The French invasion of the Isle of Wight in 1377 was a chevauchée but it also featured a siege. Carisbrooke Castle above the River Medina was the only major fortress in the island and the French laid siege to it. Because the place was extended in the 1590s to include gun-bastions, it is not clear today exactly where the French were camped. The castle had two wells, so water was not a problem, but food must have been scarce by the time the French withdrew. They did so, in part, because of a bowshot. Philip de Heynoe, the Lord of Stenbury, a local manor, commanded forty crossbowmen among the army's garrison and fired his 'silver bow' through an arrow slit (still visible today as 'Heynoe's Loop') along the west battlements. He killed the French commander, who was in the habit of inspecting his lines every morning and evening, and the army pulled up stakes to carry on with their chevauchée all over the island. There was also the matter of a sizeable bribe which the defenders paid and the French were happy to accept.

Henry V's attack on Harfleur was the first clash in his Agincourt campaign in 1415. He brought guns from Bristol and the Tower of London, with 10,000 stone cannon balls, ladders, chains, battering rams, sea coal and wood ash. Experience had taught the English that French towns were tough to take – and Harfleur was no exception. We still have his provisions list of goods gathered in Portsmouth – live animals (for food), salt beef, dried fish, bread, cheese, ale, flour and beans. Once in France, he ordered 600 casks of Gascon wine. Harfleur had 2½ miles of walls (twice as long as Southampton's) and twenty-six towers. Even if walls were scaled and fighting took place along the battlements, the garrison could still defend themselves inside the towers and fire on the fighters below them. The River Lézarde had been dammed to flood the area, limiting the use of Henry's engines.

As the siege dragged on, the weather worsened and sickness broke out in the English camp. More men died from disease than battle injuries in every war before the twentieth century and Harfleur was no exception. Shellfish, sour wine and rancid fruit led to gastric problems and eventually dysentery; 2,000 died in weeks, including the Bishop of Norwich and the Earls of Suffolk and Arundel. English attacks were beaten back by showers of arrows, boiling oil and water, sulphur and quicklime, but eventually the garrison were worn down and surrendered, Henry filling Harfleur with Englishmen exactly as Edward III had at Calais. The Peacock Inn, which still stands in the town, was given to Richard Bokeland, who had provided two ships for the invasion. It is notable that the garrison he left behind was made up of three archers to each man-at-arms.

Henry's progress through Normandy followed the playbook of the free companies. He agreed to leave various towns alone in exchange for 'protection money' and food.

In 1417, with Agincourt under his belt, Henry laid siege to Caen, establishing his headquarters in the Abbaye aux Hommes built by

William the Conqueror four centuries earlier. Caen was defended by a moat on three sides and thirty-two towers. To detect the presence of miners burrowing under the walls, the defenders placed bowls of water on the battlements and watched for vibrations. Henry took the town easily and an estimated 2,000 people were hacked to death in the market place, many of them no doubt the victims of the Goddamns. Not for nothing were the bowmen the most feared of the English. Not only was their impact on the battlefield devastating, survivors in towns remembered who did the actual throat-slitting when a settlement was taken.

At Falaise in the following year, the weather became so atrocious that rivers froze. Henry built huts for his bowmen and men-at-arms and not until a freezing February did the garrison surrender. It was from Cherbourg in that year that we have a unique letter from a common soldier. Whether he was a bowman is unknown, but he was a rare example of a literate peasant. He described the 'long time we have been here and of the expenses that we have had at every siege we have come to and have had no wages since that we came out of England, so that we have spent all that ever we had'. At Cherbourg, groups of two or three bowmen went out together to scavenge in the woods; all the game had gone.

At Rouen, Henry proved that he was not the chivalrous commander that Edward III had been. He unleashed 'Welsh knifemen' (almost certainly bowmen) to kill and steal in the surrounding countryside. This was as near to total war as it was possible to come in the fifteenth century. Reinforcements were sent from London – 2,500 drinking cups, 30 butts of wine, 1,000 pipes of ale – and, more importantly, 500 bowmen.

In the beleaguered city, a mouse cost 6d; a rat could fetch five times that amount. Prostitutes were paid in bread. While Edward III let the starving of Calais leave, Henry herded Rouen's paupers into a ditch and only gave them a little food, reluctantly, over Christmas. Most prisoners were hanged. And yet again, it was probably the bowmen who did the honours.

With the brief alliance over between France and Burgundy, Henry's successes in 1419 seemed endless and he entered Paris in 1420, which, in other wars, would have ended the conflict completely. Ironically, it was probably a siege that killed Henry V. Meaux was the only fortress left to the French in the north, straddling the River Marne and garrisoned by English and Irish mercenaries. Such was the nature of warfare by this time that it was not unusual to find Goddamns facing each other over some parapet in the middle of nowhere. The town's commander was the Bastard de Vaumes, a sadist who hanged people on the elms outside the walls. Their bodies were rotting there when Henry arrived, along with whatever was left of a pregnant girl who had been tied to a tree and had become food for scavenging wolves.

It was winter and the English bowmen were in huts again, but the camp was near the river and the water was contaminated. In the end, the garrison abandoned the town and the townsfolk themselves tried to defend the marketplace. That proved a waste of time and the slaughter was appalling.

The death of Henry V and the succession of lacklustre English commanders who came after him was a decisive turning point. Thanks to du Guesclin and the free companies, France had found a new way to fight, one that avoided full confrontation with the arrow storm of the bowmen. They also found renewed heart to drive the English out of France and at Orleans in 1429, excellent tactics and the enigma that was Jeanne d'Arc combined to signal what some have seen as the beginning of the end of English ambitions.

In October 1428, the Earl of Salisbury dug in around the city on the River Loire. Over time, the English built no fewer than seven forts, of stone and timber, in their attempt to force surrender. The chronicler Jean de Waurin refers to underground houses being built by the English 'according to their custom'. These must have resembled the trenches and dug-outs of the First World War and were designed to minimize the impact of French artillery, growing more powerful and accurate by the day. The garrison was 2,400 strong; the city's population perhaps ten times that. Salisbury was killed by a lucky cannon shot early on and command fell to John Talbot, Earl of Shrewsbury, probably the best general the English still had in the field.

We have no idea what the Goddamns on the Loire's bank made of the peasant girl in her armour, with her banner fluttering, who sailed up the river on a barge and rode around the city on a grey. Systematically, the relieving French army took the fort of St Loup east of Orleans, then the Tourelles, the fortified bridge head over the Loire. Jeanne herself was wounded, but her magic lasted long enough for Talbot to withdraw and the French ascendancy began. On 12 February 1429, a bizarre clash took place that came to be known as the Battle of the Herrings. Sir John Fastolf with 2,000 bowmen and men-at-arms were attacked by a French force over twice the size led by Jean, Count of Dunois. The Duke of Bedford had sent 300 wagons of supplies and food (mostly herrings) for the English army, but the caravan was hit near Rouvray. In a move that the Hussites in Germany would use in the next century – and which would be familiar to anyone of a certain age who enjoyed Western films – Fastolf circled his wagons and drove the French off with heavy losses. In this particular tactic, the skill and speed of the bowmen was paramount.

There was one major siege to come, one that ended in a battle of sorts, although it was not one in which the bowmen shone. That was at Castillon in the Dordogne in July 1453. It would be the last clash of arms in the Hundred Years War.

We saw in Chapter 6 that French raids on the south coast occurred before any clashes happened in France itself. In most cases, although they were serious assaults, involving murder, rape, theft and destruction of property, there was no attempt to occupy territory with a full-scale invasion.

The Isle of Wight was different, as it is in so many respects. Because of its geographical position, it was possible for an invading force to occupy the island and use it as a base for future operations along the south coast. And, as so often happened in the Hundred Years War, chevauchée and siege flowed effortlessly from one to the other.

The first attack happened in 1340, despite the English naval victory at Sluys, with St Helens on the east coast targeted. Fighting on the beach was vicious, if short-lived and resulted in the death of the island's governor, Theobald Russel. Beacons had been erected on the island's high ground since 1324 and these were manned day and night. From 1335, the old feudal levy of the local de Redvers family was replaced with a kind of conscription, involving all men between 15 and sixty. Divided into nine units, they amounted to about 1,000 men and trained regularly with longbows, bills and swords. How many of these were expert bowmen we do not know, but the island had its share of forests and no doubt, foresters. In 1339, following attacks on Southampton and Portsmouth, 150 mercenaries, including bowmen, were brought over from the mainland and stationed in Carisbrooke Castle.

It was from the Isle of Wight that Edward III issued orders for his forthcoming invasion of Normandy in 1346 and the island contributed 22 cogs and 220 men for the siege of Calais. According to one Spanish source, the destruction of the English fleet off La Rochelle in 1372 encouraged another attack on the island two years later.

On 21 August 1377, the beacons blazed on the hills and everybody prepared for the worst. Two months earlier, Edward III had died, leaving his grandson Richard, aged 10, as the king of England. It was the perfect time for a renewed assault and added to the mix were the Castilians of Enrico of Trastamara, smarting over their defeat by the English ten years earlier at Najera. They were commanded in the summer of 1377 by Juan de Roux and their fleet comprised galleys, low, sleek ships that could land easily, disembark troops and row away, independent of the wind. The larger French force was led by Jean de Vienne.

The attack came, perhaps oddly, from the west, past the treacherous Needles rocks and the French army landed on the north-west coast, somewhere near the town of Francheville (now known as Newtown). This force had raided along the mainland's south coast since late June, ransacking Lewes and hitting Rottingdean, Folkestone, Portsmouth, Dartmouth and Plymouth. Poole only survived destruction because the Earl of Salisbury had assembled a large force, including massed bowmen on the beach and the French realized that trying to land would be tantamount to suicide. Yarmouth fell easily, both its churches burned to the ground. Francheville was next.

It was a relatively new town, having been founded on church land by Aymer de Valence, the Bishop of Winchester, in 1256. In 1377, it had a flourishing harbour, the largest on the island. About sixty families lived there, mostly along Gold and Silver Streets (the names reflecting the area's prosperity), perhaps 300 people. How many of them had time to run to the safety of Carisbrooke Castle we do not know but certainly there were no militia there to save the town. It was destroyed, never to recover. Today, it is a bird sanctuary, the ghostly outlines of the streets the only reminder of its past.

Only St Thomas's Church survived the destruction of Newport and then the chevauchée became a siege. The French probably had enough men (we have no numbers) to surround Carisbrooke Castle entirely. Bodies found years later at Noddy's Hill (today Nodehill in Newport) imply serious fighting involving trebuchets, mangonels and bowmen. In the castle museum are four crossbow bolt heads discovered in the walls over a period of time. Peter de Heynoe's marksmanship in killing the French commander probably turned the tide.

It was now September and the prospect of wintering in an alien, hostile island did not appeal to the now leaderless French. In exchange for an old-fashioned bribe of 1,000 crowns, they upped stakes and went home.

Chapter 9

Crecy: 26 August 1346 St Maximilian's Day

'Then the English archers stepped forth one pace and let fly their arrows so wholly and so thick, that it seemed snow.'

'There is no one, even among those present on that day, who has been able to understand and relate the whole truth of the matter.' This is Jean Froissart, the chronicler, talking about Crecy, the first pitched land battle of the war and his wise words apply to any battle at any time. Froissart's own account of the Hundred Years War was illustrated years later by an anonymous artist and is typical of the battle scenes of the day. The armour is pure fifteenth century, with no attempt to depict soldiers as they actually looked in 1346. The scale is appalling, with ridiculously steep hills in the background and the ubiquitous castle that virtually every battle picture shows; the men are taller than the ramparts.

In trying to capture the exciting sweep of a battle like Crecy, the artist falls between two stools. He either tried to cover the entire field (as eighteenth- and nineteenth-century artists tried to do) in which case we have scale problems and rows of identical men like poor early CGI in the film industry; or to focus on one aspect, in which case the scope is lost.

In any battle, at any time, a soldier, whatever his rank or specialism, has two overlapping priorities. One is to kill the enemy, rather as local volunteers in the Crecy area ran about the countryside rattling their farm implements and shouting 'Kill! Kill!'; the other is to stay alive.

Both objectives preclude a balanced view. In the press of infantry in any of Edward III's divisions ('battles') a man was only aware of those on each side of him and those immediately ahead. The heraldry of the day helped. The royal banners of France and England floated above the heads of their respective owners. The Earl of Pembroke's maunch and martlets would have been easily identifiable, so would the leopards of Henry of Lancaster. The Black Prince's royal arms with his white label to identify the first-born son was distinctive too. Edward Despenser's trellis design and the Earl of Oxford's star marked their positions on the field.

The French likewise could pinpoint their leaders – the black lion of Louis de Nevers, Count of Flanders, the golden dolphin of the Duc de Bar, the spread eagles of Charles de Montmorency, Constable of France. These standards were rallying points. They were designed to show that their owners were still alive and to bring scattered followers to them. Once a standard was down, however (like John of Bohemia's three feathers), the rallying point had gone and chaos reigned.

Commands were issued by trumpet calls, the trumpeter standing or sitting with the standard bearer and his lord, but in the deafening noise of a Medieval battle, much of that communication must have broken down.

The countryside around the village of Crecy was gently rolling grassland. Modern photographs show fields under the plough and sown with crops. As in England, there were no walls or hedgerows in 1346 to impede troop movement, but marshy ground was always a problem and the River Maye, meandering to the south of the village, was a potential death trap. Edward drew up his three divisions, his standard depositions, with himself (the largest body of men) furthest back, at once forming the van and the reserve. To his right, nearest to the road (actually a weather-beaten track) Edward the Black Prince commanded. He was only 16 and had been knighted by his father when the army landed in France. The Black Prince was furthest ahead of everybody, but he had high ground behind him and the village and forest of Crecy to his right. Both acted as a natural defence and it is probably here that the baggage train was drawn up (contemporary accounts are unclear). To the king's left, near the village of Wadicourt, William de Bohun, the Earl of Northampton, watched the enemy deploying to the south-east. All three English commanders would become knights of the Garter two years later, part of the close-knit fellowship that would serve together for the next twenty years.

In front of the Prince's division, the French had positioned their Genoese crossbowmen. All Medieval armies hired mercenaries, in part because the traditional forty-day length of service under the feudal system was too short for most campaigns. The essential difference between French and English mercenaries is that the Welsh, Irish and Scots who fought for England were paid regular wages. The Genoese crossbowmen were paid differently and Frenchmen, especially the nobility, despised them. It is those men that most Medieval artists depict, well-armed and equipped with plate armour. The crossbow was heavy and slow to load and its range no more than 100 yards. Less than that and the wooden flighted bolts were devastating, easily thudding through plate, mail and flesh. At Crecy, they were commanded by the condottiere captains Carlo Grimaldi and Otto Doria.

The crossbow had a chequered history. In 1139, the papacy had banned its use in wars between Christians as being too horrendous. Anna Comnena, the Byzantine chronicler and one of the very few female commentators on military matters, wrote: 'The crossbow is a weapon of the barbarians [Western crusaders] …' and she goes on to describe how it is loaded and fired. 'Such is the crossbow, a truly diabolic machine.' She then claims that a man hit by a crossbow bolt 'dies without feeling the blow', rather akin to the later notion that no one hears the gunshot that kills them. It is difficult to see how the weapon caught on because it was slower, less accurate in the early years and far more expensive to make.

The common name for the crossbow was *arbalest* and a crossbowman was an *arbalestie*. At the siege of Jaffa during the Third Crusade (1189)

Richard I had his crossbowmen firing in pairs – one to load and one to shoot. Able commander though Richard was, this seems a particularly cranky, not to say foolhardy, tactic.

The French, of course, used longbowmen too, but the reason they relied on the Genoese was one of pure snobbery. A man with a bow of any kind was beneath contempt; the winners of battles were the mounted knights and the only weapon of value was the sword.

Crecy was the first full-scale encounter of the war and nobody quite knew what to expect. What would have been clear to participants is that the majority of the English were dismounted – even the Black Prince was on foot. To the south-east, the French knights dominated, jostling forward and taunting their opponents, trying to control their high-spirited destriers, bright with the coloured devices of their riders.

Behind the crossbowmen, on the French left, facing the Black Prince, was a huge contingent led by Charles, Duke of Alençon, the king's brother, an arrogant and bad-tempered man who had none of the attributes of a general. In the centre, and a little way back, the double cross of Lorraine marked the division of the duke of that territory. The right wing was still arriving when the action began and so huge was the French army that perhaps a third of them were straggling back along the road from Abbeville, where they had spent the night. It is not clear where King Philip was in the melee that followed, but it would make sense for him to command this division, had it been ready.

It may have been a nifty piece of psychology on Edward's part that his entire army were sitting on the ground as the French advanced. To a man, they rose as one, whether they had heard Philip's command to attack or not. Knights buckled on their great helms over their bascinets or arming caps. Their view would have been slightly limited, but who could miss the vast array of the French moving towards them? Billmen and spearmen grasped their weapons. It would be several minutes before the two sides clashed, but after that, it would be hacking and chopping with swords and daggers, aiming for their enemies' faces with their pole-weapons. The longbowmen planted their arrows in the ground in front of them or swung their quivers to their fronts. Each man was an expert, a steady shot made so by years of practice at the butts. In numbers they were devastating. Even the humblest of them wore a leather jerkin over his padded tunic. The better off wore brigandines, padded jackets reinforced with iron strips and studs. Their bows were encased in cloth to keep them dry and they threw these down now, fitting the first arrow to the bow, ready for the word of command. Many of them would have been wearing mail coifs (hoods) which gave the head *some* protection, but the broad-brimmed iron 'kettle hats' belonged to later phases of the conflict. *Every* man in the Middle Ages carried a knife and some of the archers at Crecy had swords too and small circular leather shields called bucklers. There would come a time, all arrows spent, that the battle would consist of hard knocks at close quarters.

The exact position and formation of the bowmen is conjecture. Military historians have argued for years over the precise meaning of 'tierce' to describe this formation. It means 'harrow', a farming implement that was roughly rhombus-shaped, in essence, a wedge. These wedges were placed between the Prince's and Northampton's divisions, although the king would have had his own, such was the range of the bow.

As the French were screaming 'Dieu et St Denys' marching forward to the attack, the rain started. Some, perhaps, saw it as an omen; at very best, it was an inconvenience. At least the Genoese were not hampered by their heavy pavises, their wooden shields which they usually placed in front of them as a temporary wall; they were still at least 2 miles away with the baggage train. 'After the rain, the sun'; the downpour was short-lived and the sun, late in the afternoon, was dazzling in the crossbowmen's eyes. They opened fire first, so they were probably nearly 100 yards from the Prince's line. Their bolts thudded into the shields of the knights, bounced off bascinets. Some must have struck home and the ranks were closed by the living.

The return fire of the English archers was a defining moment, not just in the Hundred Years War, but in Medieval history itself. While the

Genoese bent forward to reload (without the defence of their shields) they were hit by ash arrows with iron tips that rained down on them like a hailstorm. We do not know how many English bowmen there were at Crecy, but a reasonable guess would be 3,000. In the next two minutes, that meant that 250,000 arrows smashing into the Genoese. Even those across to the left could have swung their bows to join in the attack.

Perhaps now the English cannon were unleashed. Crecy saw the first recorded use of 'handgonnes', probably little more than iron tubes that fired stone shot. Some accounts have these positioned with the baggage carts, to the Black Prince's right. Their range and accuracy were pathetic by later standards, but the sheer noise they made and the novelty of their appearance, was the last straw for the Genoese.

Before they could get out of the way of the English archery, however, the impetuous French cavalry broke forward. Alençon gave the command but his own knights and Lorraine's were already moving. There was no command, no cohesion, just a headlong charge to ride the English down. In the process, the Genoese were trampled, hundreds of men battered into what had become mud made by the hoofs of the heavy destriers. The chronicler Geoffrey le Baker takes up the story:

> When they saw that their crossbowmen were not harming the English at all, the French [knights] on young warhorses and agile coursers rode down the crossbowmen, standing to the number of 7,000 between them and the English, crushing them under the feet of their horses to show how brave they were …

There is no doubt that the Goddamns were all good shots, but there was no time to use this skill in battle. The volley, all bows fired together and repeatedly, inflicted far more damage – Wellington's redcoats and Napoleon's grognards were still using the tactic 400 years later. If troops on foot (the crossbowmen) were easy targets, knights on horseback were easier still. Because of today's sensitivity towards animals, we do not see warhorses going down in battles in movies. Mel Gibson's *Braveheart* (1995) for instance ends at the start of the battle of Bannockburn, when hundreds of English horses were impaled on stakes hidden in underground traps, so we, the audience, never see it – and it was never filmed.

In reality, a horse is a bigger target than a man and the longbowmen now turned their deadly attention on them. The destriers were colourful sights in their heraldic horse bards, but the only armour they wore were chamfrons, iron plates covering their heads; the rest of the body was exposed. Bring down a warhorse and you bring down its rider and quite possibly riders and horses on either side of it. A cavalryman on foot was very exposed; shocked, possibly wounded, he had to avoid the horses of the rear ranks stumbling all around him before he could even think of taking stock and advancing on foot.

For decades, there was a myth, reinforced by Laurence Olivier's film of *Henry V* (1944) that a knight on the ground was like a beetle on its back, unable to get up because of the weight of his armour. The full plate armour of Henry V's day (Agincourt was fought in 1415) was heavier than the combined mail and plate of Crecy and the heaviest suits ever made, for the lists in sixteenth-century jousting, were no heavier than the weight carried by British infantry in the Falklands War (1982).

Le Baker's accounts suggest that the English had dug pits in front of their positions – a trick they had learned from the Scots under William Wallace and Robert the Bruce – which would have slowed the attack still further. The reality was that the French charges – fifteen of them in all as they rallied and re-rallied – were possibly delivered at little more than a trot, giving the bowmen ample time to reload and fire again. Such was the chaos across the field, with panicked horses floundering and whinnying that there was total confusion and little hope of King Philip co-ordinating the action.

In a scene which no film director would contemplate as being too corny, King John of Bohemia, who was blind, insisted on being taken forward by his bodyguard to land a blow against the English. After the battle, he and his knights were all found together, their dead horses still roped in a line. It is not specified, but it is likely that English bowmen got them all.

At last, some of the pressure told and the French under Alençon and the Count of Flanders hacked their way to the Black Prince's line. There was now a problem for the Goddamns; in the melee in front of them, it was as easy to hit friend as foe and the firing must have lessened. It may also have been the case that they were running out of arrows (which would actually happen at Agincourt, sixty years later). Essentially, the English stood their ground and waited for the impact of the French attack. Had they advanced, they could have retrieved their arrows from their targets and reused them – recycling long before it became the trend!

The Prince's division became the target as the summer's day darkened and twilight brought its own confusion; banners, shields and jupons, so bright in the sun, were just so many muddy (and bloody) scribblings now. Edward of Woodstock may only have been 16, but he was big and strong and brought up all his life in the use of arms. He hacked back at the enemy, denting helmets and smashing skulls. The first Medieval battle of which we have detailed *archaeological* evidence is Towton in Yorkshire in 1461. Of the dozens of excavated bodies near the field, nearly all had fatal head injuries. The same would have been true of Crecy. With the Prince were John Chandos, the warbler of Sluys, and Reginald Cobham, protecting him with their lives. Beaten to his knees as he was at one point, his own standard bearer, Richard Fitzsimon, brought his attacker down and saved the boy's life.

The Earls of Northampton and Arundel, on the other wing, sent men-at-arms across to stiffen the Prince's division and Godfrey de Harcourt (whose brother, incidentally, fought for France that day) sent Sir Thomas Norwich back to King Edward, begging for help. The conversation between them, as recorded by Froissart, seems a little *too* courteous, given the circumstances of the moment. The king's division had not moved yet, commanding, as it did, a clear view of the whole field. Edward himself, probably still unhelmeted, was watching from the highest viewpoint, a windmill.

'Sire,' Froissart has Norwich say, 'the Earls of Warwick and Oxford and Sir Reginald Cobham, who are with the Prince, are meeting a very fierce attack by the French. So they ask you to bring your division to their support, because if the attack grows any heavier, they fear it will be about as much as your son can deal with.'

Edward asked if the boy was dead or wounded. The answer was 'No'.

'Sir Thomas,' the king replied, in what must be the harshest comment from father to son in the Middle Ages, 'Go back to him and to those who have sent you and tell them not to send for me again today, as long as my son is alive. Give them my command to let the boy win his spurs, for if God has so ordained it, I wish the day to be his and the honour go to him and to those in whose charge I have placed him.'

If this was a piece of psychology from Edward, it worked. Exhausted as the Prince and his people were, the message from the king kick-started them and they fought back with a vengeance. Known only to a few, however, Edward sent twenty battle-hardened knights under the command of Thomas Hatfield, the fighting Bishop of Durham. They found the Prince's banner still flying.

With night coming on and a horrendous casualty rate among the French, the attacks lessened and the deafening noise died down. King Philip, who had had two horses killed under him and may have been wounded in the face, reluctantly left the field, with a knot of horsemen. The exhausted staff reached the gates of Labroye Castle, locked and shuttered now that it was fully dark.

The captain called down from the ramparts, 'Who comes calling at this hour?'

'Open your gate, captain,' Philip, bleeding and in pain managed to call back. 'It is the unfortunate King of France.'

Back on his ridge at Crecy, Edward kept his men in check. There was a natural tendency in battle, as the enemy broke and fled, for the winning side to give chase. The bowmen, who could now retrieve their arrows, were a natural group to make this happen. The exception, according to Froissart, were Welsh and Cornish irregulars who, with their long knives, swooped down on the piles of dead and slit the throats of anyone still struggling. In internal conflicts like the Wars of the Roses that followed the Hundred Years War, the proximity of battlefields to settlements meant that scavengers from the immediate vicinity (often women) went about the site robbing the dead. These people at Crecy *may* have been local French. We know that Philip's army had huge numbers of them, untrained and poorly armed, who would play no part in the fighting but could be relied upon to inflict murder and mayhem in the aftermath. The fact that Edward was appalled by this indiscriminate slaughter implies that most of this group were, in fact, English, some of them, no doubt, his bowmen.

To the screams and groans of the wounded, the English lit campfires and torches. They had no idea whether the French were still capable of a night attack (they were not) but clearly were not taking any chances. Apart from the guard appointed to keep watch, most men slept where they had stood, the sweat from their armour and brigandines drying on their bodies.

The next day, with no further attacks likely, Edward sent his heralds and clerks to find bodies and record individuals recognizable only by the coats of arms on their jupons. This was an inexact science. To begin with, we have Englishmen recording French heraldry and although heraldic devices were largely generic, the genealogical rolls were highly complicated and often obscure. In the case of men whose crests had been smashed from their helmets, who had lost their shields and whose jupons had been torn from their backs, there was unlikely to be any method of identifying them. Because of that, we have widely differing numbers of casualties. Richard of Wynkeley, one of the

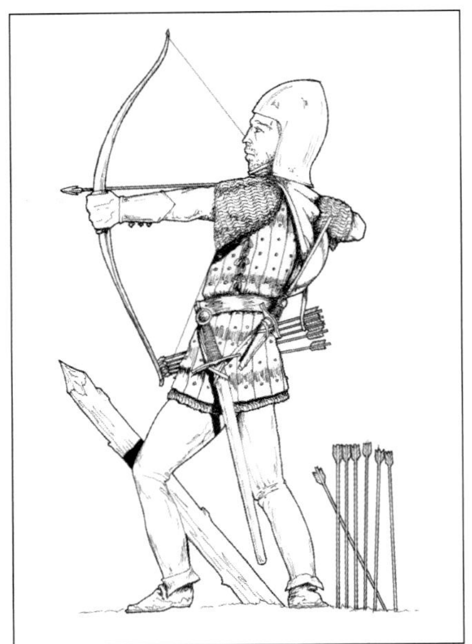

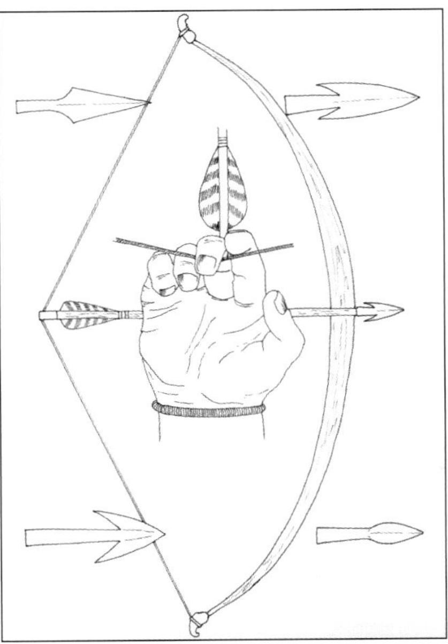

Above left: For most of the Hundred Years War the English bowman was the 'secret weapon'. The speed and accuracy of the archers destroyed both French cavalry and infantry in all the major battles, except for the last one at Castillon in 1453. The archer shown here has arrows at his belt and in the ground for speed of loading. The wooden stake was used to deter cavalry. Once an archer had loosed all his arrows, he could then fight with sword and dagger.

Above right: A montage showing the four most common arrowheads used in the Hundred Years War. The position of the fingers around the bowstring is perhaps the origin of the 'V' sign, which the English may have used during the conflict.

Above far left: Ash – *Fraxinus* – was used extensively for long bows. The tree had an ancient history. The Vikings knew it as Ygdrasil (Odin's Gallows).

Above middle left: The laburnum – a member of the pea family – are small trees now mostly confined to gardens, the tree grows naturally and was an excellent substitute for the crème de la crème of bow woods, yew.

Above middle right: Yew – *Taxux baccarta* – was the best and most popular of bow woods, to the extent that it almost reached extinction in Britain in the Middle Ages. Vast amounts of yew had to be imported from Spain.

Above far right: Wych hazel – *Hammamelis* – is today associated with herbal medicine, the 'wych' has nothing to do with the occult. It meant 'supple' or 'pliable' in Old English.

Above left: The River Downey near the battlefield of Nevill's Cross, where a combined Franco-Scottish army was defeated. King David of Scotland hid under a bridge along this river. (*Author*)

Above right: The new defences of Southampton, built by Edward III in the 1340s. These are the machicolations, or murder holes, through which the garrison poured boiling water, hot oil or hot sand onto the attackers below. (*Author*)

Above left: The groove in the centre of the photograph marks the place where a portcullis once stood. This was a wooden and iron grille operated on chains that could be lowered to keep out attackers. Several of these were built along Southampton's walls. (*Author*)

Above right: After the French attack on Southampton in 1338, Edward III ordered the walls to be improved and reinforced. Houses and shops were demolished (as in this filled-in archway) and no compensation offered. (*Author*)

Now the Duke of Wellington pub, this house, with shop below it, was one of several sacked by the French in 1338. (*Author*)

The latten-gilt tomb of Edward III in Westminster Abbey. A determined and highly able commander in the early years of the war, he increasingly passed the baton to his son, the Black Prince. Edward outlived the prince by nearly a year.

The latten-gilt tomb of Edward of Woodstock, the Black Prince, in Canterbury Cathedral. The prince died in 1376 but had never quite recovered from the grim Najera campaign almost ten years earlier. (*Robin Whitehead*)

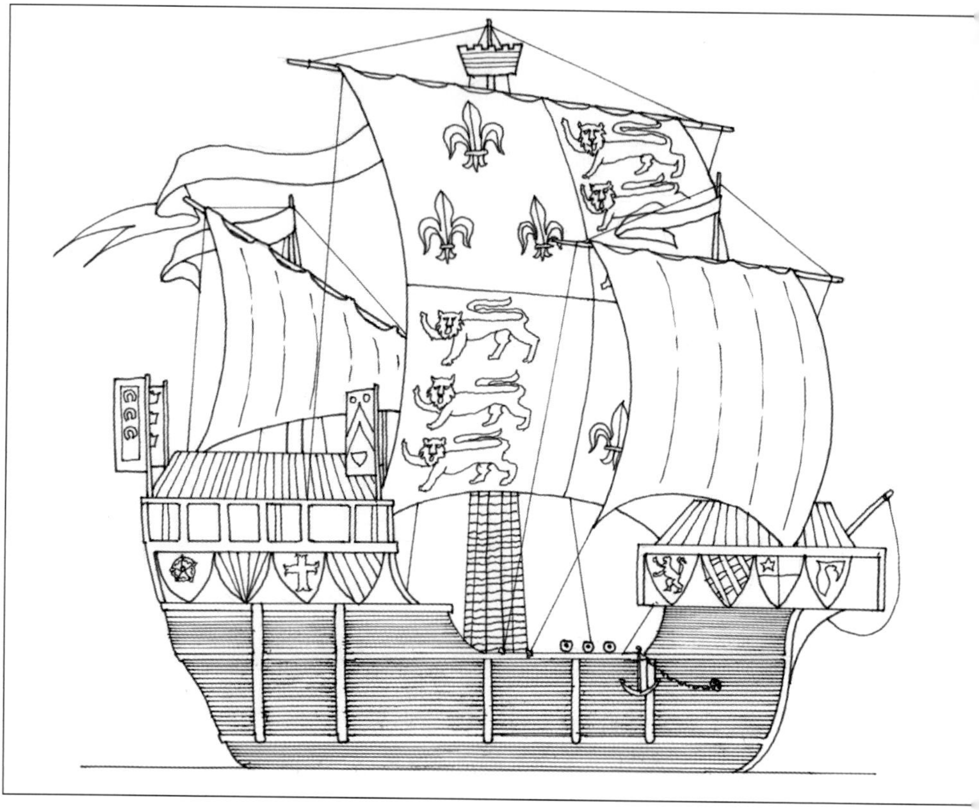

Above: Edward III's flagship was stolen by the French in 1338 and won back again at Sluys two years later. Bowmen crowded in the aft castle and forecastle and naval engagements were basically land battles on the water. The position of the cannon amidships is conjecture – we do not know where they were actually placed.

Left: Heynoe's Loop, Carisbrooke Castle. According to legend, De Heynoe fired his crossbow through this arrow slit and killed the French commander below the walls. (*Author*)

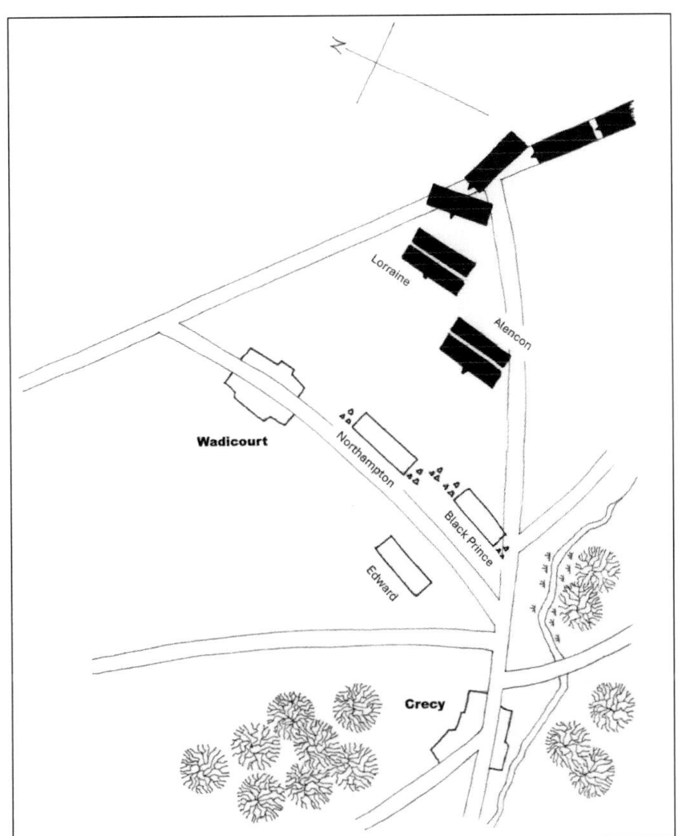

Battlefield of Crecy, 26 August 1346. The Black Prince's division was hardest hit and had to be reinforced. King Edward was positioned further back on a hill topped by a windmill. The French army was so large and slow that some divisions were still on the road when the battle was over.

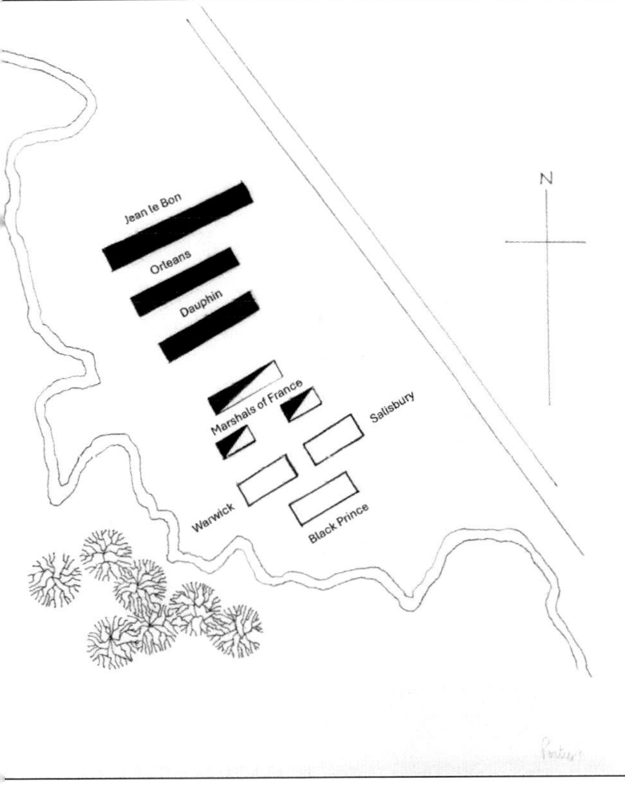

Battlefield of Poitiers, 19 September 1356. A more complete English victory than Crecy, the Black Prince showed his skill as a general. England's ally, the Captal de Buch swung round towards the Poitiers road to outflank the French. King Jean was outmanoeuvred.

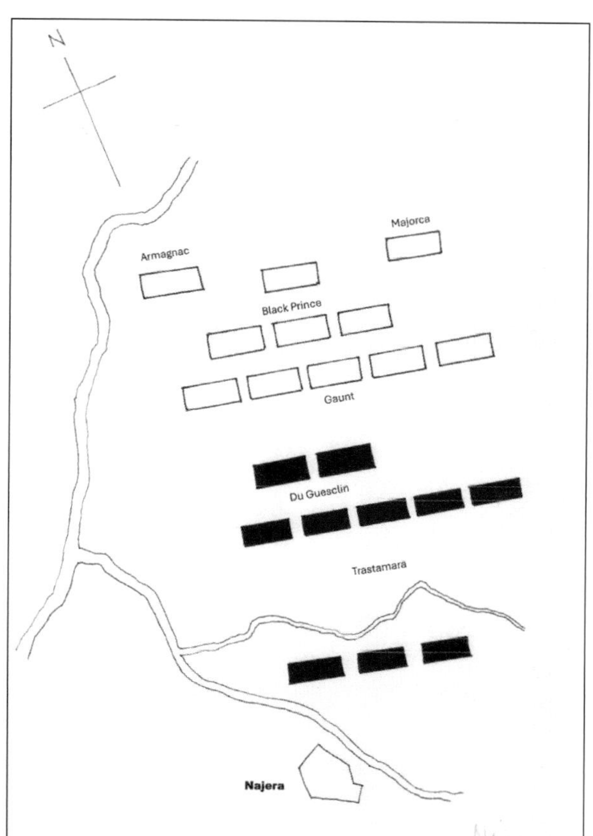

Battlefield of Najera, 3 April 1367. Though not technically a battle of the Hundred Years War, forces on both sides had fought in that conflict. The Black Prince fought for King Pedro and this was his finest battle.

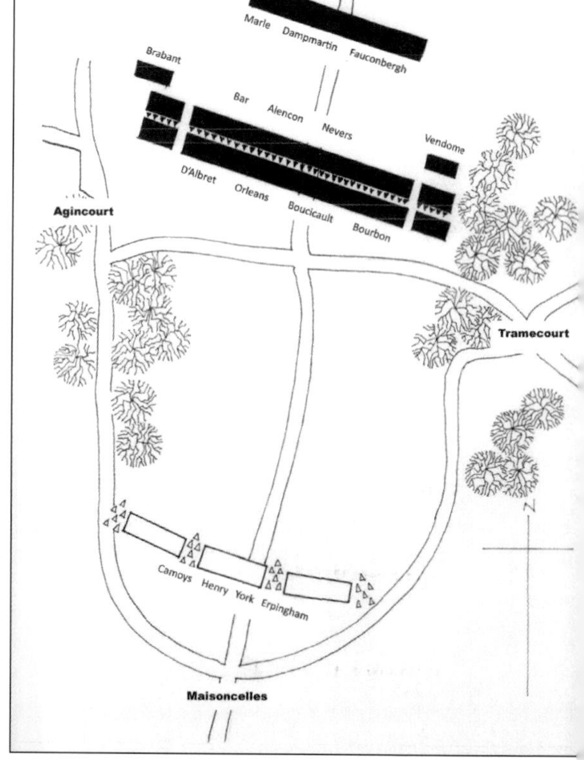

Battlefield of Agincourt, 25 October 1415. The armies fought in narrow fields between two woods and the rain had churned the ground into mud. The French cavalry had learned nothing from their earlier mistakes in the war and were cut to pieces by the bowmen in the woods to the right.

Right: Arguably Britain's best royal general, Henry V fought his first battle at Shrewsbury at the age of 16. This portrait, a Tudor copy of an earlier original, shows him from the left, because his right cheek was badly disfigured by an arrow wound received in that battle.

Below left: The only contemporary portrait of La Pucelle (the Maid), Joan of Arc, who led the French at the siege of Orleans in 1429. Two years later she was burned for heresy in the marketplace at Rouen at the age of 19.

Below right: Taken from the memorial brass to John de Northwood and his wife in Minster Sheppey, the style of armour dates from 1330, shortly before the Hundred Years War began. It shows a mixture of mail and plate armour. Note the chain over the left shoulder which secured the great helm (not shown) to the head.

Above left: The memorial brass of Hugh Hastyngs, Elsing, Norfolk, 1347. The legs are now missing from the tomb and the shield and jupon show the manche (sleeve) of the family. Hastyngs fought at Crecy the previous year.

Above right: From the memorial brass of the Earl of Warwick and his wife, St Mary's Church, Warwick, 1406. The great helm does not appear on the tomb but would have carried the bear and ragged staff crest on the battlefield.

Left: From the memorial brass of John Gaynesford, Crowhurst, Surrey, 1450. Compare this with the tomb of John de Northwood and the development of plate armour is obvious. This was largely in response to the impact of the longbow, although the French did not use the bow in the same numbers or with the same efficiency as the English. Note the 'Henry V style' haircut!

heralds turning over the bodies in the Valée aux Clerks, as it came to be known, the scene of the bloodiest fighting around the Black Prince's position, estimated that the day began with 12,000 mounted knights, 6,000 crossbowmen and 60,000 infantry (billmen and longbowmen).

There had been no noisy celebrations, on the king's orders, and a thick mist on the morning of the 27th must have added to the eeriness of the scene. Edward sent a force of 500 men-at-arms and 2,000 bowmen from his own division to reconnoitre. The inhabitants of Abbeville and St Roquier, the nearest towns, seem to have been blissfully unaware of the French defeat, even though fleeing soldiers must have been streaming through their streets throughout the night and when they saw the English, the assumed they were their own victorious army. The Goddamns quickly disabused them of that, killing an estimated 7,000 in the hedgerows along the road to Rouen. A more substantial force led by the Grand Prior of France and the Archbishop of Rouen, met the same group and suffered the same fate. No one was spared. No one was captured alive. No ransoms were taken. The churchmen, like their followers, died in the fog of war.

The herald's report to Edward that night spoke of 11 dead princes, 80 bannerets, 1,200 knights and about 30,000 'other men'. Michael de Northburgh, who had fought at Crecy, wrote home a few days later, talking of the deaths of 1,541 'good men-at-arms'. He gives no overall figures because the rank and file, including the bowmen, were not considered worth counting. Modern authorities contend that Froissart's figures were about three times too high.

The chronologically closest battle we have for which there has been modern archaeological studies was fought at Wisby on the Swedish island of Gotland in 1361. Of the 1,185 bodies studied, many had hacked legs. The leg armour of the foot soldier (and that went double for bowmen) was more or less non-existent and in an effort to defend his head, a man had little choice but to leave anything below the waist to luck. Skulls were particularly damaged (as at Towton a century later), some split in two. The tell-tale square holes of crossbow bolts are very much in evidence, some passing right through the head. Arrows, whether from cross or longbow, penetrated deep and carried filthy cloth and rusty iron into the wounds, which would lead to infection and ultimately death.

It was infection, especially gangrene, that finished off many Medieval soldiers, the men of Crecy being no exception. Because the bowmen had the habit of placing their arrows point down in the soil for speed of firing, inevitably the arrowheads were covered with germs and other debris from the earth. This was not, as some commentators have contended, a deliberate ploy to poison the enemy. The careful work of medical innovators like Ambroise Paré lay years in the future. There was no medical corps in any English army before the nineteenth century and wounds were treated by anyone with any kind of experience, trying to keep a friend alive. It was of no help at all that even actual doctors relied on the balance of humours to treat wounds, hoping that ancient Greek remedies would still work after 3,000 years.

One of the few medical men with military experience was John Ardenne, surgeon to Henry of Lancaster, Earl of Derby, who had fought at Crecy. In the 1370s, as the English were losing ground to the French, he wrote a treatise on surgery involving battle wounds, some of which is still in use today. Dressing should be clean, but not changed regularly and, as far as possible, wounds should be allowed to heal on their own. Clearly, King Philip's face wound did him no harm; he lived and reigned for four years after Crecy. In the later period, Henry, Prince of Wales, hit in the face by an arrow in 1403, went on to become Henry V and to win the battle of Agincourt. He did not die until 1422, of dysentery. As we have seen, David II of Scotland, hit by two arrows at Neville's Cross, lived on for two decades.

It was also possible to survive apparently life-threatening situations. Guilbert de Hannoy, wounded in a siege in 1412, carried a crossbow bolt in his thigh for nine months without much more than a hobble.

Whatever numbers we agree on for the casualties, no one disputes that Crecy was a devastating shell-shock to France. Its nobility, the rulers of the realm, were badly mauled to the extent that any future clash of arms with England was likely to be a lopsided affair. However many details we may yet unearth about the battle, this was a crushing blow to the concept of the heavily armoured knight as the winner of battles. Although Edward III never actually said so, the men who won Crecy were his bowmen, his Goddamns.

Chapter 10

'The Flower of Knighthood': Edward of Woodstock

Two of the most magnificent tombs in Medieval England date from the Hundred Years War. One is the latten-brass figure of Richard Beauchamp, the Earl of Warwick, a close friend of Henry V, who died in 1439. The other is that of Edward of Woodstock, Prince of Wales, in Canterbury Cathedral. It too is of latten-gilt, life-sized and shows the Prince in the armour and jupon he wore at Poitiers and Najera. His 'achievements', that is, his sword, helmet, jupon, gauntlets, spurs and shield stand in a glass case next to the tomb itself and in the 1960s exact replicas were made which are also on display.

Edward was not known as the Black Prince in his lifetime. I have used the term throughout this book to avoid confusion, but the first use of it was by John Leland in the 1540s, '*Edwardi Principis cog Nigri*'. Certainly, by Shakespeare's time, the phrase was a commonplace. Theories still fly as to its meaning. The simple idea, that it referred to darkened armour, was long ago dismissed by a careful study of his achievements. The Prince's 'arms for war' were the leopards and lilies of his father, suitably differenced by a white label, the emblem of the eldest son. His 'arms for peace', however, were the three feathers of the King of Bohemia in silver on a black field. A third interpretation relates to the kind of man he was; on the surface, the finest example of chivalry and knighthood of his day, yet callous and bloody underneath the veneer.

Edward was the eldest son of his father the king and Philippa of Hainault. He was born at the royal palace of Woodstock on 15 June 1330, was made Earl of Chester at the age of 3, duke of Cornwall at 7 and Prince of Wales at thirteen. The boy was educated as befitted a future king of England, with a strict regime involving Latin, Greek, logic and mathematics, taught by Dr Walter Burley of Merton College, Oxford. By the time he was Duke of Cornwall, he was already excelling in military arts, swordsmanship, riding, even the use of the bow. Three years later, stung by French raids on the south coast, King Edward moved his family to Nottingham Castle for safety and went to war, leaving his 10-year-old as Regent of England. The actual power was given to John Stratford, Archbishop of Canterbury.

After Sluys, the king wrote his own account of the victory in the battle which was sent, not to Stratford but to the young Edward. Some historians today see this as the first example of a naval dispatch. How much the boy, working through Stratford and a number of lords, helped raised funds for Edward's army in France is debatable. Throughout his life, he had a shrewd sense of the importance of cash, buying expensive jewellery in good economic times, ready to sell when necessary.

In early summer 1346, the Prince of Wales sailed from Portsmouth with his father and an impressive army. He landed at St Vaast-de-la-Hogue on 12 July and was knighted by his father in the church of Quettehou. The accolade, which followed spending all night in prayer before being dubbed with a broadsword tap on each shoulder, was a milestone in a young man's life, perhaps the most important.

We noted the Prince's performance at Crecy in the last chapter. Romanticized as it has become, there is no doubt that the boy won his spurs that day. As men in the late eighteenth century said of the younger William Pitt and his father, 'This is not a chip of the old block; it is the old block itself.' In the weeks before the battle, Edward roamed the Cotentin, raiding villages and towns and took Caen. He clashed with a French army under Godemar du Fay who tried to stop the English advance across the Somme at Blanchetaque.

It is the Prince's behaviour after Crecy that began the legend of his chivalry. With his father, he paid homage to the dead King John of

Bohemia and perhaps took his three feathers as his own emblem then. The German motto *Ich dien* (I serve) has resonance with Bohemia (which became Czechoslovakia) which had a large German-speaking population. The alternative theory (and with the Black Prince there are always alternative theories) is that the feathers were part of his mother's coat of arms and that Hainault also had affinity with the Germans. And there is a third theory; that the motto is actually *eich dyn*, Welsh for 'here is the man'. It would be nice to think that the Prince of Wales adopted this phrase, but the notion of Welsh-speaking Princes of Wales is purely twentieth century.

After Crecy, the Prince besieged Calais and burned the surrounding countryside in a 30-mile radius, bringing unprecedented amounts of booty back with him. In the celebrations back home in 1347–8, Edward took part in umpteen tournaments and was made a founder member of the Order of the Garter. The following year, he was on campaign again, rescuing his father in a tight situation, waiting on him as a chivalrous son and refusing to sit with the king at dinner as a mark of respect.

We know that he was in the thick of things at Winchelsea in 1350 when his ship was holed and eventually sank, by which time the Prince and his crew had boarded another one. Putting down a revolt in Cheshire in 1353 (such risings were an annual event throughout Europe, usually over taxation and/or local grievances) he went to France again two years later with the full powers of a king. In fact, in some circles he was already being referred to as Edward IV! In June, taking advantage of the 'rich and fertile' (his words) country around Avignon and the fact that the locals were 'good, simple and ignorant of war' (his words again) he led a devastating chevauchée that set southern France back for decades and must have put the fear of God into the Pope. By January 1356, the Prince had taken five towns and seventeen castles, all of them with the help of his Goddamns.

By 1359, in the company of his father, Edward negotiated the Treaty of Bretigny, a landmark in the on-and-off warfare we call the Hundred Years War.

As well as warfare, the duty of a Prince of Wales was to marry to continue the family line. Various attempts by Edward III to link his eldest boy with a European house had failed and in October 1361, the Prince shocked everybody (even his father) by marrying, apparently for love, the widowed Joan, Countess of Kent. As she was Edward's cousin, special dispensation had to be granted by Pope Innocent VI and the wedding took place at Windsor, presided over by Simon Islip, Archbishop of Canterbury. The couple (Joan already had three children by her previous marriage) lived at Berkhamsted Castle in Hertfordshire, which the Prince converted into a vast and impressive hunting lodge. His even larger residence at Bordeaux was a court to rival Edward III's at Windsor.

In exchange for the normal feudal rent of one ounce of gold a year, Edward received all his father's lands in Aquitaine and Gascony. The redoubtable John Chandos was his second in command, but the excesses of the free companies (mostly English bowmen) caused such havoc that Edward III had to tell his son to rein them in. After Poitiers, as after Crecy, the man who let his heavies slaughter his way across France was courtesy itself to the captured Jean le Bon, even hosting the French king at Berkhamsted from time to time.

The free companies' action continued and Charles V called Edward to appear in Paris to answer charges of what today we would call war crimes. The Prince announced that he would go 'but it shall be with our helmet on our head and 60,000 men in our company.' Charles V did not push it!

When Pedro of Castile asked Edward's help in defending his kingdom against his half-brother Enrico of Trastamara, the Prince obliged and won the spectacular victory at Najera in April 1367. This campaign was not the Black Prince's last, but it was his most costly. John Chandos died on 1 January 1370 and the Prince himself became ill, probably with dysentery from which he never quite recovered. He was seriously out of pocket since Pedro reneged on a payment and if Edward got the famous ruby (actually a spinel) out of him rather than being offered it, as some accounts contend, it was only a fraction of what the Spanish king owed him.

Increasingly ill, unable to mount a horse and carried on a litter, the Prince insisted on continuing the war with France. Perhaps because of his illness, his temper worsened as he aged. Furious that Limoges had been lost to him because of the duplicity of its bishop whom Edward had trusted, he mined the walls in October 1370 and ordered the slaughter of the inhabitants. The over-exuberance for a bloody tale got the better of the chroniclers as usual, who claimed that 3,000 died, among them women and children. Recent research has revealed that the figure was closer to 300 and they were nearly all members of the town's garrison. The Black Prince retired to his Berkhamsted estate and lingered, a decaying hulk like his father, until his death.

'He made a very noble end,' wrote the chroniclers, 'remembering God his Creator in his heart' on 8 June 1376 and was buried in the magnificent tomb in Canterbury Cathedral. For all we have a great deal of information on the man, he remains an enigma and it is difficult to see the reality behind the brass mask of Canterbury.

'Such as thou art,' reads the Latin inscription around his effigy, 'sometimes was I. Such as I am, such shalt thou be …'

Chapter 11

Poitiers: 19 September 1356 St Januarius' Day

Ten years on from Crecy, Edward III again pressed his claim to the throne of France and intended to coordinate his armies to bring the whole of western France under English control. After a successful chevauchée as far south as Carcassonne and Narbonne, the Black Prince, now 25 and in full command of the army, marched north to meet Henry of Lancaster's army in Normandy.

The French king now was Jean le Bon, as courageous as his predecessor but twice as reckless. With an army of nearly 50,000, he could afford to be cavalier and boxed the Prince, with his mere 8,000, into a corner. Working through Cardinal Talleyrand de Perigord (the family was still advising French political leaders up to and beyond Napoleon's time) Edward offered far too much territory to avoid a battle. This was probably a ruse, because bringing the French into the field was exactly what he had been trying to do for months. To surrender the hard-won towns of Calais and Guines would have been ludicrous; Edward knew that Jean would not accept it, but would insist on total surrender.

By 18 September, the English army had found a good position on a slope above Poitiers (referred to by Froissart, rather grandiosely, as a city – probably on account of its cathedral). They camped on high ground between the Poitiers road and the meandering river of Miausson, with the woods of St Pierre beyond that.

The French high command, led by the king, comprised two marshals, Arnoud d'Aydrechou and Jean de Clermont, and William Douglas, the Scots renegade who had fought against the English for years and had been given a bloody nose at Neville's Cross in 1346. It was Douglas who advised the king not to expose his cavalry to the English bowmen – he had seen them in action once too often. Many of the Frenchmen were hobelars, light cavalry who fought from the saddle. Douglas suggested they fight on foot and shorten their lances to make 5ft spears. As in previous engagements, the French were divided into three divisions, all dismounted, with a cavalry screen across their entire front. The idea was for the cavalry charge to open proceedings and knock out the English bowmen. This had failed spectacularly at Crecy; why should it work now?

The first division was led by the Dauphin, Jean's eldest son, a 19-year-old with no battle experience at all. The second was commanded by Duke Philippe d'Orleans, the king's brother. The third division was led by the king himself.

The Black Prince's army was composed of Englishmen and Gascons, the 'French' part of his inheritance. His position, on 18 September, had a large hedge across his entire front, enabling him to manoeuvre freely behind it, while the confused French could only look on. There was a protective marsh to the east and at the army's back, the Grué de Homme, the road south to Bordeaux. The Gascon troops, less trusted perhaps than the English, were split into three to bring up the numbers in other units.

The left wing, nearest the marsh and river, were led by the Earls of Warwick and Oxford. On the right, the honours went to Suffolk and Salisbury. Salisbury's men had the protection of a waggon barricade and a series of trenches, hastily dug while Talleyrand was carrying out his manoeuvres.

In the English army, it almost went without saying that everyone fought on foot, a move that, as at Crecy, drew shouts and whistles of contempt from the French. Edward's chivalry, especially after his gutsy performance at Crecy, was widely known, but he was also a pragmatic, realistic soldier. He had probably been prepared to break off before actual battle was joined and to do a runner. The French noticed that the bowmen held the hedge, a brilliant natural line of defence for them and the Prince was pulling back with his division towards the Grué de Homme. Again, we have no clear idea of where the bowmen were. Each division had them, standing at the front and between the infantry, but Froissart hints at a particular concentration, 'in harrow form', in front of the hedge as well as behind it. It is noticeable that the French did not contemplate taking out the bowmen with their own; only French cavalry could do that.

The marshals selected the most experienced and strongest knights from each division and they formed a unit, possibly in three mini divisions. Horse armour had not changed since Crecy and the animals' heads remained the only part of their bodies protected by iron. It is doubtful, for reasons of expense, that the horse archers employed by the French and the English (Edward III had 3,000 of them on the battlefield at Crecy) had any armour at all.

It is not true, as many historians have maintained, that the French had learned nothing from Crecy. Apart from the opening attack by the cavalry, specifically designed to terrify the bowmen, all the French, of whatever rank, fought on foot, like the English. The only exception was the German contingent, led by the Counts of Saarbruck, Nidau and Nassau. According to Froissart, there were nineteen knights wearing the king's colours, the gold fleur de lys on the blue field and even had coronets buckled to their bascinets. This was a ploy often used in Medieval battles, to add to Jean le Bon's safety but also to confuse the enemy. In Shakespeare's *Richard III*, the king, on the field at Bosworth (1485) says, 'I think there be six Richmonds [Henry Tudor] in the field today. Five have I slain instead of him.'

The Black Prince made a speech to his men, standard practice at the time. Specifically, he told his bowmen, 'Follow the standards, obey implicitly in body and mind the commands of your leaders. If victory shall see us still alive, we shall always continue in firm friendship together, being of one heart and mind.'

The bowmen, along with everybody else among the rank and file, were jeering at the enemy, no doubt using their bow fingers in the air in the symbol that would carry down the centuries. The gesture said, 'Look, we've still got our fingers and they are going to kill you in the next few minutes.'

Fearing that the English would pull back even at this late stage, the marshals Clermont and d'Aydrechou launched an attack. D'Aydrechou hit Warwick's division on the English left and Clermont went for Salisbury on the right. The bowmen of both wings opened up, the arrows thudding into man and horse and in this context at least, Poitiers was a replay of Crecy. The Earl of Oxford ordered his bowmen out to the far wing, so that the next wave of arrows hit the French in the flank, the side not protected by their shields. As the cavalry swept past them, they found themselves riddled with arrows from behind.

Clermont was soon in trouble. He had not expected bowmen behind the hedge. They stood up and fired, perhaps only once before throwing their bows down and dragging French knights from their saddles, ramming their dagger blades into the eye-sockets of helmets and cutting throats. Clermont was killed in this way.

King Jean now sent his first division forward. Its royal commanders – the Dauphin and his brothers Anjou and the future Duke of Berry – were all in their teens and they did not have that essential something which characterized the Black Prince. They were moving uphill, but were well armoured, so the showers of arrows had less effect on them than had been the case with the cavalry. The English line was composed of the hedge, hastily dug ditches and overturned baggage carts; hundreds of hand-to-hand duels broke out all along it. The French could not break through, however, and the Dauphin lost his standard, always regarded as an ill omen.

Edward had ordered his men to stand their ground and not pursue a wavering enemy. The only notable warrior who disobeyed in a moment of exuberance was Sir Maurice Berkeley. To take the Dauphin prisoner would be a huge feather in his cap and would bring, literally, a princely ransom. He ended up being taken prisoner himself!

There was a lull in the fighting. Hand-to-hand combat is exhausting, given the weight of swords and pole-weapons and it is impossible to keep it up for more than minutes at a time. The bowmen ripped their spent arrows from bodies and the ground and drank from the Miausson trickling to their left.

Jean le Bon now made the second poor decision of the day and ordered his sons off the field. No doubt, the viciousness of the attack had rattled everybody and the king wanted to keep the boys alive, but to see the princes, complete with their entourage, effectively fleeing action was a psychological bomb-burst. It was only made worse when the Duke of Orleans, not yet engaged, wheeled his division and led them away.

Jean was understandably furious with all this and advanced the oriflamme (the sacred standard carried by French kings in battle) sending his massive division down the slope from the right. The English must have been dreading this. The superior numbers of the enemy were now painfully obvious. Exhausted, in some cases wounded, men, rested on their bows, their halberds, their sword hilts and watched Jean's glittering forces marching towards them to the beat of what sounded like 1,000 drums. One soldier standing near the Black Prince is supposed to have muttered, 'Alas! We are beaten.' Edward snapped at him, 'You're lying, you bastard, if you're saying we can be beaten while I am alive.'

He gave order to attack along the entire front, anyone with a horse mounting. One contingent under the redoubtable Burgundian ally Jean III de Grailly, the Captal de Buch, was sent to the east to outflank Jean's advance, and Walter Woodward, the Prince's standard bearer, raised his flag and shouted, 'By God and St George.' 'Ride forward, sire,' John Chandos said to him. 'Today you will hold God in your hand.'

There are moments in every battle when a particular event stands out. The charge of the English knights led by the Black Prince was one of them. Whether he wore his great helm with the fur-mantled cap of estate and the golden leopard crest is unknown, but the leopards and lilies on his horse bard were unmistakeable. Edward had no doubles on the field to fox the enemy. There was only one of him and no doubt there were several thousand Frenchmen there that day who were glad that that was the case.

At Poitiers, we have a reverse of the usual situation. Now, Edward's cavalry was crashing into French foot soldiers and the bowmen, having exhausted their arrows a second time, joined the billmen hacking and slashing. Swords, clubs, knives, stones, *anything* was a weapon in these desperate moments. King Jean's division alone outnumbered the English. This was Edward's one and only chance to get it right. The Captal de Buch hit the French in the flank, trampling foot soldiers and throwing the whole advance into confusion. Sir James Audley, regarded as the bravest of the English knights, smashed into the king's right flank so that Jean's division was hammered from both sides.

The Prince himself scattered the German contingent and all the time, according to Froissart, 'No one could face the heavy, rapid fire of the English archers, who, in that encounter, killed and wounded many who found no chance of offering ransoms or pleading for mercy.' Douglas, realizing that the French had been fought to a standstill, turned tail. In terms of ransom, it was the done thing for titled men to surrender in exchange for an agreed sum, but Douglas was not of their class; he could expect the rope and did not relish the prospect. This was the second time he had run rather than face the Goddamns.

Geoffrey de Chargny, carrying the oriflamme, was hacked to death. The Count de Tancareville was captured, so was Lord Jacques de Bourbon and Lord Jean d'Artois. Lord Charles d'Artois with several knights surrendered to the Captal de Buch and the king's division cracked. They were driven back, stumbling over each other, to the walls of Poitiers itself. Slaughter took place under the masonry and Frenchmen dropped their weapons at the mere sight of an Englishman. 'Never before,' Froissart wrote, 'had there been so disastrous a rout.'

One of the most extraordinary survivors was the Frenchman Guichard d'Angle. Left for dead on the field, he recovered, went over to surrender to the Black Prince and ultimately became tutor to his son, the future Richard II and was made Earl of Huntingdon. King Jean himself had lost his shield and was swinging his battle-axe with both hands. There was an unseemly squabble now over who should take the king prisoner. In the end it was, ironically, a Frenchman, Denis de Marbecque, who had been exiled for killing a man in a duel years before. Jean would have preferred to surrender to the Black Prince himself, but short of that, was happy to pass his gauntlet to de Marbecque.

Not far from Poitiers, the Prince halted the rout, trumpets sounding for the killing to stop. He raised his standard as a rallying point and, for the first time that day, unbuckled his helmet. A crimson tent was put up and Edward and his lords drank to their success before the complicated business of sorting out ransoms. The most unedifying of these was King Jean. He was seen to be dragged and jostled by a mob of Gascons, de Marbecque having lost him in the melee. Loud arguments broke out as to who should get the ransom money. Not until he reached Edward's tent was his life out of danger. And years of delightful imprisonment followed.

> So that battle was fought [Froissart wrote] in the fields of Maupertuis … on the nineteenth day of September 1356. It began in the early morning and was finished by mid-afternoon … There died there that day, it was said, the finest flower of French Chivalry, whereby the realm of France was sorely weakened and fell into great misery and affliction.

One constable and two marshals were dead. One archbishop, thirteen counts, five viscounts, twenty-one barons and bannerets and some 2,000 men-at-arms were captured or killed. Extraordinarily, there are no figures for the English dead. 'That evening,' wrote Froissart, 'the Prince of Wales gave a supper for the king of France.' Nobody did generous chivalry like Edward of Woodstock.

Chapter 12

The Jacquerie and the Free Companies

In Chapter 2 we looked at the impact of the English Peasants' Revolt on the 'hurling time', the chaotic years of the fourteenth century. But the causes of the Revolt were largely economic and went far beyond the pressure put on society by war. In France, the situation was different. Both the Jacquerie and the free companies came into being directly as a result of the war itself.

Jean Froissart hated the Jacquerie. 'There were very strange and terrible happenings in several parts of the kingdom of France ... They had chosen a king from among those who came ... and they elected the worst of the band, this king was called Jacques Bonhomme [Jack Goodman].' What the French chroniclers called *les effrois* (the terror) began on the last week of May 1358, less than two years after the Black Prince's victory at Poitiers. The history of France over centuries has been one of rebellion, from the Fronde of the seventeenth century to the gilets jaunes of recent years, but in the 1350s, such behaviour was largely unprecedented and came, certainly to the nobility, as a complete surprise. One chronicler, Jean de Venette, wrote:

> The peasants living near Saint-Leu-d'Esséront and Clermont in the bishopric of Beauvais, seeing the wrongs and oppression inflicted on them on every side and that their nobles gave them no protection but rather oppressed then as heavily as the enemy [the English] rose and took arms against them ... They massacred without mercy all the nobles they could find, even their own lords ... they levelled the houses and fortresses of the nobles to the ground and ... they delivered the noble ladies

> and their little children … to an atrocious death … wherewith they clothed themselves and their peasant wives luxuriously.

While the ever-slippery Dauphin did his best to rally his nobility after Poitiers and got the backing of the Pope, Innocent VI (himself, of course, a Frenchman), the ordinary peasant had a very different view of life. As de Venette wrote:

> No cock crowed, no hen called to her chicks … The eye of man was no longer rejoiced by the accustomed sight of green pastures and fields covered by growing grain, but saddened by the nettles and thistles springing up on every side. The pleasant sound of bells was heard, not as a summons to divine worship, but as a warning of hostile incursions, in order that men might seek out hiding places.

De Venette, like most chroniclers anywhere at any time, was prepared to believe the worst of avaricious landlords. The nobility refused to stump up the cash for the Dauphin to keep fighting, taxes were raised and coins clipped (a physical devaluation). Such money, moaned de Venette, 'was all spent for the useless practices of pleasures, such as dice and other unseemly gains'.

Froissart went further. Without naming places or people, he tells of a peasant mob that, armed with pikes and daggers, broke into a knight's house and killed him and his family before torching the place. In another fortified manor house, they tied the owner to a post before raping his wife and daughter in front of him.

According to most contemporary accounts, the peasants of Beauvais numbered fewer than 100, but their numbers grew alarmingly as they scoured the countryside. And their violence was unparalleled. The English Peasants' Revolt was largely an agrarian movement; townspeople joined in only when their own homes were threatened. In France, the social mix, of town and country, was there from the beginning. And whereas, via the sermons of John Ball, Wat Tyler's men could claim some sort of ideological stance, even demanding equality with their social superiors, the Jacquerie were simply intent on destruction and violence for its own sake. They had no plan to reform society, not even to make Jacques as good as his master. Their wholesale theft of property and burning of homes is proof of that. The nobility had failed at Poitiers, their arrogance smashed in the mud by the arrowstorm of the English – men like themselves, but victorious.

'I would not dare,' wrote Froissart, 'to write or speak of the dreadful and revolting things they did to women.' He does, however, recount one story of a knight being roasted on a spit like a suckling pig and his wife being forced to eat some of the flesh.

Whether there was ever one, single leader of the revolt is debatable. Wat Tyler emerged in this role in England in 1381, but he had the academic clout of John Ball behind him and an able lieutenant in Jack Straw. *Jacques Bonhomme* was a generic catch-all for a peasant, rather as the soldiers facing each other in the American civil war in the nineteenth century were 'Billy Yank' and 'Johnny Reb'. The only actual name that emerges is Guillaume Cale, who had a seal made for himself to give a certain authority and had lieutenants in the Jack Straw mould. More so than Tyler, Cale seems not to have been able to control his people, even if he had wanted to, and the slaughter continued.

For Froissart, the real villain of the story was Etienne Marcel, Provost of the Parisian merchants, roughly equivalent in rank to the Lord Mayor of London. The burgesses of the city, fearing the sudden ferocity of the mob, paid for mercenaries belonging to the king of Navarre who sat around in St Denis largely ignoring the problem. There were Englishmen with the Navarese, men largely unemployed since Poitiers and no doubt several of them were bowmen. The archers of Edward III's bodyguard were paid 6d a day but the rank and file from the shires got no such benefits and their pay was often in arrears. The prospect of booty had an obvious appeal for them.

When fighting broke out between the mercenaries and the townsfolk, some 60 soldiers were killed and Marcel had a further 150 imprisoned in the Louvre, not yet the cultural centre it has become. Wanting to keep the English sweet, he let them all go after dark. This led to a state of war, with bowmen wandering the city's suburbs butchering anybody who was rash enough to be out in the streets. Under pressure from the merchants, Marcel led an army of 2,000 townsmen to St Cloud to confront the Goddamns. Half of those, having spent an exhausting day and finding nothing, were attacked and massacred at sunset. Froissart estimated over 700 deaths but worse was to come. The next day, the families of the dead brought carts to take their bodies for burial and the English attacked them too. Marcel now made a pact with the devil (in fact, the king of Navarre) and set up a plan to let the English into the city via two gates and let them kill anybody whose door was not marked with a secret sign.

The plot was rumbled and on 31 July, Marcel was beaten to death by the mob as were six of his followers. Their bodies were displayed, naked, in the courtyard of St Catherine's Church and then thrown into the Seine.

How much of this actually happened is debatable, but Froissart was all too ready to lay the blame at the door of the English, rather than mercenaries and disgruntled peasants who were far more local.

The Dauphin, fearing that the Parisians would join the rabble, fled with his court to Meaux, 20 miles from the capital, but was away when the Jacquerie struck. The town's garrison was hopelessly outnumbered and there were an estimated 900 ladies of the court in the beleaguered town. Luckily for them, galloping to the rescue came two of the very class the peasants despised – the Captal de Buch, who had fought for the English at Poitiers and Count Gaston Phoebus, a golden-haired knight errant who looked as though he had just stepped out of an Arthurian romance, popular all over France at the time.

The Jacqueries attacked Meaux on 9 June but were held at the town's narrow bridge by de Buch and Phoebus, whose professional men-at-arms re-enacted Horatius defending Rome 'in the brave days of old'. As with Tyler's peasants at Smithfield twenty-three years later, faced with well-armed experienced soldiers, the peasantry halted. Hacked and battered, they fell back on the mob behind, stumbling over each other in panic. 'They mowed them down in heaps,' wrote Froissart, 'and slaughtered them like cattle.' An unknown number drowned in the river Marne that circled the town. Froissart gives the number of dead as in excess of 7,000, which seems unlikely, but there was no doubt about the outcome of the day. Anyone suspected of alliance with the Jacquerie (and there were several) were walled up in their own homes and burned alive. The mayor was hanged. De Venette wrote that the victors:

> Went raging through the … countryside … and slew … all the peasants, not only those whom they believed to have harmed them, but all they found, whether in their houses or digging in the vineyards or in the fields. The misery caused by the nobles reached such a pitch … that before the English who had been the chief enemies of the realm before, could not have done what they did.

'The memory of these bloody executions,' wrote the anonymous author of the *Chronicon Angliae*, 'still causes inhabitants to weep.' Perhaps as many as 20,000 peasants were hanged or cut to pieces by a vengeful aristocracy and their retinues

'The English … could not have done what they did.' But the English were doing just that, not merely in Beauvais and Meaux but all over France. They were members of the free companies.

Mercenaries have acquired a bad reputation in recent centuries but in fact, men who fight for pay have always been part of military organizations throughout history. Since all soldiers serve in exchange for pay (usually little and late) it can be argued that *all* fighters are mercenaries. The distinction comes between nationals and foreigners. In eighteenth- and nineteenth-century Britain, fighting for another country was treason and that carried the death penalty. In the fourteenth and fifteenth centuries, the calling was altogether more honourable and even though 'free lances' and 'freebooters' were universally feared and detested, their commanders were treated with the same respect afforded to lords and knights, especially when some of them were actually given titles or had them already.

In 1891, Arthur Conan Doyle wrote *The White Company*, based very loosely on a real mercenary outfit that operated mostly in the Italian states in the 1360s and 1370s. Its leader was the Englishman John Hawkwood and a study of his career sheds considerable light on the chaos that reigned in France during the Hundred Years War. He was born in Suffolk about 1323 and was apprenticed as a tailor in London. He joined Edward III's army as a bowman, although why, when and where is unknown. Bearing in mind his later fluidity, it is not likely that he was part of a noble entourage, but a freebooter from the beginning. Legend has it that he fought as a bowman at both Crecy and Poitiers, but since we have no accurate lists of archers for either battle, it is impossible to tell. Legend also has it that he was knighted for his prowess by the Black Prince himself after Poitiers, but again, there is no record. Certainly, the Italians for whom he usually fought assumed he was a knight, because their own *condiottieri* (mercenaries) were.

It is in the period after Poitiers and especially the Treaty of Bretigny in 1360 that the free companies became particularly notorious. The obvious thing to do was to send troops home after a campaign, if only to reduce expense, but the Companies had been used to pillage and slaughter and refused to go. Often Castilians, Genoese, Flemings and even Germans (with more than a smattering of Frenchmen) they were universally called 'English' by the peasants who were their usual targets.

Hawkwood joined the largely Italian White Company in 1361 and had become its commander two years later. It is likely that because of this, disenfranchised English soldiers flocked to his standard, so that by 1366, the group was generally called the English Company. How many members of the free companies were actually bowmen is debatable. Probably each man was a general fighter, handy with long or crossbow, sword, dagger and bare hands. It is also likely that most of them were mounted, able to cover long distances quickly.

We do not have records of the pay given to these men, which would no doubt have fluctuated wildly depending on what services they were asked to provide, but we knew that Hawkwood earned between 6,000 and 80,000 gold florins a year, at a time when a Florentine craftsman was lucky to earn thirty. How much of this filtered down to the rank and file is anybody's guess.

Men like Hawkwood – and the free companies generally – had no compunction when it came to attacking churches and other religious houses. He took the Pont d'Esprit near Avignon and held it for three months despite pleas to leave from Pope Innocent, who promptly excommunicated the whole Company. Excommunication was a serious and heavy penalty to people brought up in the Catholic faith, but the Company shrugged it off – after all, many of them were the Goddamns! Hawkwood also burned the Abbey of San Gilgano in Tuscany and slaughtered the monks he found there.

John Hawkwood's tactics were those of Bertrand du Guesclin. He was actually a highly competitive general but preferred to avoid open battle, relying on feigned retreats, false flags and ambushes. Murder, rape and dismemberment were routine among the orders of the day.

Today, Hawkwood and his Company stand as war criminals, as brutal as anything we have seen in the Balkans, the Middle East and Africa in our own time, but in *his* day, he was honoured by the Italians who seem to have taken him to their hearts. Although he was not allowed to enter Florence in his lifetime, a lavish funeral was held there for him in March 1394 and he was buried with full honours in the duomo. Forty years after his death, the Renaissance artist Paulo Ucello designed a tomb for him, which still stands. The Latin on the fresco reads 'John Hawkwood [Giovanni Acuto (the sharp)] knight of Britain, most prudent leader of his age and most expert in the art of war'.

As we have seen, looting during a chevauchée was a widely accepted practice. All the free companies were doing was to extend this policy and make it their raison d'être. After Poitiers, they roamed Aquitaine and central France, robbing and killing at will. Armed to the teeth and wearing leather brigandines, they were responsible for giving the world a new word – brigand. They were irresponsible gangs, but all the more dangerous because they recognized no masters other than their own captains (men like Hawkwood, the Englishman Robert Knollys and the Frenchman du Guesclin) and did not confine their murder and rapine to their own backyard. Knollys himself had a company of 500 bowmen, a unit still in service with him at Smithfield in the year of the English Peasants' Revolt.

There is no doubt that while the Jacquerie were born of desperation and confined to a limited area geographically and in time (the spring and summer of 1359) the Companies were organized robbers, planning their attacks like military operations. The Jacqueries only hit the aristocracy and their retainers; the Companies targeted everybody! They ran what came to be called in the twentieth century 'protection rackets'; they would take a castle and demand cash from the locals to avoid *le feu et leurs corps* (fire and corpses). It worked. Knollys himself made 100,000 gold crowns in this way over less than a year. Froissart describes what happened if locals did not pay:

> On occasion, and that was often, they would select a good town two- or three-days' journey distant. Twenty or thirty brigands would … set out, by day or night, keeping to secluded tracks and enter the place at dawn. A house would be set on fire. The inhabitants would think that a thousand men-at-arms had come … If they fled, so much the better. The brigands would break into the houses, smash open coffers and chests, take what they found there and be off, laden with booty.

Jean de Venette saw events unfold north of Paris. 'The enemy [the Companies] seized many castles … and captured the men who dwelt nearby. Some they held for ransom; some they slaughtered miserably. Nor did they spare the monks and nuns.' In some cases, the minor nobility actually joined in!

Safe conduct was given to merchants who were all too glad to keep their businesses intact, albeit with a depleted profit. Company captains like Peter Audley, Hugh Calverley, Walter Hewitt, Robert Brickett and the Gascon Bertucat d'Albret held 60 castles between them and each had 2,000 soldiers, many of them bowmen, in their pay. It seems extraordinary that the Companies, even of professional, hard-bitten soldiers, could have taken so many castles. They were probably largely fortified manor houses and the lack of defence of them makes clear just how badly France had been mauled at Poitiers.

We shall probably never know how badly the peasantry were hit. Bearing in mind that, as in England, the pestilence raged in various localities from time to time and there was no defence against the Companies, they must have been desperate and often facing starvation. One Company commander is quoted by Froissart:

> The villeins [peasants] of Auvergne and Limousin supplied us, bringing corn to our castle, flour, baked bread, fodder and bedding for the horses, good wine, cattle, goats and fat sheep, along with hens and game. Our clothes were regal and when we went riding, the whole country trembled before us. By God, it was a good life!

The bowmen did well too. Henry Knighton's *Chronicon* (1358) reads, 'Many who had gone out as boys and valets returned very rich … There was not an Englishman so poor but soon had his fill of gold and silver, jewels and precious stuffs.'

Among the oddities in the commanders of the free companies, Hugh Calverley, from Cheshire, stands out. It is interesting that he hailed from a county known for its bowmen, although there is no proof that he was an archer himself. He was a giant of a man with red hair and a prodigious appetite and it says a great deal about the complexity of the age (some would say hypocrisy) that while he was happy to condone and oversee wholesale plunder, he insisted on the booty being sprinkled with holy water. Some of the booty he collected from France went into building the church at Bunbury, where he is buried.

It was Calverley who captured Bertrand du Guesclin at Juigné Bridge and ransomed him for 30,000 crowns. Such was the fluidity of warfare that he later found himself fighting *for* the Frenchman:

> Myself will keep you in good company. By God who created the world, I will go everywhere it may please you to go. I will fight against the whole world, on this side and on the other side of the sea, except the Prince of Wales, to whom I have pledged allegiance.

Godfrey de Harcourt led a large company of brigands including Navarese in the Cotentin, putting enormous pressure on the government in Paris to do something about the absence of King Jean after Poitiers. And such brigandage was a two-way street. A French force under the 'Archpriest', Regnault de Cervoles, led a mixed force through Provence and forced the pope to grant him concessions. All his Company's sins were remitted and 40,000 crowns changed hands. In the north, between the Seine and the Loire, a Welshman named Ruffin (probably Gruffydd) carried out raids as far as Paris, making himself a fortune in the process. No one opposed him.

France, never as unified a state as England, became more fragmented than ever under the free companies, each captain using his bowmen and men-at-arms to carve out a slice of territory for himself. Eustace d'Aubriecourt ruled in Champagne, crossing both the Seine and the Marne with up to 1,000 troops on innumerable chevauchées. At the height of his powers in 1360, he held twelve castles and policed dozens of roads, claiming tolls on all of them.

Fighting between the free companies was frequent, much like the internecine gang wars of later times and places. For Peter Audley, Jean de Ségur, Jean de Picquigny and Lus de Bethien, read Al Capone, Bugsy Siegel, Dion O'Banion and 'Lucky' Luciano. De Picquigny and de Bethien, for example, were both murdered by their servants.

Historian Roger Vercel sums up the free companies admirably:

> If they have terrified people and history, it is because they were in every sense of the word men of war. They practised war with a terrible sincerity. They divested it of all vain ornament; they displayed it in its frightful reality, in its bestial nudity. They had the only qualities that war requires, bravery and discipline … That is why even their enemies … sometimes admired these handsome, brutal soldiers. The pope called them *doctiores in excitione armorum* [teachers of war]. Men make war only to take what they can. Those who do not covet do not make war; they endure it. Repudiating all hypocrisy, the … Companies always proclaimed this primordial aim. Their enemy was he who owned what they wanted. They pillaged with a fierce impudence in every camp. They did not trouble themselves with excuses, they did not cloak themselves with flags or principles … As for the other virtues that are held up to men of war – magnanimity, respect of property and persons – the bandits rejected them as nonsense or betrayal.

As ever, we have no written record of the bowmen who joined the free companies. It is only their commanders who had the status to appear in print. One of these was Bascot de Mauléon who was interviewed by Froissart at Christmastide 1388 while he was a guest at Orthez, the estate of Gaston Phoebus of Foix who had fought the Jacquerie. How much we can believe of de Mauléon's reminiscences is debatable, but it is a fascinating insight into the mindset of a mercenary who had Frenchmen, Englishmen, Genoese and Castilians in his Company.

De Mauléon was in his mid-fifties and had plenty of followers and baggage. They all stayed, presumably the rank and file in yards and stables, at the sign of the Moon, where Ernauton du Pin was the host. They ate off silver plate and de Mauléon had as many packhorses as any baron. While waiting one night for Phoebus to start his supper (he never dined before midnight), the Freebooter sat drinking by the fire, reminiscing with his cousin and Froissart, who committed the conversation to memory.

De Mauléon had fought under the Captal de Buch's banner at Poitiers and had taken a knight and two squires prisoner, which brought him in 3,000 francs. He was on his way back from a crusade in Prussia (the East Germans were then still pagan) with the Captal and took part in saving the ladies of the court from Jacquerie outrages (see above). 'We killed more than 6,000 of the Jacques,' de Mauléon told Froissart. 'They never rebelled again.' During the Anglo-French truce after 1360, de Mauléon fought for the King of Navarre against the Dauphin. 'We became masters of the farmlands and the rivers … and won a great deal of wealth.'

The truce caused problems for the free companies whose captains called a meeting. De Mauléon had over 12,000 men, English, Gascons, Germans, Scots and Spaniards, and 'they had to live somehow.'

The victory at Brignais was a Godsend; it provided riches from the archbishoprics of Lyons and along the Rhone. At Pont-Saint-Esprit, the English, Germans and Gascons, led by John Hawkwood – 'a fine English knight' – were bought off by the pope for 60,000 francs. Most of the French commanders stayed put, however, taking nearly sixty castles and manor houses and holding the south to ransom. Throughout this period, the Companies had the blessing of the King of Navarre.

Acknowledging that the thrill of battle was part of the Companies' raison d'être, de Mauléon followed the Captal to fight for du Guesclin at Cocherel in 1364. He was taken prisoner there, by his cousin, who promptly gave him safe conduct to freedom. Three years later, de Mauléon was in Spain under Hugh Calverley, fighting for du Guesclin and Enrico of Trastamara.

De Mauléon's account is almost all about battles, not marauding, rape and pillage, but there is no doubt he sanctioned much of this too. He also admits that he lost as often as he won various encounters and sometimes did not even have a horse to ride, 'but I have always held the frontier and fought for the King of England, for my family estate lies in the Bordeaux district.' In a tale that reads like a bad script from a 1950s Hollywood movie, he and his Companies disguised themselves as women to sneak into the castle of Thurie which brought de Mauléon a very nice annual income. In the mid-1360s, so many French lords were still imprisoned in England while their ransoms were arranged that the Companies had a free hand in their reign of terror.

'Well, my dear sir,' the Freebooter said to the chronicler, 'I've done a lot of talking to while away the time. But it's all true.'

Hmm.

Chapter 13

Najera: 3 April 1367 St Richard's Day

Jean Froissart writes briefly about the battle of Najera and he covers the reasons for it: a succession struggle in Portugal between Pedro the Cruel and Enrico Trastamara, his half-brother. Froissart also writes about the battle of Monteuil in 1369 and John of Gaunt's ill-advised attempts to take the Portuguese throne in 1386. With hindsight, Najera was the last great victory of Edward, the Black Prince; after it, his slow decline coincided with that of England.

Najera was an important station for pilgrims taking the 'French way' over the Pyrenees to the shrine of Santiago (St James) of Compostela. It was also in the high sierras of Castile, unbearably hot in the summer and just plain unbearable in the winter. Men froze to death in their saddles during the winter months.

The interminable feud between Pedro and Enrico was a squabble over power not unlike that between John and his barons in England that led to Magna Carta. Enrico was the Castilian barons' hero and the epithet 'the Cruel' that they gave to Pedro could have been applied to any of them. Edward III had wisely told his eldest son to keep out of Castilian politics, but as ruler of Aquitaine, the Prince could see huge advantages in gaining Castilian support. The Castilian navy was regarded as the best in Europe in the 1360s, far in advance of anything the English or French could offer. Every leader involved shared the ongoing problem of the free companies whose uncontrolled chevauchées in various areas continued to cause problems in terms of civilian morale and local economics. If gang warfare could be channelled, however, … and this led both Castilians to hire mercenaries.

Pedro's army crossed the Pyrenees at Roncesvalles, following the pilgrim's way. The little way stations that provided food and shelter for pilgrims were swamped by the Black Prince's retinue, who proceeded to help themselves to whatever southern France and northern Spain had to offer. Roncesvalles held a special place in the mythology of chivalry, because the *Song of Roland*, who was killed there in a battle in 778, was the stuff of immortal legend. The minstrel Taillefer was reputed to have sung it to William of Normandy's knights before the battle of Senlac in 1066 and it was a staple of royal court entertainment throughout Europe. A sword called Durandal, allegedly belonging to Roland, was found wedged into a rock in the pass, rather like Arthur's Excalibur. Its replica was stolen from its position as I write this book.

Earlier accounts of the battle that followed, after Froissart, who was not there, give Pedro and the Black Prince's army about 24,000 troops; the French and Enrico 76,000. Both figures are unrealistic, but the accuracy of numbers is not helped by the mixed make-up of both armies. Pedro, along with his loyal Castilians, had the Englishmen, Gascons and Poitevins of the Black Prince, most of them, in this campaign, fighting for money. Enrico had Castilians loyal to him, Aragonese crossbowmen and men-at-arms, and a sizable contingent of Frenchmen, mostly freebooters. They were commanded by Bertrand du Guesclin.

The Prince had met with Pedro in August 1366 to agree terms for the campaign. Desperate, the king had promised Edward a huge cash bonus as well as chunks of Castilian territory to be added to Aquitaine. What could go wrong? Among the Prince's leading captains was Robert Knollys, who had fought with him at Crecy and Poitiers and had recently made a fortune looting with his Companies in the Loire (and whose bowmen would scatter Wat Tyler's revolting peasants in 1381). With him rode a regular contingent of 1,500 men-at-arms and 4,000 bowmen. Because of the distances involved and the rugged nature of the Sierras, nearly all the archers in the Najera campaign were mounted. This probably did not come naturally to the Goddamns. A horse, even a palfrey, was an expensive outlay and only a knight could afford a destrier, the 16 or 17 hands war horse of the day. Years of the chevauchée in France had meant that bowmen had had to become cavalrymen. Unlike the Moors in Al-Andalus to the south of Spain, however, they still dismounted to fight, using the same battle-winning tactics they always had. Knollys was a man after du Guesclin's heart, foraging, skirmishing, stealing as he went, but his knights, keen for personal glory and feats of arms, were not always happy. Having burned villages in front of Paris, with no one from the city's garrison coming out to their rescue, one English knight galloped up to the city gate and hit it with his lance. The challenge went unheeded. Knollys was blamed for shameful episodes like this. According to the *Chronicon Angliae*, written in St Albans, he was known by his younger followers as *vispillionem veterium,* the old brigand.

With the Prince too was John Chandos, everybody's hero, as impressive to the French as he was to the English. He was blind in one eye after a hunting accident in Bordeaux, but was probably the most experienced of the generals in the English army (he was actually from Hainault and had come to England in Queen Philippa's retinue). Hugh Calverley, like Chandos, we have met already. A captain of freebooters and a champion of the famous Battle of the Trinity (a tournament fought over territory in March 1351) he was as ambivalent as any free company commander and changed sides in this campaign as soon as he knew that the Black Prince was commanding Pedro's army. He had already told du Guesclin that he would never fight against the Prince. The youngest leader with the English was Edward's younger brother, John of Gaunt. His odd name comes from the fact that he was born in Ghent, in 1340 and, like Knollys, he had a contingent of bowmen with him, perhaps 400 strong. Gaunt's experiences in Spain must have kindled his ambition because he spent the next twenty years negotiating to become king of Castile. In the end, he had to settle for being, in Shakespeare's words, 'time-honoured Lancaster', altogether less glamorous.

There is no doubt that the Najera campaign was tough, probably more so than the Goddamns had faced in France. Added to the weather, the strong local wine 'burnt their livers and lungs and all the entrails of their stomachs'. Spanish white wines, like Lepe and Osey were available in England and cost the same as red wine from Bordeaux, but there is a suggestion that the local stuff available in Castile was rather more rot-gut.

The Black Prince camped for a month at Vitoria (the site of a much later battle in Wellington's Peninsular War) but the cold and incessant rain forced him back to more sheltered areas. What the weather did to archers' bows and more importantly their bowstrings will be discussed in the Appendix. At the end of March, Edward crossed the River Ebro over the old Roman bridge built when Hispania was part of the empire. This was at Logroño and he was marching to Navarrete, 10 miles from Enrico of Trastamara's position.

On the night of 2/3 April, the Prince swung to the west, carrying out a march in darkness with as little sound as possible. He used the existing hills to confront Enrico's army from the left, throwing the man into confusion because he had expected a frontal assault. Luckily for Enrico, his van was composed of du Guesclin's veterans and with his usual speed and efficiency, the Constable charged front to face the Prince. Enrico had been warned by the French to avoid a battle with the English, but taunting letters from the Prince had forced him into it. Du Guesclin too had had a bloody nose from the Goddamns before, but on that April morning it was too late to do anything about it.

The Prince's vanguard was led by John of Gaunt, backed by Chandos, Steven Cushington and Guichard d'Angle. Each of the Prince's divisions was made up of dismounted men-at-arms with bowmen on their flanks. We cannot be sure of numbers, but the usual balance was two or three archers to every billman. Du Guesclin did not wait to be attacked, but by pushing forward, he was walking into the customary English trap – bowmen packed solidly in a defensive position. Even so, the Bretons with him had faced the arrow storm before and du Guesclin's men pushed John of Gaunt back before they rallied and held firm.

In the second division, the Black Prince himself watched events unfold. His Gascons and English bowmen were the largest contingent on the field, strengthened with battle-hardened freebooters, Castilians loyal to Pedro, the Count of Armagnac and the Captal de Buch. Most of the Aragonese, who had joined the enterprise despite the wavering of the king, were in this division too. The Black Prince ordered them forward – 'Advance banners in the name of God and St George' – to perform a pincer movement that crushed du Guesclin's struggling soldiers.

So far, the battle had been an infantry slog, pike to pike and jaw to jaw, punctuated by the ever-deadly arrows. Now, Don Tello, Enrico's brother, decided it was time for the cavalry. The ginettes or *genitors* to give them their Latin name, were light horsemen created after centuries of warfare against the Muslims of Al-Andalus. When the kings of Castile were not squabbling among themselves or with Aragon, they continued the ongoing *Reconquistada* (reconquest) to drive the Moors out of Spain. Their national hero, St James (he of Compostela) was called the 'Moorslayer' for obvious reasons. The ginettes were in many ways the face of modern war, with light-armed horsemen riding Arab horses, faster than the destriers of the heavy cavalry. The problem was that the ginettes wore padded jerkins (like the brigandines of the bowmen) and minimal leg armour, usually mail. Their horses were not armoured at all. When Don Tello ordered his horsemen forward, he was horrified at the result. The arrow storm utterly destroyed them, men and horses going down in their hundreds. They had never faced the bowmen before and were thrown into chaos. This in turn led to mass – and instant – desertion; hundreds of men turning their horses and riding off the field. There is a psychological moment in battle when doubt creeps into an army, followed by panic, indiscipline and finally a rout. And it is contagious. Infantry, who had taken no part in the battle yet, saw the cavalry turn tail and the banners go down and they too broke and ran for the river.

An experienced commander like the Black Prince wasted no opportunity here. He ordered the cavalry reserve of King Jaime of Majorca to chase them, hacking them down with their swords. Many drowned in the stream of the Falde; many more in the River Najerilla. Most of the slaughter that happened that day happened there.

The Prince stayed on the field that night and received the casualty list from his heralds. Perhaps 5,000 of the enemy were dead, nearly half Enrico's force, but the man himself had got away, running to France for help. As Edward said when he heard this, '*Non ay re fait* (then, nothing is done).' With both contending kings of Castile still alive, the feud would continue; two years later, Enrico of Trastamara had Pedro the Cruel murdered.

In the aftermath of Najera, Pedro tried to live up to his nickname by ordering the execution of captured nobles, including, it is said, Bertrand du Guesclin himself. Only the intervention of the Prince saved their lives. Apart from any sense of chivalry involved, the captives were worth their weight in gold in ransom money. It must have given his old arch-enemy John Chandos a great deal of smug satisfaction that du Guesclin had surrendered to him.

Najera was the Black Prince's greatest victory, surpassing Poitiers and Crecy (in which of course his father was in command). The cool handling of battlefield manoeuvre and the devastating impact of the bowmen were too much for whatever Spain could throw at them. Today, largely because Najera is not technically part of the Hundred Years War, it is, ironically, the forgotten battle, remembered only among wargamers and a handful of devotees of the Black Prince. In the long term, it achieved nothing. Pedro reneged on the payment and the land that he owed to Edward and was dead before the Prince could enforce it. Edward himself almost certainly contracted dysentery, which would ultimately kill him, on this campaign and the next nine years of his life saw only a shadow of the great warrior.

As for the Goddamns, they had fought and won in Spain as they had fought and won in France. Perhaps a handful of them stayed, as their counterparts did five centuries later in the Peninsular War. Some of them were buried there, their graves unmarked and now forgotten. Some of them returned to France to carry on their private wars with the free companies.

Some of them, and we have no idea of numbers, went home.

Chapter 14

'The Hog in Armour': Bertrand du Guesclin

Bertrand du Guesclin was a street fighter. In an age where the leaders of armies prided themselves on their chivalry and their sense of honour, du Guesclin had more in keeping with the riff-raff, the peasantry who filled the lower ranks, even the Goddamns themselves. He belongs to the middle years of the protracted struggle, when the early spectacular victories of the English were becoming a nostalgic memory and French strategy and tactics were gaining the upper hand. This did not merely coincide with du Guesclin – as Constable of France, it was largely because of him.

One biographer wrote of him:

> There was none so ugly from Rennes to Dinant … Wherefore his parents hate him so sore that often in their hearts they wished him dead. Rascal, fowl or clown they were wont to call him; so despised was he as an ill-conditioned child that squires and servants made light of him.

Du Guesclin was born near Dinant to a Breton nobleman and was described as an ugly baby. He developed into an equally ugly man, bull-necked and broad-shouldered, which partly explains the description of him that is this chapter's title. As a child, he had a fascination for all things military, in a period when childhood games grew into practice for actual warfare. He was probably born in 1320 and in 1337 won a championship in Rennes when he was staying with an aunt. Later embellishments of this story have turned the local contest into a tournament, a full-scale run at the tilt, but in fact, it was a wrestling match. Since this was at a time when wrestling was confined to the lower orders, he is said to have promised his aunt that he would never fight again without a knightly weapon in his hand.

For several years, du Guesclin was a captain of freebooters but was knighted by Charles of Blois and took his battle cry 'Notre-dame-Guesclin', his arms a spread eagle. There is no doubt that many knights in the Hundred Years War, on both sides of the conflict, were bullies and thugs. Training in what today we would call the martial arts gave them an edge over most of their contemporaries.

In the period before the victory at Poitiers, du Guesclin led his company in support of Charles of Blois for the duchy of Brittany. His stock-in-trade was subterfuge, as when he invaded the Fongeray estate with his men disguised as wood-cutters, ambushing the English lord, de la Poole, who held it. Du Guesclin was a guest at the castle of Montmirail in 1354 when word reached the garrison that an English company, led by Hugh Calverley, was on its way to take the place. He led thirty archers, probably a mixed force of long- and crossbowmen, to ambush Calverley, destroyed his retinue and made a small fortune out of his ransom. It was this that earned him the accolade from Charles of Blois.

The one-to-one combat at Rennes between du Guesclin and the English knight Thomas of Canterbury went down in legend. So impressed was he by the Frenchman's reputation as a fighter that John Chandos, perhaps the Black Prince's best commander, lent du Guesclin his own horse so that it would suit the occasion. Du Guesclin won, but it was a messy contest in which the Frenchman resorted to wrestling moves and his fists to bring his opponent down – so much for the promise to his aunt!

By 1357, the tottering government of the Dauphin Charles (his father, the king, was in prison, however genteel, in England) granted du Guesclin an annual income of 200 *tournois pieds* for his part in the Rennes siege. He now offered his services to the Dauphin, who was Duke of Normandy, against a rival claimant, Charles 'the Bad', King of Navarre. He nearly came to grief mounting a scaling ladder at Melun when the timber cracked under him and he fell into the moat, dragged out by his men in the nick of time.

The Treaty of Bretigny in 1360 brought a fragile peace but led to the chaos of free companies ransacking whole swathes of the countryside. The Dauphin hired du Guesclin to sort the problem out, which was rather like putting a fox in charge of a hen-coop. As *capitaine souverain* of the Duchy of Normandy, he had carte blanche, funded by the government, to do more or less as he liked.

In a major clash at Cocherel in 1364, du Guesclin commanded a multi-national force of Bretons, Gascons, even Englishmen. Froissart describes his opponents (the Navarese) as 'archers and brigands' as though they were the same (low) thing, but du Guesclin's troops were just as bad. In intense heat, with thirst being a major factor, the French enticed the Navarese off their hill and attacked them with ferocity. An English attack had worked at Poitiers; it would not work at Cocherel. A screen of English bowmen stopped the French charge in its tracks, but du Guesclin insisted his men fight on foot and without horses to bring down, the carnage of Crecy could not be achieved again. It became a series of hand-to-hand clashes all over the field. The English knight John Jonel's attack on du Guesclin failed and he was captured, to die later before he could be ransomed.

The 'hog in armour' was 44 by now, an age when many men would have hung up their swords. Du Guesclin was Count of Longueville but the succession problem in Brittany had yet to be settled. As Charles of Blois' staff-officer, he formed the first division against the force of Jean, one of the Brittany claimants. It was du Guesclin's misfortune that his actual opponent in the field was John Chandos whose archers cut down the cohorts of the Count of Auxeurre before hacking his way through the Bretons and taking du Guesclin prisoner. Charles of Blois was cut down. The Breton succession was decided by the Dauphin (now technically Charles V) and the free companies were free to rampage over the countryside again.

As we have seen, the Spanish adventure involving Pedro the Cruel and Enrico of Trastamara was too good an opportunity for the Black Prince to pass up. The same applied to du Guesclin, who, naturally, fought for the rebels under Enrico. He led a 30,000-strong army over the Pyrenees, backed by the Pope at Avignon and slaughtered his way across Castile, taking the opportunity to butcher an unknown number of Jews along the way. In the case of the Najera campaign, Enrico was eventually crowned but no one believed that would be the end of things.

At Najera, the rampage of du Guesclin's mercenaries came to an end and he was taken prisoner on the field by John Chandos, the pair having a grudging respect for each other. Both armies, as we have seen, fielded bowmen that day. Du Guesclin's ransom was fixed at an unbelievable 100,000 francs and he teased both Chandos and the Prince by saying that was not enough, but the king of France would pay it anyway. He duly did.

After further fighting, in which du Guesclin continued to give his military advice if not actually his services to Enrico, the Breton was made Constable of France, the highest accolade possible and the equivalent of commander of the army. In terms of status, this potentially created problems. The whole structure of western Europe was based on a strict, still feudal, hierarchy. Du Guesclin was not sufficiently high-born to give orders to royal dukes, but Charles V told him to do it anyway.

From 1370, as Edward III sank into his dotage and the Black Prince was frequently ill, the Constable went to war in Poitou, re-capturing Poitiers and La Rochelle. Duke Montfort in Brittany fled to England and the death of John Chandos in a skirmish was a huge coup for du Guesclin. He may have honoured the man, but he was glad that he was out of the way. When the English sent an army to Calais in 1373, du Guesclin used evasionary tactics and avoided battle. He refused to fight, even when directly challenged by the English heralds – which was regarded as shameful but it worked – until a truce was declared in 1375. The Black Prince died the following year and Edward III the year after that. The head and the heart of the English war machine had melted away. There were still bowmen able to bring a French army to a bloody standstill, but they had to catch them first. Emboldened, there were further French raids on the English coast.

Brittany remained a problem for the hog. As a Breton, he wanted the territory to be independent, not part of the kingdom of either France or England, but he had nailed his colours to the French mast and many Bretons regarded him as a traitor. While besieging the town of Chateauneuf-de-Randon, du Guesclin, now nearly 60, fell ill and died

I am not as impressed by Bertrand du Guesclin as other military historians have been. The French, always ready to big-up their heroes to a ridiculous degree, ranked him among the Nine Worthies, along with Julius Caesar, King Arthur (fictional) and their very own Charlemagne. He was a hugely popular commander, able to speak the language of his men and to slog beside them on campaign, but his strategy was to avoid battle, not seek it and when he had no choice but to fight, for example against John Chandos and the Black Prince, he lost.

There is one other aspect to du Guesclin often overlooked, especially by military historians. He believed implicitly, as did most of his contemporaries, in prophecies and the mysticism of the planets, putting great faith in the ancient wisdom of Merlin, the magician of Arthur's court at a time when Arthur was lauded as the epitome of the chivalrous king. We know today that the Arthurian cult was based on little more than wishful thinking, but that was not how du Guesclin saw it and he made few moves without consulting the movements of the heavens.

Chapter 15

Agincourt: 25 October 1415 St Crispin's Day

By the end of the sixteenth century, when English control of France was an increasingly distant memory, there was a huge nostalgic revival of the interest in the reign of Henry V, focusing on his astonishing victory in the mud of Agincourt in October 1415. Not only did William Shakespeare devote an entire play to him in his history cycle but Michael Drayton, his Warwickshire contemporary, wrote *The Ballad of Agincourt:*

Fair stood the wind for France,
When we our sails advance,
Nor now to prove our chance,
Longer will tarry;
But putting to the main,
At Caux, the mouth of Seine,
With all his martial train,
Landed King Harry.

And taking many a fort,
Furnished in warlike sort,
Marcheth towards Agincourt,
In happy hour;
Skirmishing day by day,
With those that stopped his way,
Where the French General lay,
With all his power.

Which in his height of pride,
King Henry to deride,
His ransom to provide
To the King sending.
Which he neglects the while,
As from a nation vile,
Yet with an angry smile,
Their fall portending.

And turning to his men,
Quoth our brave Henry then,
Though they to one be ten,
Be not amazed.
Yet have we well begun,
Battles so bravely won,
Have ever to the sun,
By fame been raised.

Poitiers and Cressy tell,
When most their pride did swell,
Under our swords they fell,
No less our skill is,
Than when our grandsire great,
Claiming the regal seat,
By many a warlike feat,
Lopped the French lilies.

The Duke of York so dread,
The eager vaward led;
With the main, Henry sped,
Amongst his henchmen.
Exeter had the rear,
A braver man not there,

O Lord, how hot they were,
On the false Frenchmen!

They now to fight are gone,
Armour on armour shone,
Drum now to drum did groan,
To hear, was wonder;
That with cries they make,
The very earth did shake,
Trumpet to trumpet spake,
Thunder to thunder

Well it thine age became,
O noble Erpingham,
Which didst the signal aim,
To our hid forces;
When from a meadow by,
Like a storm suddenly,
The English archery
Struck the French horses,

With Spanish yew so strong,
Arrows a cloth-yard long,
That like to serpents stung,
Piercing the weather;
None from his fellow starts,
But playing manly parts,
And like true English hearts,
Stuck close together.

When down their bows they threw,
And forth their bilboes drew,
And on the French they flew,

Not one was tardy;
Arms were from shoulders sent,
Scalps to the teeth were rent,
Down the French peasants went,
Our men were hardv.

This while our noble King,
His broad sword brandishing,
Down the French host did ding,
As to o'erwhelm it;
And many a deep wound lent,
His arms with blood besprent,
And many a cruel dent
Bruised his helmet.

Gloucester, that Duke so good,
Next of the royal blood,
For famous England stood,
With his brave brother;
Clarence, in steel so bright,
Though but a maiden knight,
Yet in that furious fight,
Scarce such another.

Warwick in blood did wade,
Oxford the foe invade,
And cruel slaughter made,
Still as they ran up;
Suffolk his axe did ply,
Beaumont and Willoughby
Bare them right doughtily,
Ferrers and Fanhope.

Upon Saint Crispin's day
Fought was this noble fray,
Which fame did not delay,
To England to carry;
0, when shall English men
With such acts fill a pen,
Or England breed again,
Such a King Harry?

As with many of his history plays, Shakespeare has done a great deal of damage with *Henry V.* Anxious as he is to take the action out of the 'wooden O' he encourages his audience to imagine 'the vasty fields of France'. Cue Laurence Olivier's 1944 filmed version of the play which shows the French knights trotting, cantering, galloping, across rolling green countryside under a dazzling sun. That was Ireland and utterly unlike the actual battle site between the villages of Agincourt and Tramecourt. In fact, recent photographs of the site give an expanse of open spaces, but the Agincourt of 1415 was a narrow defile between two woods. It was a wet October and the ground had been churned to a quagmire by prancing horses. It is very telling that this area – Artois – is not far from Picardy, across which the trenches of 1914–18 were dug.

Henry's army was smaller than the Black Prince's at Poitiers – perhaps 6,000 men. A sixth of these were men-at-arms; the rest, bowmen. The French had 20–30,000. Most of these were men-at-arms, mostly mounted and included Italian mercenaries. As they had done before, they hacked their pole-arms down to make them easier to wield in the confined space. Such was the complacency and arrogance of the high command (Poitiers was a long time ago) that the Constable. Charles d'Albret, turned down the offer of 6,000 crossbowmen from the Paris militia because he felt sure they would not be needed. The crossbowmen he did have were sent to the rear, perhaps so that there would be no repeat of Crecy. Their impact on the battle would have been negligible. Days earlier, a high-level conference at Rouen had decided the battle formation when and if they faced the English. As St Crispin's Day developed, however, this was forgotten by over-zealous young knights all clamouring to be in the first division. Not all the French units had arrived when battle was joined and overall command seems to have been in the hands of the Duke of Orleans, not yet 21, who was certainly no Black Prince.

Henry was up before dawn and heard Mass, already wearing his armour. He wore the Garter below his left knee and fitted to the crown aventail around his helmet was the Black Prince's ruby, still part of the crown jewels today. The dented helmet he may have worn over this that day formed part of his funeral achievements in 1422 and can still be seen in Westminster Abbey. He rode among his troops on a grey palfrey as his three divisions formed up. He had spent the wet, miserable night in a house at Maisoncelle. Most of his men were camped in the open, trying to keep dry under trees and carts. Many of them were still suffering with dysentery, with high temperatures and sudden cold shivers. And they were all hungry. It was this last fact that dictated what form the battle should take.

Just as they had been ordered to be silent all night, so now, as the divisions took up their positions, they made no sound. In contrast, the French had been heard laughing and joking throughout the hours of darkness, confident that they had the English at their mercy. In keeping with tradition, the bowmen formed their wedges on the wings and between each division. The appearance of these men would not have changed much since Poitiers. Most wore a brigandine, reinforced with studs and metal strips. Some wore caps of boiled leather (*cuirboulle*) or tarpaulin stretched over a wicker frame; others had *chapel-de-fers*, or *sallets*, rimless iron helmets that made visibility easy and did not impede the movement of the neck. The traditional green and white tabards of Crecy had gone and most bowmen had a red cross stitched to their sleeves or chests. Everybody carried a dagger, sword and buckler for hand-to-hand work. The widespread dysentery meant that many men went into battle naked from the waist down. Highly dangerous though this obviously was, it was less trouble than constantly unlacing hose to relieve oneself at the roadside. There is no evidence that the bowmen wore any leg armour at all. Knights' legs were encased in steel by 1415 and most crossbowmen wore *genouilles* (knee defences). On the march from Harfleur, the bowmen had carried wooden stakes hacked from the forests they travelled through. The branches were lopped off and both ends sharpened, one to ram into the ground to act as a hedge defence and the other to impale the horses in a cavalry charge.

The left wing was commanded by Thomas, Lord Camoys, whose magnificent brass tomb stands in the church at Totton, Sussex. Newly appointed to the Garter, Camoys was one of the oldest men in the field at 60 and with a wealth of experience. Henry himself commanded the centre and the right was led by Edward, Duke of York, the king's cousin.

The harvest had not been gathered at Agincourt and the English stood up to their knees in corn. Behind them the baggage carts had been left at Maisoncelle, together with the sick and the boys who carried all kinds of impedimenta. They were protected by ten men-at-arms and twenty bowmen, which was clearly not enough. Henry's baggage included part of the crown jewels, King Arthur's Excalibur and a piece of the True Cross. The symbolic power of these icons was immense.

The French army was in disarray before first light. Unlike the English, they made a great deal of noise, drinking, eating, allegedly dicing for who would take the most important prisoners that day. Unlike Crecy and Poitiers, there was no king in command because Charles 'the Mad' was indeed insane and spent much of his reign buckled to his bed. Command of the first division, therefore, was split (never a good idea on a battlefield) between the Constable, d'Albret, Marshal Boucicaut and the Dukes of Bourbon and Orleans. The Counts of Eu and Richemont backed them up. The second division, perhaps twice the size of the first, was divided between the Dukes of Bar and Alençon. Supporting them were the Counts of Nevers, Vaudemont, Blamont, Salinès,

Grandpré and Roussy. Each of those divisions had cavalry on their wings, the traditional deployment of European armies. One of these was commanded by the veteran Clignet de Brabant, whose job it was to break the English line. There was also a scattering of crossbowmen, led by their Master, Lord Rambures and a rope of cannon. These were too far back to be of much use, their trajectories obscured by their own men and dense forest.

The third division, half a mile behind the others, was composed almost entirely of cavalry. Led by the Counts of Marle, Lenroy, Dampmartin and Fauconberg, the rank and file were inferior troops from Gascony, Brittany and Poitou. They were in the third division for a reason; the assumption being that they would probably not be needed.

Henry's oration before the action began has been totally hijacked by Shakespeare:

> This day is called the feast of Crispian. He that outlives this day and comes safe home, Will stand a tip-toe when this day is named and rouse him at the name of Crispian … then shall our names, familiar in his mouth as household words, Harry the king, Bedford and Exeter, Warwick and Talbot, Salisbury and Gloucester, Be in their flowing cups remembered. We few, we happy few, we band of brothers. For he today that sheds his blood with me Shall be my brother, be he ne'er so vile, This day shall gentle his condition. And gentlemen in England, now abed Shall think themselves accursed they were not here, And hold their manhoods cheap whiles any speaks That fought with us upon St Crispin's Day.

He rode from division to division, exhorting them in a variety of ways. Chroniclers have different versions of this. Whether any of them are accurate is unknown. Some claim that Henry asked the time. Being told it was prime (six o'clock) he said it was a good thing because at home people would be at prayer. In fact, it was over four hours before the fighting began. The French writer Juvenal de Ursins (who was not there) claims that the king told his troops that:

> he had not come as a mortal enemy, for he had not consented to burning, ravaging, violating or raping girls and women as [the French] had done at Soissons [and elsewhere] but he wished to conquer gently [?] all that belonged to him, not to cause any destruction at all.

Nobody would have heard much as he trotted past, but the *sight* of the king was more important than what he said. To the bowmen, he specifically pointed out that they would lose their right-hand fingers if the French overwhelmed them, which is as much recognition of their importance in the field that any of them would ever get. This version is realistic. The chronicler Lefevre was with the army at Agincourt.

Henry prowled his lines until about eleven o'clock. His men were tired, ill and starving. Like the Black Prince at Poitiers, he had to strike now or the French could wear his army down without loosing a single arrow. He sent a message to old Sir Thomas Erpingham with the archers to launch an attack. The man was 58 at Agincourt, a veteran in every sense in the fifteenth century, and he scanned his lines of bowmen. Perhaps half of them had abandoned their hose but put their boots back on – running over rough ground in bare feet was not a good idea for anybody. They had sheaves of arrows in their belts and pouches, their bows were primed and ready. Some of them were hidden in the Tramecourt woods, effectively an ambush.

'Nestrocque!' he roared, the time-honoured command that everybody understood, throwing his white baton in the air. 'Now, strike.' It was answered by a cheer. The army, that had been effectively been silent all night, now roared into action. Erpingham wheeled his horse away, dismounted and stood beside the king. His green and white banner flapped overhead. Erpingham's order may have been given to the bowmen who saw off a pointless little sortie by French knights anxious to get the action going.

'Banners advance!' Henry bellowed. 'In the name of Jesus, Mary and St George!'

The whole army fell to its knees, crossed themselves and crammed a handful of French mud into their mouths. Then they slogged forward. Revisionist historians like Jim Bradbury and Tim Newark have played down the impact of the bowmen, claiming that they were only effective in massed numbers holding defensive positions. Yet this was true only of Crecy, Dupplin Moor and Halidon Hill. At Poitiers and Agincourt, the bowmen attacked first, shooting as they went. This was a risky manoeuvre and it meant upping the stakes and replanting them again 700 or 800 yards nearer the French lines. *And* they had to do it through the rain-washed mud of a ploughed field. It is likely that Henry had seen the manoeuvre against Owain Glyndwr in Wales and it had proved successful at St Cloud in 1411 when the Earl of Arundel had destroyed a French army with his bowmen alone.

Each time the army halted, for the men-at-arms to catch up, the bowmen in their wedges shot volleys of arrows into the enemy, drums and trumpets drowning out the chants of 'St George, St George!'

D'Albret was rattled by this. The tiny army, perhaps a fifth of the size of his, was dictating the pace. Perhaps 200 yards from the French line, the bowmen hammered the stakes they had dragged from the Somme, their points poking upwards like a murderous hedgehog. Then they pulled back and fired again.

The French cavalry on the right wing, commanded by Guillaume de Saveuses, charged, but in the wet mud of a rainy October, could barely manage a walking pace. Even so, a horse could cover the ground in seconds, not minutes and the rate of fire from the Goddamns was never more crucial. The arrow storm decimated them and they hesitated, then turned back. In the end, only de Saveuses and two knights rode on and they all died long before they reached the English stakes. Thoroughly unnerved by this reversal, d'Albret ordered an advance along the whole front, exactly as the Black Prince had done at Poitiers, sure that he could crush the English through sheer weight of numbers. Three columns advanced, making for each of the three English divisions. There was no doubt who was there – the banners of York, the king and Camoys gave the game away. An estimated 8,000 men-at-arms were slogging through the mud in tight-packed formations.

Again, it was the bowmen who slowed the advance. Firing about 1,000 arrows a minute, they hit the French head-on and from both wings. As the Frenchmen went down – 'lopping the French lilies' as Drayton put it – their broad front narrowed and they lost cohesion, stumbling over the fallen bodies, knocked off balance by wounded and dying men. The piles of men and horses were higher than a man and movement had slowed to a standstill. Such was the crush that men were unable to use their swords. Commanders like the Dauphin and the Count of Vendome were screaming at their men to retreat, but the chances of hearing any of that in that maelstrom of chaos were remote. The closest we can come to it, on a microcosmic scale, is two scrums locked in a rugby match. The pressure to advance comes from behind and often, those at the front are forced sideways or off their feet as the whole thing collapses. Something like this was happening at Agincourt; the end result was not a penalty or a try but death.

At this point, the archers dropped their bows (no longer needed in the slog) and hacked away with their swords alongside the billmen. Ian Mortimer says they used a new weapon, the pole-axe, but this was a two-handed staff with a steel head and men already carrying a bow, armour, sword, buckler and stake could hardly have managed this too. Lethal weapons lay everywhere – axes, maces, clubs, swords and daggers – even without recourse to their own. Misericords, with narrow blades and razor tips, were jabbed into the eye-holes of helmets. The bowmen went for throats, armpits, groins, anywhere where plate armour was limited and a man was most vulnerable. Many men must have drowned in the mud.

The Duke of York was hacked down in this chaos, crushed or asphyxiated. Three times the king was battered to the ground, the crown all but bashed off his helmet and his standard bearer, John Codrington, had to work feverishly to keep the man alive. Three of Henry's squires, including the Welshman Dafydd Gam, were killed alongside him.

With the first French division attack brought to a halt, the second wavered. Their commanders, the Dukes of Bar and Alençon, were begging their men to hold their formations and carry on the advance. Alençon himself fought his way to the banner of the Duke of Gloucester and caught him with his sword. He was swallowed up by the king's bodyguard and raised his hand in surrender. But it was all too late for chivalry in moments like that and one of them smashed his helmet and skull with a battle-axe.

The Duke of Brabant died too, probably in this same attack. He was the youngest brother of Jean Sans Peur (the fearless) Duke of Burgundy and had been at a wedding 30 miles away at Lens when he heard the news of the battle. He outgalloped his people and had to borrow armour and weapons from his chamberlain, Groblet Voskin. When his body was found, he had wrapped a banner around himself as a jupon.

After perhaps two or three hours, the French had nowhere to go. The woods on each side were still full of bowmen, ready and eager to cut them down, although they were fast running out of arrows. Ahead, the English line had broken nowhere. The French folded in on themselves and stumbled backwards over their own dead, to escape as best they could.

Henry did not have the men or the strength left to mount a pursuit. In fact, he had an impossible number of prisoners. There is an odd, some would say inexplicable, moment in Olivier's film when he catches sight of mounted knights on the horizon – 'Take a trumpet, herald. Ride unto those horsemen on yon hill. If they will fight with us, bid them come down. Or void the field; they do offend our sight.' This was the

French third division, whose massed cavalry had seen no action all day and were unlikely to make much of a dent in the solid (if exhausted) English line. They backed off, although there was always the possibility of their looping behind the woods and launching an attack from the rear.

What happened next is one of those imponderables, a stain on an otherwise unblemished reputation. In keeping with the common notion of looting at the time, a number of French knights, backed by local militia from Heslin, attacked the baggage and grabbed the valuables. 'Kill the poys and the paggage,' sobs the Welsh captain Fluellen in Shakespeare's take on it, and he is horrified by the deed. In fact, Henry had left the baggage under-guarded and his own retaliation was far worse. It may have been that the French attack was part of a plan, like the Black Prince's at Poitiers, to cause disruption with a flank attack, but the greed of poor men had got in the way and they went for expensive trinkets rather than victory. Henry ordered all prisoners executed. Their helmets were ripped off and their heads bounced, adding to the many already lying in the Agincourt mud.

Today, this act of slaughter would be regarded as a war crime, with all kinds of pinko-liberal outrage underpinned by the Hague Convention and other humanitarian milestones. It caused outrage at the time because of the huge loss of ransom money to the victors and serves as a reminder in L.P. Hartley's phrase, that the 'past is a foreign country'.

Henry's losses in the battle were relatively low, though not as low as those given by Shakespeare – perhaps twenty-five, he says! The Duke of York was dead and the Earl of Suffolk. So were Thomas Fitzhenry, John de Peniton, Walter Lord, Richard Kyghley and Dafydd ap Llewellyn ap Hywel – Shakespeare's Davy Gam who had been knighted by Henry shortly before he died. It was he who had been sent to reconnoitre before the battle and had ridden back to tell the king that there were 'enough to be killed, enough to be taken and enough to be chased away'.

This list is known as the Agincourt Roll, in which Shakespeare casually says, 'None else of name'; in other words, nobody important.

Henry probably lost about 600 men, most of them the nameless foot soldiers and bowmen who had given him his victory.

In fact, from a variety of sources, over recent years a smattering of names have been found. I include all of them here because otherwise, we have no tangible record of the Goddamns, as if they are merely ghosts that float over battlefields. There was William Bretorum, Matthew Bromfield, Morgaunt Filkyn, Jankyn Fustor, William Gladewyne, William Glyn, John Grfton, Yevan ap Griffith, Thomas ap Griffith Grogh, John Hert, John Hertford, Lewis Hunte, John ap Meredith, David Tailler, Thomas Tudor, Richard Walsh, David Whitecherche and Richard Whityington. From their names at least, half of them were Welsh.

By comparison, the French losses were horrific. It was an action replay of Crecy. Constable d'Albret, the Dukes of Bar, Alençon and Brabant were the most senior but hundreds of lesser nobility and knights also lay naked and barely recognizable in the mud. Even allowing for those whom Henry had had killed, high-ranking prisoners included Charles, Duke of Orleans, the Duke of Bourbon, Marshal Boucicaut and the Counts of Vendome, Richemont and Eu.

Henry gave thanks in the church at Maisoncelle that night and his exhausted, but victorious, army marched to Calais.

Theirs would be the last great victory in the Hundred Years War.

Chapter 16

'Such a King Harry': Henry V

Our image of Henry V is pure Shakespeare. As such he is a one-dimensional puppet, brilliant at speeches before battles, fearless and heroic as the underdog.

We only have one portrait of him and that is a Tudor copy of the original. The face is narrow, determined and humourless, the hair cropped in the fashionable 'pudding basin' cut of the time. The portrait is singularly left facing (most English monarch's portraits are not) and this is almost certainly because of the nasty arrow wound he received at Shrewsbury in 1403 when he was 17 and fighting in his father's army against the Welsh rebel Owain Glyndwr. It was Henry V who began the long-lasting tradition of not looking the king directly in the face (it was still going on under George III in the 1790s); put simply, Henry was embarrassed by the disfigurement. It may be because of that that we hear nothing of the man's love life. There is no mention of a mistress and his marriage, to a French girl half his age, was for political convenience only.

Henry was born in Monmouth Castle on the Monnow in the summer of 1387. His mother, the 17-year-old Mary de Bohun, became an accomplished scholar, if she was not already, but she was dead by the time Henry was eight. His father was Henry Bolingbroke, the Earl of Derby, but he was not there when the boy was born. Bolingbroke was preparing for another rumoured French attack on England and, as the grandson of Edward III (through his son John of Gaunt) he was expected to do his bit. He did it well. For all the failures of Bolingbroke (who became Henry IV in 1399) he was an excellent general, scholar, politician and crusader.

Bolingbroke fell foul of Richard II, his cousin, over a number of issues in which Richard was accused of 'bad governance'. There was nothing new in this – the barons had been resisting royal 'tyranny' since long before Magna Carta in 1215 – but Bolingbroke was exiled as a result of his outspokenness. It says something of Richard's goodness of heart, however, that he kept young Henry as a ward of court so that his education was that of a prince. From the age of 7, he learned to fire a bow (he was actually a crack shot with a crossbow, ironically) and to ride at the quintain with lance and shield in practice for the tilt and the real business of battle.

Young Henry travelled with the court, spending time, for instance, at his grandfather John of Gaunt's new castle at Kenilworth. At such venues, in the setting of the hunting field, the lists and the sumptuous banquets, the boy would have heard stories of his great-grandfather's time, the early battles of Sluys, Crecy and Poitiers. He was brought up in a paternalistic military tradition that is still the way for British princes today. And he was brought up to be a devout Christian. When the threat of Lollardy, pouring scorn on the Church and raising tricky questions of the Bible, became an issue early in Henry's reign, he quashed it vehemently. John Wycliffe had no place in Henry V's scheme of things.

By the age of 10, he was a tolerable harpist and had developed a love of music. Like his father he wrote in French, English and Latin, although he never became a scholar in the accepted sense. In a way, the politics of the day prevented this. Bolingbroke's ten-year exile in 1398 must have made life difficult for his son. John of Gaunt died the next year. Henry was still more adrift, especially when his father's exile was extended to life. That year, too, Richard II took an army to Ireland to put down a rebellion there; he took 13-year-old Henry with him.

In the king's absence, Bolingbroke came back from France, to claim his inheritance as Duke of Lancaster and a descendant of Edward III. Interestingly, in the context of this book, the king's Cheshire bowmen, then the best in the country, tore off their white hart livery and deserted in droves. Richard was overthrown, abandoned by almost everybody and for the rest of his life Bolingbroke, now Henry IV, was a usurper. More than that, he was a murderer, because he undoubtedly ordered Richard's death in Pontefract Castle sometime in 1399/1400.

Young Henry and his brothers, who would go on to become the Dukes of Clarence, Bedford and Gloucester, became a force to be reckoned with. Clarence would die at the battle of Beaugé in 1421; Bedford would be Regent of France in the years after Henry's death and smashed the French many times; Humphrey of Gloucester protected England during the minority of Henry VI and had a torture instrument – 'Duke Humphrey's Daughter' – named after him.

For twelve years, the Welsh ruler Owain Glyndwr fought a stubborn guerrilla war against Henry IV. Partly, this was because the Welsh had always backed Richard and partly because Glyndwr claimed (with *some* justification) to be the rightful Prince of Wales. Legally, from the English viewpoint, that was Harry and he spent his mid-teens effectively fighting for his birthright.

One of Henry IV's many failings was that he had favourites and his favourite son was not the eldest, Henry, but Thomas, Duke of Clarence. The brothers had been rivals all their lives and as often happens, the 'playground' spats of childhood became serious and nasty as the boys grew. As the king grew old before his time, brooding on his usurpation of Richard and ill with an unspecified disease, two camps grew up. Clarence was busy controlling a rebellious Ireland and Henry was running a rival council until his father stepped in and stopped it. A tearful rapprochement in 1411 did little to alter this situation.

It was in this period, with Henry in his late teens, that vague rumours spread of the Prince's roguery. Falstaff, Bardolph, Nym and Doll Tearsheet are all part of Shakespeare's imagination, but it seems that the straitlaced lad who had done little but fight all his life did sow a few wild oats at this time.

Henry IV's death in the Jerusalem Chamber of Westminster Palace in March 1413 catapulted 'Hal' into the hot seat. If he had ever been Shakespeare's 'Jack the lad', which is unlikely, all that stopped now and he was at once focused and earnest. In terms of foreign policy, he opened the can of worms of his right to Gascony and then all France. Taking advantage of the squabbles among the French nobility involving Burgundy and Armagnac, Henry prepared for war. A popular king, he never found it difficult to raise money or find men. One indenture for 1413 has a list of Welsh bowmen for what would become the Agincourt campaign. Bedford handled it all with efficiency.

In the hectic last days of the campaign's organization, a plot was discovered to kill the king and his brothers and to put Edward Mortimer, the Earl of March on the throne. Fourteen years after the deposition of Richard II, the crime still rankled. The conspirators involved some of the highest in the land, led by Richard, Earl of Cambridge and unknown numbers of Lollards, Welshmen and Scots, all of whom had no reason to love King Harry. The plot was a farce and a tremblingly guilty Cambridge confessed all to the king. There was the briefest of trials, kangaroo-style at what today is a pub in Southampton, and all the leaders faced the executioner's axe.

Both Portsmouth and Southampton claim that Henry sailed for France from their jetties on 11 August 1415. Troops did indeed embark from both ports, but the king himself was on board the *Trinity*, his flagship, moored between the two.

The outlines of the campaign are covered elsewhere in this book – the bloody siege of Harfleur and the 'miracle' of Agincourt – but Henry had to spend another four years in the saddle to make sure the promises of the battle's aftermath came about. The Treaty of Troyes in 1420 gave Henry's full claim to the throne of France. To cement it, he married Katherine de Valois on 2 June in the cathedral of Troyes. Their son, who went on to become Henry VI, was to be ruler of both kingdoms, except that Henry V's death two years after his marriage left a child king and all the unease that always accompanied that situation in the Middle Ages.

Even after Troyes, the war went on, largely because the Dauphin refused to accept the grovelling stand taken by his deranged father,

Charles. Much of the fighting was led by Richard Beauchamp, Earl of Warwick, one of Henry's most loyal supporters, but by late 1421 the king was back on the campaign trail again. He fell at the siege of Meaux and was unable to ride against the Dauphin. Carried on a litter to his castle at Vincennes, he died on 11 August 1422. The exact cause is unknown, but it was probably dysentery – 'the bloody flux' – which had affected so many of his men in the Agincourt campaign.

In the tradition of the time, the king's body was dismembered and boiled to remove the flesh. Everything was sealed in a lead coffin with spices and carried in state, first to St Denis, the burial place of French kings, then to Rouen, his own capital. Four black horses dragged the coffin onto the ship at Calais, the Duke of Bedford making sure that everybody remembered the passing of 'Henry the Conqueror'. His funeral at Westminster Abbey was the most spectacular in two centuries.

Chapter 17

'The Maid'; Jeanne d'Arc

The best description of Joan of Arc comes from the French nobleman the Lord of Gamaches. According to him, she was 'a girl who came from no one knows where and has been God knows what.'

While Gamaches was exaggerating (we know exactly where she came from, for example), his sheer inability to understand and explain the phenomenon of 'the Maid' says it all. Almost everything we know about her comes from biased sources and her role in the Hundred Years War is such that she is either a heroic saint (the French angle) or an evil witch (the English perspective). Much of the information comes from the account of her trial at Rouen in 1431 where she faced charges of heresy. The whole thing was, in modern criminal parlance, a 'stitch-up', none of the charges reasonable even by the standards of the time. Many of them were added to the charge sheet after her death and her signed 'confession' was meaningless.

The death of Henry V had not slowed down the English intention to force the French to abide by the Treaty of Troyes and acknowledge the infant Henry VI of England as their king. Things were going well. Lords Salisbury, Suffolk, Talbot and others were taking town after town in a continuation of the chevauchées of Edward III and the Black Prince.

Into the middle of all this stepped the 'miracle' that was the Maid. Jeanne was born to Jacques Tart (which formed over time into d'Arc) and his wife in the village of Domremy in Lorraine. It is difficult to fix Jacque's status. He is usually referred to as a peasant, but he seems to have held land of his own, had a flock of sheep and was highly regarded by the locals. According to her own words, Jeanne began to hear voices at about the age of 12, especially when playing near a certain tree, the Tree of the Fairies, near the village.

Such victims of religiosity are not uncommon. They are found all over the world, usually in the context of the Catholic Church. We often overlook the fact that during the Hundred Years War, *everything* was attributable to God and his angels; victories, defeats, plague, fire and destitution – all this was not due to men's work but God's or his nemesis, the Devil.

Today, Jeanne would undoubtedly have received psychiatric help, but the fifteenth century did not think like that and had no such remedy. What was disturbing was that the barely teenaged girl came to believe that God had called her to rid France of the English and to see Charles VII, himself mentally unstable, crowned at Rheims. An uncle (her parents would never have gone along with this, experts agree) advised her to put the situation before Robert de Baudricourt, the local lord. The man laughed at her (as did many others) but a member of his court bought her story and took her to Chinon to meet the king.

The story goes (and such fables litter Jeanne's actual life) that Charles disguised himself among his glittering courtiers, but she picked him out immediately, even though she had never seen him before. Intrigued, the king had the girl interrogated, questioning her faith (and perhaps her sanity). A physical examination revealed that she was a virgin, which ruled out her being a witch because witches copulated with the Devil.

Charles was hooked and Jeanne received a modified suit of plate armour and was given a horse and the holy sword called Fierbois, associated with a local saint. From this moment on, Jeanne was a pawn in a political game she could barely understand. How a peasant girl, barely literate, could follow the murderous intrigues of the civil war between the Burgundians and the Armagnacs, both vying for control of the French throne, requires an explanation that we simply do not have. She was given nominal command of the army, although the real leaders were tough fighting men like the freebooter la Hire and the supposed devil-worshipper Gilles de Rais. Jeanne's army would march on the English force besieging Orleans and end the war once and for all.

To that end, a letter was sent to the English lines:

> King of England [Henry VI was never with an army in France personally] and you, Duke of Bedford, who call yourself Regent of the kingdom of France; you, Guillaume de la Pole, Earl of Suffolk; John, sire de Talbot; and you, Thomas, Lord Scales … do right before the King of Heaven. Hand over to the Pucelle [Maid] who is sent from God … the keys of all the towns which you have taken and ravaged in France …

Specifically, she singled out the bowmen:

> And you, archers, soldiers, gentlemen and others who are now besieging the town of Orleans, get you back in God's Name into your own country … And if you do not believe the message of God and the Pucelle, I inform you that, wherever we find you, we will fight you and will make so great a hay-hay [hoo-ha?] there that not for a thousand years has France had one so great …

The letter is clearly a polemic, in fact a challenge written by men who knew their business. By mentioning the bowmen, they knew where the heart of the English military strength lay. Jeanne never called herself 'La Pucelle'; neither did she, as another part of the letter states, refer to herself as a 'chieftain of war'.

With Jeanne at their head and her specially designed banner held high (in fact, three were made for her), the French army smashed into Bedford's camp and destroyed it. The de la Pole brothers, William and John, were taken prisoner and a third brother, Alexander, was killed at a follow-up skirmish days later. We have already seen that the siege of Orleans was a bitter one and that the English fortresses built were difficult to take. No wonder that French troops, from nobleman to billman, regarded Jeanne as a saint and an avenging angel. She stands uniquely in the story of the Hundred Years War – neither side produced anyone else remotely like her. That said, Bedford's troops were ill and desertion was rife.

On 29 April, she crossed a swollen river wearing her white armour (the full plate armour now worn by knights on both sides) and brought food and freedom to Orleans. People prayed and kissed her feet; they had found their saviour. On 8 May, as the last of the English were pulling out, Jeanne was wounded by an arrow. Ironically, it was a crossbow bolt and hit her shoulder. Knowing what a talisman she had now become, she remounted and fought on until dusk. Orleans was free – another nail in the coffin of English aspirations in France.

Charles VII was crowned at Rheims and Jeanne went on to another victory at Patay. The following year, however, her fortunes changed. She was captured during a skirmish at Compiegne against a combined Anglo-Burgundian force and was dragged by a bowman from her horse. The Duke of Luxembourg sold her to the English for 10,000 gold crowns.

Incredibly, we have a virtual transcript of Jeanne's trial. In effect, it was a court of the Inquisition, presided over by Pierre Cauchon, the Bishop of Beauvais. Courts like this bore no resemblance to modern justice. Jeanne had no counsel and had to do her best to fend off questions from an assortment of clerics, all male, of course, who had clearly made up their minds of her guilt before they started. There was no jury in the modern impartial sense. The charges against her were heresy, idolatry, conjuring the Devil and blasphemy. Jeanne mentioned throughout weeks of cross-examination that she was regularly visited by Saints Catherine, Margaret and Michael who told her that it was God's will to drive the English out of France. Much was made of the girl's banner, itself seen as a token of blasphemy and the fact that she wore men's clothing, an abomination, according to the Inquisition, in the eyes of the Lord. Much of what we know about Jeanne's extraordinary life comes from the trial records, but no witnesses appear to have been called and Cauchon et al let Jeanne condemn herself with her own admissions. It seems likely that a number of charges were not actually levelled in court, but added to the indictment afterwards.

She was taken to the churchyard at St Ouen to be burned (the conventional execution method for heresy), where she cracked and recanted. This recantation she later withdrew, saying that she had been coerced and because of this was burned in the marketplace at Rouen on 30 May 1431. She was nineteen.

Her abandonment by Charles VII and the French nobility was shameful. However briefly, her presence in the field won battles for them and only one, the Maitre (Chancellor) of the University of Paris, spoke out in her defence. In 1456, with the Hundred Years War over and the English clinging on to Calais only, an ecclesiastical court ruled Jeanne's trial 'irregular'. It was not until the twentieth century that the girl from Domremy achieved sainthood. Declared Venerable in 1904, Blessed in 1908, she officially became St Jeanne in 1920.

Chapter 18

The Thunderers: Artillery

On 30 April 1524, long after the Hundred Years War ended, a man was killed in battle at Sesia, in the service of his king, Charles VIII of France. He was Pierre Terrail, Seigneur de Bayard and has come down to us as the knight 'sans peur and sans reproche', the epitome of chivalry, above ordinary men and the perfect example of knighthood. Bayard was mortally wounded by an artillery shell and for three centuries after his death, he was a cult figure who represented the heroism and dignity of the old ways of warfare being brought down by the heartless operation of a machine.

This is hopelessly romantic stuff, partly because there is no evidence that Bayard despised artillery and partly because bows too, whether long or cross, were also military machines, used to kill indiscriminately. What is certain, however, is that artillery marked the beginning of the modern age of warfare and although bows, even longbows fired by the English, were still in widespread use in the time of Elizabeth and the Armada, their days were numbered.

The alchemist Roger Bacon was probably the first Englishman to experiment with gunpowder, at Oxford in the 1250s. It was black and composed of charcoal and sulphur, so that with such hellish connotations, it was called the 'Devil's Invention'. Potentially, it could do far more damage than, for example, the crossbows outlawed by the Papacy in the twelfth century.

The first known use of 'gonnes' comes from Edward III's war with the Scots in the 1330s. The king obtained his charcoal, saltpetre and quick sulphur from York, although how many such weapons he had is unknown. Time and money were spent on providing stone balls for siege engines, as the tried and tested implements for siege warfare. Guns came in all shapes and sizes and fired all kinds of missiles. Their range, at first, was limited and they were notoriously unsafe, liable to explode and kill the gunners operating them. With such a deadly – and unstable – weapon, it is hardly surprising that umpteen countries were credited (and damned) for inventing it, in much the same way as disease. In the early sixteenth century, tuberculosis was called the 'English fever' by the French. At the same time and for the same xenophobic reasons, venereal disease was the 'French pox'. In North Africa, gunpowder was called 'Chinese snow' and the Spaniards believed that the Moors had used it against them during the ongoing *Reconquista* in the 1340s. Not to be outdone by Western advances, Japan claimed that the Mongols had used gunpowder against them in the thirteenth century. The earliest reference in England is a manuscript of 1326 which shows an iron pot, apparently of Greek fire, firing a crossbow bolt. Over time, the bolt became a bullet (both words from the Latin *ballista*). It is possible that the French used pots de fers (iron tubes) against the flimsy walls of Southampton in 1338.

Handguns were used at Crecy in 1346, but their numbers and effect must have been negligible since the victory belonged wholly to the bowmen. Edward took twenty-two on campaign with him and some of the purpose seems to have been psychological. Guns were called 'thunderers' for obvious reasons and they rattled the nerve and composure of an enemy. For siege work, where cannon were more effective against masonry and timber, the earliest guns were called 'ribaulds'. Edward III had their tube barrels lashed together so they could be fired in rapid succession. They were used at Calais along with trebuchets and mangonels. The oldest surviving gun in England was found in the moat of Bodiam Castle, is fourteenth century in manufacture and is made of wrought iron. A fifteenth-century version found in the Marne probably came from the siege of Meaux and it seems that obsolete cannon were routinely dumped in rivers rather as supermarket trolleys are today! By the time of the siege of Orleans in 1429, cast iron had replaced the wrought iron, brass and latten of the early years.

The first guns were mounted on wooden blocks which allowed the weapon to be tilted to change aim and trajectory. The bigger and heavier the gun and shot, the more men were needed to operate it and oxen were used to drag the big siege guns into position. At the very end of the war, we have evidence that wheeled carriages were being used, the forerunner of the mobile firepower, say, of the nineteenth-century Royal Horse Artillery. Vinegar and water were thrown over the barrels to cool them down and gunners had constantly to scrape out powder residue to keep the tubes clear. Shot was loaded via the muzzle and was first made of stone; iron came later. Some handguns were probably fired like the anti-tank bazookas of the Second World War, but if they were too heavy for the shoulder, were rested on walls.

The huge guns used at Constantinople in 1453 were legendary. Mons Meg, now in Edinburgh Castle, was made for Duke Philip of Burgundy in 1449 and weighed an astonishing 15,366lb. But such weapons were for effect, very expensive and by no means the norm. In 1353, William of Aldgate made guns which cost 13s 4d, which would have broken nobody's bank. The earliest were anti-personnel weapons, hence their use at Crecy. The attacks on Southampton in 1338 brought guns that fired bolts with iron feathers; the gunsmith William Woodward made ever bigger cannons in the 1370s and the masons who made the cannonballs were paid 6d a day.

The future Henry V was already using cannon in Wales in 1407, one 4½ ton monster – 'the King's Gonne' – transported by sea. Henry was effectively the Napoleon of his day, a master of artillery and siege warfare. He had 10,000 cannon balls and 65 gunners at Harfleur, the guns, as we have seen, called *London, Messenger* and the *King's Daughter.* It was largely because of his successful artillery bombardments that earthworks became essential defences for a castle or town, with arrowhead bastions and ditches to protect stonework and bog an attacking army down.

There is no doubt that Henry's gunners were the way to the future, even though it was his bowmen who won Agincourt – 'there failed them no manner of skill and science'. Even in a siege that ultimately failed, Orleans in 1429, the Earl of Salisbury's gunners flattened whole areas of the city, including twelve parish churches. He himself, of course, was killed by gunfire.

Among gunsmiths, the Bureau brothers, Jean and Gaspard, were kings, providing a whole range of excellent weapons for Charles VII. Between 1449 and 1450, the French army took or won back sixty enemy towns. The mere sight of the big guns caused some garrisons to throw open their gates and in terror of such weapons, pregnant women were warned to stay away in case they miscarried at the sheer noise. In 1411, the Burgundians fired their bombard *Griete* against the gates of Borges. 'It shot stones of enormous weight … Nearly twenty men were required to handle it. When it was fired the thunderous noise could be heard 4 miles away and terrorized the local inhabitants as if it was some reverberation from Hell.'

By the end of the war, true handguns were in use. They were matchlocks, iron tubes mounted on a wooden block and could be fired like a crossbow, with the butt against the shoulder and the gunner looking along the barrel to line up his shot. It was perhaps unfortunate for the bowmen that this shooting method was at odds with their technique, at least in the volley fire for which they were famous on fields all over France. And in various parts of Europe, handguns were catching on. In Frankfurt in 1431, the council insisted that every man of fighting age, an estimated 2,000 of them, should own such a weapon. It was the fifteenth-century equivalent of Edward III's insistence that all Englishmen should be proficient with the longbow nearly a century earlier.

To purists, perhaps like the fearless and peerless Bayard, the use of handguns was sneaky. It proved that Jack was as good as his master and artillery went on to drive the heavily armoured cavalryman into obsolescence. Firing a handgun took skill but it took less courage than tackling an opponent with a sword or dagger at close quarters and the more accurate the gun became and the greater its range, the more that was true. Just as the French cut the bow fingers off archers in the early years of the Hundred Years War, so a worse fate awaited the gunners of the next generation. In the siege of Buti Castle in 1498, the Florentine general Gian Vitelli had the hands of captured gunners hacked off and their eyes put out.

Since the manufacture of guns was new and carried out without universal rules by individual gunsmiths and engineers, we have no overall view of the exact types of weapons. Bombards were the largest, the Ghent Bombard, used by the Burgundians at Andemade in 1382 was 18ft long with a calibre of 26in, using 140lb of gunpowder to fire a stone ball weighing 600lb. Transportation of guns of this size was a nightmare (contrast the 20 plus miles a day of the Goddamns on foot); in 1433 at the siege of Avalon it took 8 days, 100 horses, 8 carts and 70 men to cover the 90 miles from Dijon.

The breech-loading *veuglaines* (there is no English equivalent) of the Burgundians was a smaller, lighter version of the bombard, anything between 3 and 10 feet in length. They were not powerful enough to smash masonry, but useful in demolishing outbuildings and timber structures. They were in use by the 1420s. Culverins came from the German states and were certainly in operation by the time of Jeanne d'Arc's trial and death. Between 2 and 4 feet long, they were first used by German gunners, rather as the Genoese had a reputation as crossbowmen. A generation later, culverins were known as arquebuses. Serpentines were so called because of the snake-like shape of their firing mechanism and were mobile and more powerful than culverins. We first find them in the Burgundian records in 1430. The *culverines à main* are the forerunners of the musket and ultimately rifle of much later battlefields. John the Good of Burgundy owned 4,000 of them in 1411. The earliest of these had no stock to rest against the shoulder and cannot have been very accurate. Shot of iron, lead and stone was used, iron being best for penetrating the plate armour by then in widespread use.

The development of artillery in this period is most clearly shown in Burgundian, as opposed to French and English archives. The *Mâitre de*

L'Artillerie held a princely status after 1415, often acting independently even of the Duke. France had their Master of the Crossbows during the ongoing war too, but there seems to have been no similar role given specifically to any Englishman. Perhaps it was believed that the bowmen needed no such control.

Chapter 19

Castillon: 17 July 1453
St Justa's and St Rufina's Day

Shocking news reached England, as it did the rest of Europe, in the days and weeks after 19 May 1453. That was the day that a huge Ottoman army, led by the Sultan, Mehmed II, smashed its way into the city of Constantinople and brought the 1,100 years of the Byzantine Empire to an end. Three days of looting followed, an orgy of destruction which made the Black Prince's and Henry V's chevauchées look tame. Men, women and children were butchered indiscriminately. The sacred holy relics of the emperor and monks were trashed as worthless trinkets. The Greek Orthodox church of Hagia Sofia became a mosque.

If the English had time to process this news and the enormity of Christianity's loss, they were soon busy with more pertinent business. The glory days of Edward III, the Black Prince, and even Henry V were gone. Charles VII regained, with grim determination, nearly all Henry's gains before 1422. Paris was French again, so was Harfleur. Burgundy, ever vacillating, was back in bed with the French under an agreement made between Charles and Philip the Good, Duke of Burgundy. There were revolts in towns held by the English, such as Dieppe.

As we have seen, the problem for English hopes and ambitions was that Henry VI was as intermittently mad as any of the Valois kings had been and he was content to let various noblemen try to govern France. With a ferocious French wife, Margaret of Anjou, and very little grasp of what was going on (he assumed Margaret's pregnancy that resulted in Edward, Prince of Wales, was the work of the Holy Ghost!) it is not surprising that French fortunes were on the rise. The Earl of Somerset got out of Rouen at the earliest opportunity and the pay of the bowmen, often woefully in arrears, was cause for constant complaint.

At Cherbourg, French artillery proved superior and, despite the heroism of the wife of an English captain who put on armour to fight on the battlements, then billed and cooed in a provocative dress to get the best deal she could, the garrison was forced to surrender.

The action turned to the south, to the Gascon province of Aquitaine, which had belonged to the Black Prince and long before that to the Angevin kings of England. Thirty miles from Bordeaux, along the Dordogne, the English held Castillon.

By now, the French had learned to cope with the Goddamns. Attack on foot, quickly enough, having bombarded them with artillery fire first and they would not have time to release more than their first volley of arrows. This happened at Patay in 1429 where the bowmen had no flank protection and were cut to pieces. At Formigny, in April 1450, 1,500 bowmen and 3,800 men-at-arms under the command of Sir Thomas Kyriell 'held themselves gallantly' but were forced back by sheer weight of numbers. Five hundred bowmen died in a garden by the river and were buried there in a mass pit, still known as Le Champ Anglais.

Commanders like the Earl of Shrewsbury – 'Le Roi Talbot' as the French called him – still carried respect and he led 3,000 men to break the French siege at Castillon. His first attack was brilliant. As dawn came up, he routed French archers, mostly crossbowmen, and drove them back to their camp three-quarters of a mile away. Talbot knew that the strength of the French army lay in its artillery, said to be 300 guns parked between the Dordogne and the tributary of the Lidoire. His fame was legendary and he was used to the Frenchmen running at the mention of his name. It would, he believed, be like that this time too.

He had been captured three years earlier in the war and had sworn never to take up arms against the French again. Accordingly, under the letter of chivalric law, he rode a white destrier forward on 17 July, wearing a crimson gown and purple hat. He had no armour, which might alone have saved him from what was to come and he was well over 60 years old. A feint by French cavalry, apparently retreating, persuaded Talbot to attack, even though the French artillery were secure in a well-designed temporary fortress, with trenches and abutments to make it difficult to reach them. Fired up by the old boy's rhetoric – and the large vat of wine he made available to them beforehand – the men-at-arms and bowmen charged the French positions, reaching the earthworks, now riddled with arrows and trading blows with the defenders. In theory, the position of a besieging army was a hopeless one when threatened with a relieving force – they were being hit simultaneously from two directions, a war on two fronts.

How long they could have held on against the French artillery barrage is uncertain. As we have seen, it was possible to dodge cannon balls in the fifteenth century, but the arrival of *another* relieving force, this time of Bretons, fighting for Charles VII, turned the tide. They attacked from the north, splashing across the Lidoire, which was little more than a stream and taking Talbot in his right flank.

Talbot's grey was hit, probably by a culverin shot and it went down, pinning the earl to the ground. A French archer, of all the ironies, finished him off with his axe. His body was found the next day with a tooth knocked out. In common with as many noblemen as possible throughout the war, his corpse was boiled and sent home for burial, in his case in Shropshire. The tomb was opened in 1860 and the story of the smashed tooth was proved correct.

Fast forward to 1957. Another John Talbot, Earl of Shrewsbury, visited Castillon that year and at nearby Villeneuve saw some old buildings. He and his wife were told by locals that they had been built by the English during the war. 'The war?' Talbot queried. 'Bien sur!' came the reply. 'Le guerre de cent ans.' For Gascons loyal to the English, the war ended in 1453!

Perhaps a greater irony lies in the fact that, according to one French account, Talbot's body was riddled with arrows. They had not killed him and were probably crossbow bolts rather than longbow arrows, but their existence alone seemed to mark the end of a world, as surely as did the sack of Constantinople months earlier.

Now only Calais remained, more of an embarrassment than anything else. That embarrassment lingered on until April 1564. By that time, even though Shakespeare was yet to glamorize Henry V through his play, the Hundred Years War was the vaguest of memories. In England, only the tombs of the great and good remain as a reminder in stone and brass. Half-heartedly fighting – and still using longbows against the sporadic French attacks – the garrison was hit by the plague and was forced to surrender. There is a tragic déjà-vu about all this. The same disease had hit Western Europe two years after Edward III's victory at Crecy. And Calais was officially lost under the terms of the Treaty of Troyes (11 April 1564), a very different arrangement from the one signed by a triumphant Henry V in 1420.

Chapter 20

The Goddamns

'It all depends,' Arthur Wellesley once said, 'on that article there.' Arthur Wellesley was created Duke of Wellington in 1815, 400 years after Agincourt. The 'it' he referred to was his six-year campaign against Napoleon in Portugal and Spain. The 'article' was the British infantryman, the heart of the only army that the British had against the extraordinary military might of Napoleonic France.

In the same war, George Hennell of the 94th Foot wrote in April 1812:

> Soon after daylight, the bugle sounded for two hours plunder … One of our officers saw a man go among a number of women and force off all their ear-rings. Those that would not give way [he] broke off a bit of their ear … and, oh, shame to the British soldiers, the fatigued officers could not get the men moved all day from their plunder and intoxication.

This was Badajoz, stormed by Wellington's army and the men that Hennell was writing about wore scarlet coats and carried flintlock muskets. Such a man may have been able to read the recruiting posters that urged him to join and he certainly subscribed to the patriotism of one nation state fighting another. 'You should hate a Frenchman,' Admiral Horatio Nelson said, 'as you hate the Devil' and most Englishmen went along with that. By Nelson's and Wellington's day, the French and the English had been at each other's throats, on and off, for 700 years.

Wellington had contemptuously written off his own men. They were 'the scum of the earth' and 'the sweepings of the gaols', but he did concede that life in the army had 'made men of them'. Most of them, in what was not yet a fully industrialized society, were agricultural labourers who were lured into 'taking the king's shilling' (the daily pay of an infantryman) at the mops or hiring fairs for farmworkers all over the country. The 'bringer', the crafty old recruiting sergeant who provided the ale in the taverns, told tall tales of the exciting life, the glitter of the regiment, the adoring women. A shilling a day was not a fortune, but it was regular and with it came a suit of clothes, a warm barracks and three meals a day. Civilian life could offer nothing so dependable. It was a lie, of course, but by the time the 'Johnny Raw' had taken the shilling, it was virtually impossible to back out and he was committed, in theory, to twenty-one years' service.

The fourteenth century was not quite like that. In Wellington's day, several of his officers wrote their memoirs, giving us fascinating glimpses of what war was all about in the opening years of the nineteenth century. It was rare, but there are instances of Other Ranks doing the same, famously *The Recollections of Rifleman Harris*. But in the days of Edward III, the Black Prince and Henry V, not even the kings wrote memoirs. Neither did their officers; there are no 'recollections' of John Chandos, Walter Manny, Thomas Erpingham and the Captal de Buch. The nearest we come are the chroniclers of the day and, vital though they are, they fall woefully short of first-hand accuracy.

Far and away the best known, from whom I have quoted extensively, was Jean Froissart. Intended for the Church, he began writing a history of the war at the age of 19 (in 1352) and first visited England from his native Hainault eight years later. He became clerk to the chamber of Queen Philippa during the peace of Bretigny and met David II of Scotland in 1364. Two years later he was with the Black Prince on the Najera campaign (of which he makes little) and was in Italy by 1368. Most modern commentators find him reliable and impartial, but occasionally his 'Frenchness' shows through.

Geoffrey le Baker, also known as Walter of Swinbroke, died in 1360 and was a secular clerk from Oxfordshire. His *Chronicon Angliae* written in Latin covers the entire history of England and has a detached account of Poitiers. Thomas Walsingham's *Historia Anglicana* covers the period 1328–88. He was superintendent of the scriptorium (library) at St Albans Abbey and his own experiences gave him a natural bias. He detested John of Gaunt to the extent that his work was kept hidden by his fellow monks for years in the abbey itself. Since St Albans was attacked by the peasants in 1381, he was bitterly opposed to them too. As a Benedictine, he hated John Wyclif and his Lollards and was no doubt impressed by Henry V's suppression of them. He dedicated his *Chronicle of Normandy* to the king in 1419.

Other English chroniclers, the anonymous author of the *Anonimalle Chronicle*, Adam of Usk and John Streeche, plagiarized Froissart and have no important views on the war at all.

Two outstanding French chroniclers were directly involved in military action (which makes them unusual among writers at the time). Jean Waurin, the illegitimate son of a nobleman, fought for Burgundy at Verneuil in 1424. Although this was an English victory and saw the virtual annihilation of the Scots contingent, the bowmen were off form that day and the French reached their lines. Waurin's *Receuil des Chronique de la Grande Bretagne* covers this period and is among the first to refer to the country as Great Britain. Jean Le Bel was born in Liege about 1290 and fought for the English against Scots marauders in the period of Halidon Hill. He wrote in French rather than Latin and insisted on interviewing people to confirm facts before committing them to vellum. This, in effect, makes him one of the first of the modern historians and Froissart borrowed heavily from him.

It would be nice to claim that we know a great deal about the ordinary soldier from these men, but that is simply not true. The bowmen are referred to in action, with numbers largely made up, but we have no details. Chroniclers, antiquarians and even early historians were interested in heroes and leaders, not the rank and file. Because we only have one surviving letter from a foot soldier (who *may* have been a bowman) from the period, we are left with an infuriatingly vague concept of who the bowmen were.

From a variety of sources, however, let us try to get a picture of the men who won battles without number and who, in their own way, put '*Grande Bretagne*' on the map. From the brief list of bowmen in the Agincourt campaign, I have chosen Jankyn Fustor because his name belongs so squarely in the past. If you take another one, say Matthew Bromfield, and look him up on the Internet, his profile is available on LinkedIn! We know nothing about Fustor, but let us assume he hailed from Macclesfield Forest, at the heart of Cheshire from which the best English bowmen came. We cannot be sure, but his parents were probably peasants. Let us assume too that he was 20 at Agincourt; he would have been born in 1395 and would have been a small child when Richard II was overthrown and Henry IV became king. Soon after that and not far from Cheshire, Owain Glyndwr and Henry 'Hotspur' Percy allied against the king and Prince Hal had his own baptism of fire at Shrewsbury.

The Forest was a royal one, much bigger than it is today. In fact, it extended over miles of landscape from Chester near the Welsh coast to Staffordshire in the Midlands. It belonged to the Earl of Chester and in the fourteenth century, the Earl of Chester was also the Prince of Wales. Edward I had 100 bowmen from the area as his personal bodyguard, as did Edward III and Richard II. We know from the record that a bowman called William Jaunderell was given two trees from the forest to repair his home. This was in 1356, the year of Poitiers; was the gift a bonus for his stalwart work on that campaign? Jaunderell is one of the few bowmen specifically referred to by the Black Prince. In a document dated 16 December 1355, it says 'Know all that we, the Prince of Wales, have given leave on the day of the date of this instrument, to William Jaunderell, one of our archers, to go to England.' He returned in time for Poitiers and the family, perhaps as a result of that, had a coat of arms. Jodrell Bank in Cheshire takes its name from the family.

Since the Forest was used as a hunting ground for the king, as well as pasture for sheep and cattle, it is plausible that young Jankyn's father was a forester, responsible for tending game, acting as a beater during royal hunts and conserving the forest in a hundred different ways.

In the 1380s, when Geoffrey Chaucer wrote his *Canterbury Tales*, he included a fictional yeoman. This man too was a forester, who hunted for a living. His arrows had peacock feather flights and he knew every tree by its appearance. If Fustor senior was such a man, his skill with a bow would have been taken for granted and he would have taught that skill to his son. From the age of 7, little Jankyn would have practised most days at the butts, either on his own or with friends and siblings. He would learn how to string the bow, fixing the arrow to the gut and the gut to the nocks. As he grew older, he would probably try different woods – the Forest of Macclesfield was alive with them. His father would take the boy on hunts to keep his hand in, teach him where to find the rabbits and hares and to know the habits of the king's deer. In the heart of the Forest was Wildboarclough, and although the boar had been hunted to extinction by now, kings of England still had a few roaming their hunting-grounds, presents from other kings in Europe. Jankyn would know that it was potential death to kill the king's deer, but if he had been taught to read, he might as a child have read the stories of Robin Hood, who did just that routinely. Even if he was illiterate, he would have heard the tales anyway.

Once or twice a week, the boy might go with his mother or father to the market in Macclesfield. It was 6 miles away so the venture would last the whole day. In the winter, such a journey was virtually impossible because of the snow that drifted deep in the valleys. Twice a year, the entire family would make the journey to the fairs in the town. One, the Barnaby Fair, took place on 11 June, St Barnaby's Day; the other was All Souls on 2 November. Here, they would be entertained by musicians, acrobats and conjurors, with street traders crying their wares. Here too, Jankyn and his father would enter archery competitions, for the prize of ale or a side of beef. It was all heavy to carry home but the prestige alone was worth it. On the way home, the Fustors would have walked past the castle, actually a Norman building, but being rebuilt as a fortified manor house from 1398.

The difficult question to answer is when a boy like Jankyn was old enough to enlist in the king's army. The age of maturity was very fluid in the fourteenth and fifteenth centuries. Children as young as 7 could be hanged for crimes. Girls of the same age were betrothed or even married by then, if not earlier. By the time he was 17 (in our fictionalized timeline, 1412) Jankyn was no longer under obligation to practise with his bow under the various statutes of Edward III and Henry IV; he had to own a bow in his own right and use it regularly. It would make sense for the boy to 'join up' then or soon after and Henry V was recruiting from 1413. If Jankyn's father was a forester in the service of the Prince of Wales, so too was Jankyn and there was no question of reporting to the fifteenth-century equivalent of a recruiting office; it was a foregone conclusion that he was in the king's retinue. There was, technically, no Prince of Wales in 1412, but Henry held the Earl of Chester title and Jankyn was one of his men.

As such, the status of the bowmen from Macclesfield was higher than other archers and certainly other foot soldiers. How much Jankyn Fustor would have been influenced by patriotism is debatable. There was much of this in the 1340s when Edward III was raising bowmen under the Commissions of Array but that was probably because of recent French raids on the south coast. There had been no recent examples in 1413 and much of the flag-waving we associate with the Agincourt campaign is actually Shakespearean from nearly two centuries later.

No doubt there would have been tearful farewells in the Fustor household. It is likely that in the Macclesfield Forest area there were older men who had served under the Black Prince and perhaps even Edward III. They would have experience of war and of France and no doubt their tales were as tall as most old soldiers of any generation. But, essentially, young Jankyn was marching off into the unknown. The one consolation is that he was certainly already in the company of other bowmen, either in a lance arrangement or as an independent cohort.

How far these men had trained together is anybody's guess, or what form the training took. By Wellington's day, all that mattered was the discipline and tightness of drill formation, instilled into recruits by endless parade ground manoeuvres and the use of volley fire. Unlike musket shot, arrows could be recovered and used again, so the expense of such practice was negligible. No doubt there was a need to carry out manoeuvres in a body because 'firing at will' was less effective and would not produce the arrow storm necessary to stop an enemy in the field.

As he marched south to join the king's army, Fustor would have been carrying his bow, ideally of yew, and up to fifty arrows, with hazel shafts, goose or peacock flights and iron/steel tips. He would also have his dagger at his back and even if he had never actually killed anyone with it, he had been bought up to use it for shaping bows and arrows and skinning game. He almost certainly carried a sword too, not the princely and expensive weapon carried by knights, but a simpler, shorter version that would not trip him up on the march or in action. It is unlikely that he had any other weapons other than his buckler, a circular leather shield for defence. Only crossbowmen carried the large wooden pavises to crouch behind and the stakes the bowmen habitually used were found en route to battlefields. On his left forearm, Fustor would have worn a leather brace which would reduce the risk of torn skin from the bowstring and he would almost certainly have a shirt of mail over his linen underwear. His legs would probably have been unarmoured, merely covered by woollen hose laced to his shirt. His boots would have been made of stout leather, perhaps studded with iron for a better grip.

Fustor's headgear is open to conjecture. The ubiquitous term used is chapel de fer (cap of iron) but its shape varied. The kettle hat with its wide brim gave good protection to the face but it may have limited all round visibility and caused problems when aiming and shooting.

The sallet was a simpler form, moulded to the shape of the head, with or without hinged cheek plates. This caused no visibility problems, but left the face largely unprotected. Over his mail, Fustor would have worn a brigandine, a padded jacket studded with iron and reinforced with leather.

One unanswerable question is what heraldic device he would have worn. This served a double purpose. On campaign, it was a status symbol for a lord – the more men wearing his livery, the more impressed were his contemporaries. On the battlefield, it was used as a sign of recognition, rather as the red coats of the British infantry and the blue of the French were used in Wellington's day. As a king's bowman, he could have had the royal arms, the leopards and lilies, on his chest or sleeve. Or it could be the wheatsheaf of the Earl of Chester, in whose company Fustor was marching. It is unlikely that such a prestigious body would wear the simple cross of St George on a white background, although that was what most archers wore.

I have made the assumption that Fustor was a foot archer, in which case he would have been paid 3d a day (although exactly when this kicked in is not clear). That was one and a half times what a skilled civilian craftsman could make, but not as much as mounted archers, who got 6d a day. The rate of pay also varied depending on location. Until he reached Southampton, Fustor got his 3d; after that it might increase, but there was always the risk of delay in pay actually getting through.

The men were organized into 'hundreds' (the old Roman 'century' of the legions) or 'vintaines' (twenties) led by a knight or lord appointed by the king. We have no idea who this would be in Fustor's case, because his actual lord (Henry) was already in London organizing his campaign. Whoever the leader was, he carried the men's pay and the nominal list of who was there.

Southampton is 210 miles from Macclesfield and armies were expected to cover no more than 13 miles a day. That said, Fustor's contingent would have had minimal baggage, perhaps a couple of carts carrying water, ale and spare bows and arrows. The journey should have taken nearly a fortnight but we know that many units did it in half that time. Whether Fustor had ever left the Macclesfield Hundred before we cannot know, but it is most unlikely he had ever been to Southampton. His route too is unknown. We are so used to the motorway network directing our journeys that the idea of tramping over open country is alien to us. There *were* roads, some of them the old legionary tracks, some older, but their condition varied enormously. We know that Edward III rode from London to York, covering 55 miles a day, but that was without his retinue and probably involved a change of horses. For part of his journey, Fustor would have travelled the king's highway; for some of it, he would have followed drovers' paths and local by-ways. We do not know what time of year this was, but travel in late spring and summer was obviously preferable to midwinter; dust was less of a problem than clogging mud and dangerous ice. It is possible that they travelled by sea from Chester, but that would have taken them all the way around Wales (still dangerous under the marauding bands of Owain Glyndwr), the Lizard and the south coast. Sea travel was often the cheapest and fastest means of transport in the fourteenth century, but it had its obvious hazards, not least the storms that spring up from nowhere.

Following a logical land route south and covering perhaps 20 miles a day, Fustor's unit would have passed Uttoxeter and Coleshill, then virtually villages, in three days and on to Evesham by the fourth. This was a sizeable town, with its impressive twelfth-century abbey and was the site of the battle in 1265 when Edward, Prince of Wales (later Edward I) had routed the rebel baron Simon de Montfort in a loop of the Avon. Late the fifth day would see them at Cricklade with its church, oddly, dedicated to the Welsh saint Sampson. From here it would have been possible to take a boat down the Thames, but there was no need to travel via London; in fact, it would slow things down. Day seven would see the Cheshire bowmen arrive at Salisbury with its massive thirteenth-century cathedral, still the highest spire in the country. Perhaps they looked with astonishment at the new clock, put up in 1386 and one of the oldest still operating in the world. Perhaps they gave thanks for their safe journey so far in the cathedral. Almost certainly unbeknownst to them, a copy of Magna Carta lay in the library and the impressive four-gated town walls were a sign of things to come.

Where possible, Fustor and his comrades would have slept in inns or stables and if their lord was alert, he would have prevented them from being ripped off by unscrupulous landlords. And so to Southampton. The town's walls had been completed by the 1360s and essentially what we see today is what Jankyn Fustor would have seen on arrival – a bustling city, well defended and crawling with troops. Those not billeted in the town's many inns were camped under canvas in the fields to the north and along the river banks in both directions. Southampton Water was crammed with the cogs of Henry V's navy, bright with the heraldry of the lords who commanded them. The king's own flagship lay moored off Lee-on-Solent, 2 miles from where another Henry's flagship, the *Mary Rose*, would sink in 1545.

Jankyn Fustor spoke a different language from most of the men he met here. They were all English (with some Welsh and Irish) but regional dialects were far stronger then than today and there was no such thing as received pronunciation. The bowmen would have been kept busy, practising shooting and manoeuvring in open spaces beyond the walls, but boredom must have set in during the wait for embarkation, with the risk of drunkenness and outbreaks of violence, quite possibly on a regional basis. We know that even in the hallowed halls of academic Oxford, punch-ups between northern and southern students were commonplace.

We cannot know how much ardent patriotism filled the hearts of Fustor's generation. The volunteers of 1914 were desperate for adventure and glory, confident that it would 'all be over by Christmas' and that God was on their side. But the men of 1415, even if they had never fought before, had been brought up on the stories of their fathers and grandfathers. The energy of the king was infectious, but how much of this filtered down to the rank and file?

Vast quantities of provisions were arriving daily. We still have the inventories of Henry's efficient organization. Mutton, beef and pork, rarely eaten by the Goddamns, was supplemented by cheese, peas and beans. Bread, which did not keep for long, was provided for in tons of flour and portable ovens to bake the stuff on campaign. Ale was in plentiful supply and wine, from the English lands in Gascony, added to the headiness of the atmosphere. Fish was caught locally and men like Fustor, bought up in the remoteness of the Peak District, had only ever had that (salted) on Fridays, because the Church said so. Weapons arrived too, the southern counties providing 1.19 million goose feathers for the bows. 'White' (i.e. unvarnished) bows cost 1s 6d each (12 deniers); 'painted' variants 2s or 18 deniers. Some were yew, probably better seasoned and more reliable than other types. The arrows arrived by cart or packhorse in wooden barrels, each cart covered in tarpaulin and pulled by up to eight horses. It is estimated that Henry's army took over 40 tons of arrows to France, with all the baggage problems that that entailed.

We do not know whether Jankyn Fustor had ever seen the sea before. Having lived briefly in Macclesfield Forest as a child, I can vouch for the isolation and remoteness of the place. Our tiny hamlet had two farms and a school. There was no bus service and no telephone (in the 1950s) and hot meals for the school had to be brought by van from Macclesfield 6 miles away over moorland roads. I suspect that Fustor's unit would have been transfixed by what they saw as Southampton Water widened into the Solent and the fleet sailed east.

We have no idea which ship Fustor sailed in, but the king hoisted sail aboard the *Trinity Royal* of 500 tons on Sunday, 11 August. Its master was Stephen Thomas. Eyewitnesses talked of 1,500 ships in the armada with 15,000 men and almost as many horses on board and Fustor would have seen the flock of swans trailing the fleet, hoping for food. This was an omen; Henry Bolingbroke's family had a white swan as its crest. The Macclesfield man was in good company; 8,000 bowmen were on those ships, along with their spare bows and arrows, ready for anything the French could throw at them. They had come to Southampton from all over Britain and it was time to stand up and be counted. They were probably in no hurry; they were already getting, as the wind filled their sails, 6d a day. But if the swans were a good omen, the accidental fires on board three ships were not; they all sank.

Late in the afternoon of Tuesday 13th, the fleet weighed anchor off Chef de Caux in the mouth of the River Seine. On being told what the place was called, the rank and file immediately called it 'Kidcocks' to much hilarity, rather as their successors would call Ypres 'Wipers' in the First World War; the English nobility spoke French, nobody else did. No one was allowed to land, least of all in search of booty and women. If Fustor and his bowmen had hopes of plunder on this campaign, they were to be bitterly disappointed.

The Goddamns had been cooped up on their ships for the best part of a week by Thursday the 15th, the Feast of the Assumption. As they came ashore, to set up camp on the nearest hilltop, they helped themselves to livestock and food. Buildings were burned but there is no mention of violence offered to the locals. All the men by this time wore white tabards painted with the red cross of St George.

The first target of Henry's army was Harfleur, the walled town that provides us with so much evidence of siege warfare in the Hundred Years conflict. On the king's order, the Goddamns torched the outlying cluster of houses, clearing a level field for Henry's cannon and siege engines. Most of his army were camped in fields to the west of the town, at Graville, well out of cannon and bow range from the walls.

Fustor would have heard the king's edict read out before any real action began:

> No town or manor is to be burnt, no church or holy place sacked and no old people, children or women in my kingdom of France

> are to be harmed or molested. Nor is anyone to threaten people or do any kind of wrong, on pain of life and limb.

Edward III had issued a similar order before Crecy; so did Wellington in the Peninsula. There were fifteen regulations, all designed to keep discipline. An army that is allowed to do what it likes is no army at all. We have no idea whether Jankyn Fustor was married (at the age of 20 he may well have been) or what kind of sex life he had, but the king's orders were explicit. There were to be no women in the camp at all; in fact, they were to be kept 3 miles away. If a woman was found on military premises, she would receive a warning. If she was found a second time, she would have her arm broken. That kind of punishment was often carried out by the bowmen.

By Monday 19th, Harfleur was surrounded and Henry sent his heralds to warn that he had the right, if the town did not surrender, to put the inhabitants, men, women and children, to the sword. This again would be the work of the bowmen. No doubt most of them would have found this distasteful – many had wives and children themselves – but this was 1415 and no one would have queried the order for a moment. The offer to surrender was refused. In the cannon bombardment that Henry unleashed over the next two days, he did just that, his cannonballs ripping the town's main square apart. And the bombardment continued through the night, the crashing of stone through timber and the screams disturbing everybody's sleep.

The townsfolk as well as the garrison fought back and Fustor's Goddamns found themselves replying to volleys of crossbow bolts. Hitting targets behind high walls was difficult and no doubt the bowmen were warned not to waste their arrows. On Sunday 25th (the Lord's Day clearly did not count for much during a war) the English made their first direct assault but they were beaten back by the jars and pots of inflammable material that set fire to a belfry. The bowmen were out of range of all this, but they could not make any impact either.

In Paris, the council sent out orders for their scattered army to assemble at Rouen. The archers and crossbowmen wore white, as opposed to red, crosses on their tabards. They too were ordered not to pillage nor to stay longer than one night in any one place.

On Wednesday, the bowmen were busy digging out new ditches to the east of the town under orders from Thomas, Duke of Clarence, the king's brother. He had fewer men than Henry and took the brunt of the counter-bombardment from the town.

By Sunday, 1 September, a new problem arose; dysentery. A form of the disease had killed the Black Prince; it would kill Henry V. The chronicler Thomas Walsingham wrote:

> These deaths were caused by eating fruit, the cold nights and the foetid smell from the bodies of different animals that they had killed throughout the English lines but which they had not covered with turf or soil or had thrown into the waters of the river, so they were forced to endure their decaying stench.

The Goddamns would have had their own take on the cause of the outbreak. It was a bad smell. It was the Devil's work. It was the Lord's punishment for wickedness. They thought the same about the pestilence, although up to this point, that particular plague had not broken out again. It was appallingly hot, even for a French summer and the nights only seemed cold by comparison. The attacking army was expected to hold out in terms of food supplies for three months, but after three weeks they were running low. Reinforcements were coming from England every day and everybody prayed that the corn fields in the area could cope with the extra demand. Harfleur had become a death trap and Jankyn Fustor must have been hardened to the fact that, even if he did not become ill, he might not come out of this; the 'bloody flux' was everywhere.

Two weeks later, a French counter-attack made the Goddamns wake up. The English defences were on fire and the bowmen fired their volleys to keep the townsfolk back behind their walls. The defences were rebuilt by the bowmen at dead of night, with virtually no noise. An attack the next day was beaten back, the Goddamns using flaming arrows soaked in tar to burn the roofs and timbers of the town's barbican; it took them two days to put the fires out. After a further ferocious artillery bombardment on the 16th, the inhabitants of Harfleur finally cracked, begging Henry for a truce until 22nd, St Maurice's Day. Twenty-four citizens were offered as surety, rather like the burghers of Calais in the distant days of Edward III.

Michael de la Pole, Earl of Suffolk, died of dysentery on the Wednesday. In accordance with tradition, his body was boiled in a large cooking pot until the flesh fell off the bones. The heart had been removed already and the disarticulated skeleton was collected and placed in an ossuary to be sent home. Another ghastly job for the bowmen.

By St Maurice's Day, it was obvious that no French army was on its way to relieve Harfleur and a ragged group of leading citizens made its way, flanked by English heralds, to the king's great tent. They had ropes around their necks, according to Adam of Usk, who was there. In all probability, Jankyn Fustor was too, although how much he could see of the solemn action is unknown. The town was spared, perhaps against Henry's better judgement and the flags of the leopards and lilies and of St George were hoisted over Harfleur's gates.

The next day, the king walked barefoot to the church of St Martin and looked at the ruins around him. There was damage and chaos everywhere and the Goddamns were ordered to round up all the women, children and poor and herd them into the square. There was a language barrier of course, but nobody was going to argue with a Goddamn with a sword at his hip and a bow over his shoulder. The women and children were escorted by the bowmen to Lillebonne, carrying whatever they could. The men were left behind to rebuild their shattered town as an English military base.

By now, perhaps as many as 2,000 Englishmen were dead or out of action. We know that Jankyn Fustor was not among them (or if he was ill, he recovered) because he fought at Agincourt. The deaths continued throughout September and the rank and file like Fustor had no idea of the strategic problems facing Henry and the high command. If the king wintered in Harfleur, he only had one town to show for his pains and already, the loss of perhaps a seventh of his army and nearly half his commanders. And it could only be a matter of time before a French army came to attack. If he marched on into the country in chevauchée, as Edward III had done, he risked running slap bang into a fresh French army many times bigger than his own.

Because we do not know who Fustor's lord was, we cannot know if he had survived Harfleur too. On the 26th, Sir William Butler of Warrington died and the fifty Lancashire bowmen under his command were transferred elsewhere. The king sent an unknown number of the sick and wounded back home in perhaps twenty ships. He did not have the time or the resources to care for them either at Harfleur or in the field.

By Friday, 4 October, Henry's mind was made up. He would march for Calais, following Edward III's route and he left behind him 1,200 men, three bowmen to every man-at-arms, to defend Harfleur. Jankyn Fustor was one of about 9,600 men who marched out into the unknown, 6–7,000 of them bowmen. A storm broke as the army marched out, smashing a handful of the English ships in the harbour to driftwood. To the simple, superstitious Goddamns, here was another omen; there was no way back home. And ahead of them, although the Goddamns did not know it, were 144 miles of hostile territory.

On the march, the army was divided up into three divisions as was the custom on the battlefield too. We can assume that, as a bowman of the Earl of Chester, Fustor marched with the king's central division. The Duke of York led the second but because the Duke of Clarence had gone home sick, we do not know who led the third. With the baggage train was the food supply. It would be difficult for the Goddamns to find resources in the open country. Everyone knew by now that the English army was on the prowl and a kind of scorched earth policy would have been underway, livestock taken away, corn gathered (although we know that it still had not been on the Agincourt battlefield) and, where possible, water supplies contaminated. That said, Henry's army would cross six rivers en route to Calais, so fresh water would not have been a problem. Even so, the baggage contained eight days' worth of supplies, mostly walnuts and dried beef and it is likely that the men carried some of this in bags over their shoulders. At Montvilliers on the first day, the vanguard was attacked. Henry's orders were to bypass settlements but he could not ignore an actual attack. He lost six men taken prisoner and one killed.

There was no possibility of finding quarters on the march and October was wet and cold. So they camped in the open, under canvas or trees and the king's orders were read out again to make sure the Goddamns behaved themselves. The main force marched north-east to Fauville, while the wings, largely bowmen, scavenged on the left and right in search of food. There was a brief clash of arms at Fecamp on the coast where the Lord of Rambures, the French crossbow master, had already burned the suburbs and conducted a defence from the town's abbey.

They reached Arques on the River Bethune on Friday, 11 October. The townspeople opened fire with cannon, but Henry had 10,000 men with him and the king did a deal. In exchange for wine and bread, he would leave Arques alone; it was what the free companies had been doing for years and no doubt Jankyn Fustor was grateful for the fresh produce.

Eu was next, well defended on the banks of the Bresle and a skirmish outside the fortifications had left a handful on both sides dead. The town went the same way as Arques and Fustor could wet his whistle again. On Sunday the 13th, the army struck its tents and began the march to Blanchetaque, the ford of the Somme that Edward III had found on the Crecy campaign. Rumours had spread that there was a massive French army there; and rumours among an army are dangerous. Young men like Fustor were hardened to a siege situation, the deprivations of marching and campaigning generally, but they had never faced a full-blown army in the field and they must have been painfully aware of their few numbers, however much of a 'band of brothers' they may have been. It had been seven days since they left Harfleur and the food supply was running out. Rumour had it – there it was again – that two French armies were about to capture the English in a pincer movement – 'enclosed on every side like sheep in a fold'. The men around Fustor, perhaps even the man himself, were suffering from painful infected wounds and they had removed their hose so that the effect of dysentery ran down their legs.

Given the situation, Henry swung east, away from Blanchetaque where about 6,000 of the enemy waited for him, following the south bank of the Somme. The bridges had been destroyed by the French and they camped, already exhausted, at Marevil. The bridge at Pont Remy had gone too, its stones lying smashed in the river. The anonymous author of the *Gesta*, who was with the army, wrote, 'I, the author of this, looked up in bitterness to Heaven ... and called upon the Glorious Virgin and St George ... for we were few in number, fighting with great weariness and weak from lack of food.' There may have been desertions, but it is unlikely; a man surrounded by his comrades had a fighting chance; a man on his own had none. It was now that looting began, irrespective of the king's regulations, and smoke rose into the cold autumn air.

Amiens was next and the Constable of France, Charles d'Albret, had stupidly stripped the town of its cannon and most of its crossbowmen who had joined him at Abbeville. Henry simply marched past the town. The speed of the advance had now slowed. Fustor was just about managing 10 miles a day as opposed to nearly twenty. He had not eaten and the wine and bread had long gone. Walnuts can only carry you so far. His feet were blistered. If he had dysentery he would have found walking difficult and painful. His stomach would have been grumbling with cramps. No one was paying any attention to the smell. It was raining hard and the nights were bitterly cold. At each bridge, the bowmen were sent to reconnoitre, to find a crossing point. All they found was broken stones and an armed body of men on the far side of the Somme, waiting for them.

At Boves, a miracle. The town did not fire at the Goddamns, neither did it attack them. It was Wednesday by now and, after dark, the townsfolk crept out from their walls carrying huge baskets of bread. The Goddamns cracked. A body of bowmen smashed their way into the wine press buildings in the vineyards, filling their goatskin canteens with the stuff. The king was furious.

South of the town the next day, the English found an unbroken bridge at Corbie across the River Avre. A French cavalry attack came out of nowhere and Fustor and his Cheshire bowmen fired volleys into them and drove them off. It must have been reassuring that after days of exhaustion, marching and suffering in their soaking clothes, their bowstrings were still serviceable and they had not forgotten how to shoot! It was now, and probably because of this, that Henry gave orders for the bowmen to cut themselves a stake each. It was to be 6ft long and sharpened at both ends. It added to the weight for a tired, sick man to carry, but against cavalry, it could just save his life.

It was now that Henry's bluff was called. A gilt-copper pyx (relic) had been stolen from a local church the army had passed and the king got to hear about it. He halted the advance and the captains searched their men. It was found in the satchel of a bowman who was forced to return the pyx. Then he was hanged from the nearest tree in full view of the others. It was not Jankyn Fustor but it could have been any one of his comrades and the punishment carried out was not lost on the rest. Wellington did the same thing in Spain nearly 400 years later.

This may have had a galvanizing effect because the army's march speeded up and they covered about 30 miles on the Friday. But Nesle stopped them in their tracks. Fustor saw the red flags hanging from the town's walls and knew at once what it meant – no surrender. Henry dropped all pretence of chivalry and ordered the outlying villages and hamlets torched. Fustor and the others were probably delighted – after weeks of misery, it was payback time.

They also found a ford, at last, at Betheneart over the Somme. It was a marshy area so the bowmen had to wade through the brackish water with their bows held two-handed over their heads. As soon as they were over, the Goddamns took up a defensive position with their stakes rammed into the ground to screen the bulk of the army as it crossed. The French had seen them, but they knew the reputation of the bowmen and dithered for too long, by which time they no longer had the numbers to do anything. At a stroke, morale was lifted.

On Sunday 20th, as the English rested in villages beyond Monchy-Lagache, Jankyn Fustor might have seen three French heralds galloping towards the English lines. Throughout the Hundred Years War, this had been an accepted prelude to battle and no one, least of all the Earl of Chester's bowmen, opened fire on them. He could not have understood what was being said, but this was a direct challenge, lord to lord. From the next day, the king and his knights rode in full armour and the bowmen marched with bascinets on their heads and bows slung over their shoulders. Near Peronne, a group of English knights charged a body of French cavalry who veered away rather than clash with them.

Skirmishes like this increased from now on and the English became ever more apprehensive. They had no idea of the size of the enemy army but they should have taken heart from the state of the ground in the area; it had been mashed to mud by hundreds of horses and would cause the French huge problems over the next three days. On the night of the 22nd, Henry's men camped at Acheux and he let them take whatever they could from the surrounding countryside. The author of the *Gesta* implies that the English were terrified and that Henry was diverting their attention, keeping them busy and not letting them brood too much. If this is correct, it is a rare glimpse into the mindset of the Goddamns. Since Harfleur, it had been a war of nerves rather than anything else and what with the lack of food and the sickness that followed them, it had worn them down. Men like Jankyn Fustor were not the same happy-go-lucky knarres who had set out from Macclesfield what must have seemed years ago. They crossed the rivers

Authie and Grouche, camping in the open south of Frévent. The Duke of York skirmished with a French outfit here and rebuilt the bridge with the help of his bowmen.

The English columns had retained their cohesion so that the vanguard, under York, did most of the hard work. If, as we assume, Fustor was with the king's second division, he could take life relatively easily. Seven bowmen from Lancashire were taken prisoner in one clash and Henry's strategy seems to have changed. Prepared for a battle as he was, in fact relying on one, he now seemed to back-track and to avoid an all-out confrontation, probably because his men were so weak, physically and in terms of morale.

At Blanquy, York smashed a group of Frenchmen trying to destroy the bridge and crossed it. Beyond it, however, he saw the biggest army he had seen in his life and spurred back to tell the king, 'for you are about to fight against such a huge host that it cannot be numbered'. They looked like 'a swarm of countless locusts', the *Gesta* author thought when he saw them. Jankyn Fustor may not have known what a locust was, but he was familiar with grasshoppers and thousands in their hard armour was a good analogy.

The famous line hijacked by Shakespeare – 'Who's he that wishes more [men]? My cousin Westmorland? Nay, fair cousin …' – as a muttered aside, this was actually attributed to Sir Walter Hungerford and, tellingly, he wished specifically for 'ten thousand of the finest archers in England'. Hungerford and Henry both knew that it was the bowmen who were most in demand – they were the winners of battles. The king ordered his entire army to kneel and pray, as if battle were imminent. But the day wore on and nothing happened. The men were told to sleep wherever they could in the barns, houses and orchards of the village of Maisoncelle, which, presumably, the locals had abandoned.

The rain set in before nightfall and hammered down all night. Each man coped as best he could, nursing aching feet, shivering with dysentery, hungry, cold. All of them probably prayed intermittently during the night. Very few of them had ever faced a battle like the one that would take place the following day. There was to be no noise and if Fustor was camped in the open, perhaps without a tent, he would have heard the arrogant laughter from all the French lines where the fires guttered in the rain. Any bowman or billman who made a noise in the English camp was to have an ear sliced off. At one point, there was a scare. Night attacks may have been unchivalric, but they happened anyway and the Count of Richemont advanced in the darkness with perhaps 2,000 men. The bowmen drove them back; perhaps Jankyn Fustor opened fire for the first time on Frenchmen, although in the dark he cannot have known if he hit his target.

There was no 'little touch of Harry in the night', the superb line from Shakespeare where the king goes incognito through his lines, picking up vibes from the Goddamns. He probably did not sleep but stayed in a house at Maisoncelle and, fully armed, attended a Mass sung by his priests of the royal chapel.

As he rode out with his staff, the leopards and lilies flapping behind him carried by Sir John Codrington, the companies formed up. It was a little after dawn and everybody had slept in their clothes, in many cases wringing wet. Fustor buckled the sword around his waist, checked his dagger and hitched his bundle of arrows into place at his hip. He pulled the bow out of its linen cover and checked that the string was dry. Finally, he buckled the bascinet under his chin and stepped out to collect the stake that might just save his life. Perhaps there were muttered asides, whispered jokes, *anything* to keep the spirit up. But there were no trumpets, no drums and no barked orders of command.

The king's division took its usual place in the centre, perhaps 400 yards from the French lines. Fustor would have been part of the wedge formation to the right or left of this. Let us assume he was on the king's right. Beyond the bowmen was the Duke of York's division that had seen most of the skirmishing action up to that point. To his right was the dark wood of Tramecourt, although the bowmen probably had no idea what it was called. Ahead was such a quagmire of churned mud that some bowmen took off their boots so that their feet would grip the ground better. Beyond that, although the heraldry was unfamiliar to them, the banners of the Duke of Bourbon and the dreaded Boucicaut, with mounted knights on the wing. But the French archers were well back, half-hidden by the billmen and dismounted knights at the front. Fustor probably looked at them with contempt; they were in the wrong place and nobody trembled at *their* reputation. In short, they were not the Goddamns.

The bowmen hammered their stakes into the soft ground, resharpening the ends with their daggers, ready to impale the French horses. At about nine o'clock (terce) they were told to string their bows. The moment of reckoning. There was no going back now. For the bowmen, as for the king, it was all or nothing. Then, at last, an order. Two hundred bowmen, led by a squire, were sent into the woods. The same was happening on the left, on the Agincourt side.

Whatever speech the king made, he made it now, reminding the bowmen that the French would hack off three fingers of their right hand if they were caught. Perhaps Fustor chuckled, along with his comrades, at this gallows humour. Perhaps they cheered and waved the deadly fingers in the air in the general direction of the French.

Heralds squelched between the lines, trumpets blaring to announce their arrival and brief conversations took place. All this was time-wasting. The Goddamns were ready but they also were tired and starving. There had been no food at all in the past twenty-four hours. Henry was very aware of this and gave the signal to advance. The banners around him, the leopards and lilies, the arms of Edward the Confessor, the Trinity, the Virgin, the bowmen's own cross of St George were raised and the trumpets blared. Everybody marched forward, the bowmen upping their stakes and carrying them across their chests. Their bows were slung over their backs and could be brought into the firing position in seconds. In those heart-stopping moments, as they felt the French mud squelching under their feet, the Goddamns saw Sir Thomas Erpingham canter across their front. The bowmen stopped and stood stock still. Those who had stakes rammed them into the ground again as the earth shook with the pounding of 1,000 mounted knights racing towards them. Erpingham, at 58, must have seemed ancient to Jankyn Fustor. He was wearing his green and white tabard (the colours of Edward III's archers) over his armour and may have been, at this stage of the battle, bare-headed, his white hair belying his guts and physical strength. He threw his white baton into the air, yelling to the bowmen the command they longed to hear – 'Ne strock!'

And all hell was let loose.

We do not know if Jankyn Fustor survived Agincourt. If he did not, his body was among the hundreds burned in a common funeral pyre the next day or the day after. His bow and other weapons would have been recycled into the army and there was nothing to send home to his family. The king's priests would have chanted the dirge for the dead for him in a language he could not write and did not understand. If he survived, he would have licked whatever wounds he had on Crispin's day and gone on for the rest of the campaign, perhaps in the years ahead, to 'rouse himself at the name of Crispin', tell ever taller stories to his children and grandchildren, which is the way of old soldiers.

Everything you have read in this chapter is based on contemporary evidence and Jankyn Fustor certainly fought at Agincourt. After that, I have had to invent a back story for him and guess his emotions and feelings, because we do not have a single written word from any of the bowmen of the Hundred Years War. They were vital to the ambitions of the kings of England. They won battles for them. They also looted, drank, whored and terrified the world they lived and died in.

They were the Goddamns, the bowmen of England.

Bibliography

Bradbury, Jim, *The Medieval Archer,* Boydell Press, 1985

Bradbury, Jim, *The Medieval Siege,* Boydell Press, 1992

Cantor, Norman F., *In the Wake of the Plague,* Pocket Books, 2001

Champion, Matthew, *Medieval Graffiti,* Ebury Press, 2015

Collis, Maurice, *The Hurling Time,* Faber and Faber, 1958

Duffy, Eamon, *Saints and Sinners,* Yale University Press, 1997

Durschmeid, Erik, *The Hinge Factor,* Coronet Books, 1999

Earle, Peter, *Henry V,* BCA, 1972

Elukin, Jonathan, *Living Together, Living Apart,* Princeton University Press, 2007

Embleton, Gerry and Howe, John, *The Medieval Soldier,* Windrow and Greene, 1994

Froissart, Jean, *Chronicles,* Penguin Classics, 1978

Guest, Ken & Denise, *British Battles,* Harper Collins, 2002

Hardy, Robert, *Longbow: A Social and Military History*, Sutton Publishing, 2006

Herrin, Judith (Ed), *A Medieval Miscellany,* Weidenfeld and Nicholson, 1999

Horsler, Val, *Living the Past,* Weidenfeld and Nicholson, 2003

Johnson, Paul, *Edward III*, BCA, 1973

Keen, Maurice, *Chivalry,* Yale University Press, 1984

Martin, Paul, *Armour and Weapons,* Herbert Jenkins, 1967

Matz, Terry, *The Daybook of Saints,* Mirchell Beazley, 2000

Michael, Nicholas, *Armies of Medieval Burgundy,* Osprey, 1983

Medland, J.C., *The Making of the Wight,* Isle of Wight Beacon Ltd., 2008

Mortimer, Ian, *1415: Henry V's Year of Glory,* Vintage Books, 2009

Mortimer, Ian, *Time Traveller's Guide to Medieval England*, 2009

Naphy, William and Spicer, Andrew, *The Black Death,* Tempus, 2000

Norwich, John Julius, *The Popes,* Vintage Books, 2012

Parker, Geoffrey (Ed), *The Age of Chivalry,* Time-Life Books, 1989
Postan, M.M., *The Medieval Economy and Society,* Pelican Books, 1972
Rothero, Christopher, *The Armies of Agincourt,* Osprey, 1981
Rothero, Christopher, *The Armies of Crecy and Poitiers,* Osprey, 1981
Rothero, Christopher, *The Scottish and Welsh Wars,* Osprey, 1984
Rule, Margaret, *The Mary Rose,* Windward, 1982
Sanger, Ernest, *Englishmen at War,* Alan Sutton, 1993
Scott, W.S. (Ed), *The Trial of Joan of Arc*, The Folio Society, 1956
Senior, Michael, *Richard II,* BCA, 1981
Shakespeare, William (ed A.L. Rouse), *Henry V,* The Annotated Shakespeare, 1599
Uden, Grant, *A Dictionary of Chivalry,* Longmans, 1968
Wadge, Richard, *Archery in Medieval England,* The History Press, 2024

Index

Other Works by M.J. Trow

The Pocket Hercules (2006)
War Crimes (2008)
Foul Deed and Suspicious Deaths in the Isle of Wight (2009)
Jack the Ripper: Quest for a Killer (2009)
Enemies of the State (2010)
The Adventures of Sir Samuel White Baker (2010)
Ripper Hunter (2012)
Isle of Wight in the Great War (2015)
Interpreting the Ripper Letters (2019)
Richard III in the North (2020)
The Killer of the Princes in the Tower (2021)
The Charge of the Heavy Brigade (2021)
Famous Horses at War (2022)
Scandalous Leadership (2023)
The Wigwam Murder (2023)
The Meon Hill Murder, 1945 (2023)
The Hagley Wood Murder (2023)
History vs Hollywood (2024)
The JFK Assassination (2024)
Dodging the Bullet (2024)
Failed Justice (2025)